torn

TORN

RESCUING THE GOSPEL FROM THE GAYS - VS. - CHRISTIANS DEBATE

Justin Lee

New York   Nashville

Worthy
Hachette Book Group
1290 Avenue of the Americas, New York, NY 10104
worthypublishing.com

Originally published in hardcover and ebook by Jericho Books in November 2012
Second Edition: May 2024

Worthy is a division of Hachette Book Group, Inc. The Worthy name and logo are
registered trademarks of Hachette Book Group, Inc.

The publisher is not responsible for websites (or their content) that are not owned by the
publisher.

Worthy Books may be purchased in bulk for business, educational, or promotional use.
For information, please contact your local bookseller or the Hachette Book Group Special
Markets Department at special.markets@hbgusa.com.

The author is represented by Daniel Literary Group, Nashville, Tennessee.

Library of Congress Control Number: 2023052687

ISBNs: 978-1-5460-0690-9 (trade paperback), 978-1-4555-1432-8 (ebook)

Printed in the United States of America

LSC-C

Printing 1, 2024

To my parents. Your love, faith,
and encouragement made me who I am today.
I love you with all my heart.

CONTENTS

CONTENTS

A NOTE ABOUT BIBLE TRANSLATIONS

Where not marked otherwise, Bible quotes come from the New International Version (NIV).

I've also drawn from other translations in the service of clarity, accuracy, familiarity, and ease of understanding. These are marked as follows:

- BSB—Berean Standard Bible
- CSB—Christian Standard Bible
- ESV—English Standard Version
- KJV—King James Version
- TNIV—Today's New International Version

For historical reasons, I've included a few passages from the NIV's 1984 edition that differ from its 2011 revision. These are indicated with an endnote.

PREFACE TO THE SECOND EDITION

A lot has changed since I wrote the first edition of *Torn*.

At the time, many Christians I knew were just beginning to wrestle with conflicting feelings on the subject of homosexuality. A number of them had discovered that someone they cared about was gay and were trying to figure out how to love that person and stay faithful to God at the same time. Same-sex marriage was not yet legal in most of the U.S., and nearly all major Christian denominations taught that same-sex sexual practice was sinful. To many people, it felt like a culture war was brewing between "the gays" and "the Christians," inspiring the subtitle of this book.

Today, things have gotten even more complicated. New issues have arisen, church positions have shifted, and denominations and congregations have split. We Christians are more divided—more *torn*—than ever. We're torn within the church, torn within our families, and, in many cases, torn within ourselves.

These last few decades of debate about sexuality have ripped open wounds in our hearts—and in the reputation of Christianity—that have yet to heal. And as the culture marches on, many Christians I know are struggling to find their footing. What does it look like to love our neighbors and our siblings in Christ, even if we think they've gotten things wrong? How do we maintain relationships with family and friends in the midst of such strong disagreements? And how can we apply the lessons we've learned in the sexuality debate to new and different issues that may arise?

These are questions I wanted to address in more detail in this new edition. With that in mind, I've added brand-new sections on topics like gender identity, handling disagreement in a Christlike way, and what we can do when we feel overwhelmed by it all. I've also expanded some existing sections, addressing major events that occurred after *Torn* was originally published and adding some details about my own journey that I hadn't originally included. In addition, I've updated some language and culture references and made various other tweaks throughout.

The topics in this book are personal, not just theoretical, so, as before, I've included a number of real-life stories. As I noted in the first edition, I have changed some names and personally identifying details to protect people's privacy, and in some cases I have altered event sequences or other minor details for the sake of brevity and clarity. Other than that, though, I've worked hard to ensure the accuracy of the particulars, relying not only on my own memory but also on hundreds of pages of saved emails, journal entries, and other documents—including some I discovered after the first edition had been written.

I am eternally grateful to Wendy Grisham and her team for making the first edition of *Torn* possible and to Beth Adams and the Worthy team for believing in and working so hard on this updated edition. This book would never have happened without them—nor without my wonderful agent, Greg Daniel, who walked me through the publishing process when I was a first-time writer and answered all my stupid questions. Many thanks are due, also, to my friends and family for their encouragement and to everyone who lent their stories to this book and/or offered feedback to help make it better.

The incredible response to *Torn* has been one of the greatest blessings of my entire life. Thank you to everyone who has supported this book, and thank you to everyone who has written to tell me how you've used it. I have been truly touched by every one of your stories.

Ultimate thanks are, of course, due to God, who has seen me through far more than I could ever recount here.

In all things, no matter how we disagree, may we always keep our sights set on Christ, who is faithful to heal our torn and broken hearts.

Justin Lee
2024

torn

CHAPTER 1

◆

BATTLE OF THE CENTURY

Some years ago, I was working at a Christian ministry when a call came in from a woman in tears.

"I'm calling about my son..." she began, then stopped. She seemed to be struggling to get the next words out. After a long pause, all she managed was a whispered "I'm sorry..." as she tried to regain her composure.

"It's okay," I said quietly. "Take your time."

She swallowed, took a deep breath, and started again.

Her name was Cindy. She was the mother of a fifteen-year-old boy. He was her only child, her pride and joy. He was, she explained to me, a good kid. The best kid. Kind, loyal, honest. A good student. Active in the church youth group. A committed Christian. She and her husband couldn't have been prouder.

And then, with one revelation, their whole world had changed. Late one night, their precious son had confessed to them that he had realized he was gay.

In the two weeks since, Cindy and her husband had been through a wide range of emotions, wondering what they'd done wrong and what to do next. They'd read and reread the relevant Bible passages, scoured the internet for information, and had numerous conversations with their son, hoping for some sign that he wasn't gay after all. Much to their chagrin, he kept insisting that he was.

More than anything else, Cindy was afraid for her son. She was afraid of what this would mean for his relationship with God, and she was afraid of all the hardships, dangers, and loneliness he might face as a gay man. But of all the things on her mind, there was one she kept coming back to over and over in our conversation.

Most of all, it seemed, she was afraid of their church.

The family had long been members of a rural, conservative evangelical church. "It's a wonderful church," she assured me. "They're wonderful people. But this—if they found out about this, they would never treat him the same way again. I know it."

And that possibility troubled her deeply. For Cindy, church was far more than just a weekly worship service. It was a life-giving community of fellow believers, a place of unconditional support in times of trouble, and a way to grow spiritually and become more like Jesus. It was the flesh-and-blood Body of Christ at work in our world.

Until now, she had always taken comfort in the knowledge that, no matter what might happen in their lives, the church would be a place of refuge for her and her family. Even if her son had someday rebelled and *rejected* the church, she had known that the church would always be there, ready to welcome him back. But if the *church* rejected her *son*—what then?

Whatever mistakes her son might make in life, Cindy was sure God would have mercy on him. The church, she feared, might not.

◆

Cindy's not alone. After I told her story in the first edition of this book, I heard from parents across the country who told me that they, too, were feeling less welcome in their churches after their children came out of the closet. Many described feeling torn between their love for God and their love for their child, worried that being faithful to one might somehow mean letting the other down.

And that really upsets Martin, one of many pastors I sat down with to discuss the situation. Over coffee, Martin told me how much he hated the idea of anyone feeling unwelcome or unsafe in church. He said he hoped everyone—including Cindy, her husband, and their son—would feel welcome to attend his church and hear the gospel. No exceptions.

But this is a tough situation for Martin too. Like many Christian leaders, he's worried that society is moving away from biblical teachings and taking large sections of the church with it. Yes, everyone is welcome, he said, but that doesn't mean that every sexual practice or identity is okay with God. As a pastor, he feels a responsibility to preach the Bible even when it doesn't line up with our world's changing values. Homosexuality is one area where he feels he must take a stand. He's struggling with how to do that without causing further pain for families like Cindy's.

"There's no doubt in my mind about what the Bible says about homosexuality," Martin said to me. "But I truly do want to love the gay community. I'm just trying to figure out how to express that in a way that doesn't sound phony."

I nodded. I'd been hearing the same thing from Christian leaders around the world. They felt torn too. They didn't want to contribute to hate or unkindness toward gay people or the broader LGBTQ[1] community; they genuinely wanted to love them the way God loves us all. But they couldn't disregard biblical teachings, either, and some of the things they saw in Scripture seemed clearly at odds with what they saw in the LGBTQ-affirming culture around them. They were trying to combine truth and love, but it wasn't being received the way they intended.

"What do *you* think?" Martin asked me. "You've talked to a lot of people. How does a church like mine make the gay community feel loved and truly welcomed? Or is that not possible as long as we don't agree with them?"

I took a sip of my coffee and thought about my answer.

◆

Outside the church, homosexuality is becoming more and more accepted in American society. In 2004, fewer than a third of Americans supported legal same-sex marriage.[2] By 2023, that number had risen to nearly two-thirds.[3] That's a dramatic shift in less than twenty years, and it's likely to continue; today's young people are far more gay-affirming than their parents' and grandparents' generations.

And that's created a real dilemma. Martin and many pastors like him are worried that if they don't take a strong stand, their churches could fall victim to a cultural slippery slope. Meanwhile, parents like Cindy tell me that they're worried their churches' harsh words are pushing their children away from Jesus.

And there's reason to think those parents could be right. A 2022 study by the Public Religion Research Institute found that religious negativity toward LGBTQ people was one of the biggest factors causing people to turn from God, with almost half of religiously unaffiliated Americans citing it as a reason they left their faith—more than those who cited other reasons like church scandals or politics.[4]

Of course, truth isn't a popularity contest. Jesus himself was rejected by many who found his teachings too difficult. The bigger issue is whether we are representing Jesus well as his Body in the world. Unfortunately, it seems clear that we aren't.

An early sign of this came from a 2007 study by the Barna Group, a Christian research firm. In the study, researchers asked 16- to 29-year-olds to choose words and phrases to describe modern Christianity. Among the many choices available to them were positive terms like "offers hope" and "has good values" along with negative terms like "judgmental" and "hypocritical."

Out of all of it—good and bad—the most popular choice was "antihomosexual." Not only did 91 percent of the non-Christians describe the church this way, but 80 percent of the *churchgoers* did as well.

In their book *unChristian*, Barna Group researchers David Kinnaman and Gabe Lyons explained their findings this way:

> In our research, the perception that Christians are "against" gays and lesbians...has reached critical mass. The gay issue has become the "big one," the negative image most likely to be intertwined with Christianity's reputation....Outsiders say our hostility toward gays—not just opposition to homosexual politics and behaviors but disdain for gay individuals—has become virtually synonymous with the Christian faith.[5]

That last sentence is especially troubling. It's bad enough for Christians to be more known for an *issue* than we are for the gospel. But it's even worse if we're known not for our *position* on an issue but for our *hostility* and *disdain* for an entire group of people. Issues come and go, and society's focus on any particular disagreement can be short-lived. But if we have a reputation for *treating people badly*, that sticks to us long after the controversy itself has faded.

Sadly, in the years since that Barna study, that's exactly what we've seen.

I didn't always think this. Growing up in a conservative Christian home, I knew that we disapproved of homosexuality in general, but I never thought we had "disdain for gay individuals." Now, however, I'm convinced that Kinnaman and Lyons are right: Christians don't just have a reputation for being against gay *sex* or against gay *marriage*; we have a reputation for being hostile to gay *people*.

This is disturbing news for all of us in the Christian community. Jesus wasn't known for his *disdain* or *hostility* toward people; he was known for his unconditional *love* for everyone, especially outcasts and sinners. One of the charges Jesus' opponents had against him was that he was "a glutton and a drunkard, a friend of tax collectors and sinners."[6] Surely the faith he founded should never be known for looking down on *anyone*. After all, isn't the whole message of the gospel that all of us are sinners and fall short of God's glory, and that's why Jesus had to die for us and why we so need grace?[7]

In one of Jesus' parables, a king forgives a servant's massive debt. The servant then goes out to find a fellow servant who owes *him* a much smaller sum and demands that he pay immediately or be thrown in prison. When the king finds out, he is angry and has the first servant thrown in prison instead.[8] Jesus' message is clear: We've been shown so much grace from God that we must be gracious to others.

In another parable, Jesus tells of two people who go to the temple to pray. One, a devoutly religious man, prays, "God, I thank you that I am not like other people—robbers, evildoers, adulterers— or even like this tax collector. I fast twice a week and give a tenth of all I get." The other prays only, "God, have mercy on me, a sinner."[9] It is the second man, the sinful and ostracized tax collector, who goes home justified before God. Why, then, do so many people think Christians sound more like the first guy?

Meanwhile, with Christians widely perceived to be against gays, it's no surprise that many gay people are decidedly against Christians. But in a gays-vs.-Christians world, no one wins. The gospel gets lost, grace goes out the window, and millions of people with gay loved ones—people like Cindy—suddenly feel as if they're being asked to choose a side in some kind of epic cage match.

Ladies and gentlemen! Get your tickets now for the Battle of the Century! Gays vs. Christians! Who will control the future of our culture?

With that kind of mindset, every question is a competition and every issue is the field for a new battle. Disagreements over things like sexual morality turn into shouting matches that change no one's mind, and even terrible tragedies become excuses to blame our enemies.

This has been going on for quite some time. Two days after the horrifying 9/11 terrorist attacks, influential preacher Jerry Falwell blamed gays in part for what he viewed as a sign of God's wrath on America, saying, "I point the finger in their face and say, 'You helped this happen.'"

"Well, I totally concur," televangelist Pat Robertson responded. Both men later said they regretted the exchange, but it continued to be referenced for a long time by gay people I know as proof of Christians' true feelings about them.

Years later, popular gay columnist Dan Savage—himself the child of Christian parents—angrily lashed out at the Christians he viewed as responsible for a rash of gay teen suicides:

> The dehumanizing bigotries that fall from lips of "faithful Christians," and the lies that spew forth from the pulpit of the churches "faithful Christians" drag their kids to on Sundays, give your straight children a license to verbally abuse, humiliate and condemn the gay children they encounter at school. And many of your straight children—having listened to mom and dad talk about how gay marriage is a threat to the family and how gay sex makes their magic sky friend Jesus cry himself to sleep—feel justified in physically attacking the gay and lesbian children they encounter in their schools....

Oh, and those same dehumanizing bigotries that fill your straight children with hate? They fill your gay children with suicidal despair. And you have the nerve to ask *me* to be more careful with my words.[10]

Perhaps the most visible symbol of the gays-vs.-Christians culture war is the controversial Westboro Baptist Church, a hate group famous for picketing events like Pride marches and funerals of gay people, carrying signs that read "God hates fags" along with various Bible verses.

The truth is far more complex than these examples suggest, but they still resonate in our culture as extreme illustrations of a conflict that shows up on a smaller scale in a thousand different ways, from the pulpit to the ballot box.

Part of the issue is that sexual morality is a big deal to Christians, and many Christians have been concerned that our culture's rethinking of gender and sexuality is leading people away from biblical teaching and God's will for their lives. But that's not the whole story. Whatever views they might hold on same-sex marriage or sexual behavior, I don't know any Christians who want *that* to be the primary thing the church is known for. If it is, that suggests that something somewhere has gone horribly wrong.

But how do we fix it?

It's easy to say that we shouldn't have a gays-vs.-Christians mindset. What's much harder is to determine what we *should* do. Some churches and denominations have publicly moved to affirm gay people and same-sex relationships, sparking concerns that they're abandoning scriptural truth to appease a fallen world. Others, like Martin's church, have pushed back, standing firm in their opposition to homosexuality while attempting to be more loving in their approach, but critics charge that this talk of love too often rings hollow in practice, leaving people like Cindy feeling isolated in their own churches.

Meanwhile, the situation is getting *more* complex, not less so. Conversations about gender identity and transgender people have raised a whole new set of questions—affecting even more people. To the world, *gays vs. Christians* increasingly looks like *LGBTQs and families and friends vs. Christians*—as we become more and more known for the people we're "against" rather than being known for showing the love of Jesus.

Something has to change. We need to get this right, and to do so, we need to understand what's gone wrong.

Over the last thirty years, I've been prayerfully studying and writing about these questions while God has taken me on an incredible, often painful, but ultimately inspiring journey that has shaped my views and forced me to confront my own mistakes. I could tell you what I think now, but when it comes to this debate, opinions are a dime a dozen.

Instead, I'd like to share with you what I've experienced and how it radically altered my approach to an issue I thought I knew everything about.

And it all started with the kid in high school who called me "God Boy."

CHAPTER 2

❖

GOD BOY

H ey, God Boy, I have a question for you."

Sean grinned at me from across the lunch table in our high school cafeteria. We were sixteen-year-old high school sophomores, at that wonderful age when you think you know everything.

Okay, to be fair, as a teenager I *hated* it when adults made jokes about "teenagers who think they know everything." It sounded condescending and rude. I didn't actually think I knew *everything*, and my most recent history test had just proved it.

However, I did think I was pretty smart, and (that last history test excepted) my academic record bore that out. I was a straight-A student taking challenging, top-level classes at a challenging, top-rated high school for the academically gifted. My bookshelf at home held a collection of math and computer competition trophies I had won over the years, and while I didn't brag about my academic achievements, I tended to be the kid in several of my classes who messed up the curve by doing "too well" on tests.

Yeah, I was *that* kid.

Learning had taught me that, as smart as I was, there was always more to know. But if there was any area where my teenage know-it-allness came out in full force, it was my faith.

I was a committed Christian, and everybody knew it. If I didn't have a Bible in my backpack, I at least had a church bulletin and some tracts about salvation. I was ready to witness to anybody, anywhere, at the drop of a hat. More than anything in the world, I wanted to represent my God well, and I prayed every day for the wisdom and opportunities to do so. I was confident in my knowledge of my faith and always eager to explain some minor point of theology to my friends and classmates.

Yeah, I was *that* kid too.

Sean was a friend of a friend who sometimes joined my friends at lunch. He had teasingly nicknamed me "God Boy," and he took special pleasure in trotting out the nickname whenever he was going to ask me about a controversial religious or political issue of the day. He wasn't particularly religious himself, but he enjoyed coming up with hypothetical moral quandaries to pose to me, just to see how I'd handle them.

For my part, I enjoyed the challenge. I had studied the Bible from a young age, and I knew it well. Whenever Sean called me "God Boy," I knew he was challenging me to express my faith intelligently. *Bring it on*, I silently thought. *I'm ready for you.* As I saw it, debates with Sean were a way to hone my rhetorical skills and share the truth of Christianity with a non-Christian. I knew I wanted to do ministry work in the future, so being forced to defend my faith seemed like great practice.

On this particular occasion, Sean had a gleam in his eye as he considered his question. Either he thought it would be tough, or he had other reasons for wanting to hear my response.

I put down my sandwich and met his gaze. The challenge was on. "Okay, what's the question?"

"What do you think about this big gay controversy? Whose side are you on?"

"Ah," I said. The question didn't come as a surprise. The whole school had been buzzing about it for the last few days.

The drama had started when some students anonymously taped up a poster in the school hallway. Titled "A Call to Arms," the poster handled the topic with all the subtlety and compassion of an angry bull.

"Attention all heterosexual students," it began. "Many of us have come to realize that we are in the presence of faggots and dykes!" It continued predictably into vicious hate speech, urging straight students to band together against their gay peers.

The poster was pulled down by faculty members as soon as they saw it, but it had already been seen by hundreds of students, leading to ripple effects throughout the school. Some laughed; some trembled; others dismissed it as irrelevant. But *everyone* was talking about it.

That evening, six students got together to write up a response. The next morning, they were distributing pamphlets of their own. The pamphlets mocked the language of the original poster and called for tolerance and understanding of gay students. The principal, likely seeking to avoid controversy, created one instead by suspending the six students who were pleading for tolerance.

It turned out that there was an old rule on the books that forbade the distribution of literature without prior administrative approval. The poster, with all its hate speech, had been anonymous. But the six students calling for tolerance had put their names on their work. They hadn't known—none of us had—that it would be against the rules for them to pass out something they had written in an attempt to do good.

The local media had a field day with the event. It was a juicy story: Students who wanted to combat hate speech with compassion had been suspended for their efforts! The fact that the story also touched on hot topics like school safety, free speech, and teenage sexuality only made it that much more controversial. As debate raged in the community, it became less and less about the actual school rules and more and more about taking a position on "the gay issue." Some students began protesting by wearing black armbands as a sign of support for their unnamed gay peers. Others wore white armbands to protest the protest.

Many of us didn't know, or didn't think we knew, anyone gay. It was the mid-1990s, a time when comparatively few people were out of the closet. Surveys showed that most Americans disapproved of homosexuality, but also that opinions were changing, and on both sides, there was a sense that something must be done—either to hasten that change or to prevent it. For some people, this was about freedom or diversity; for others, it was about faith and taking a moral stand.

It was a perfect storm of outrage and indignation on all sides. Sean took great pleasure in raising the subject just to see how God Boy would weigh in on it all. What could be more controversial than the much-hyped cultural battle of *gays vs. Christians*?

LOVE THE SINNER . . .

As far as I was aware, I had never met a gay person. I had seen them on TV and I had read about them in the newspaper, but I didn't know any personally. If there were gay people at our school, I had no idea who they were.

As a Christian, though, I did know a thing or two about homosexuality. For one thing, I knew that the Bible said it was a sin. I didn't have the passages memorized, but I remembered that it was called an abomination, and I knew that it was outside of God's design for our sexuality. God had created men and women for each other, and sex was supposed to be part of their lifelong bonding in marriage. I thought of sex like fire: Used properly, it was a beautiful and awesome thing. Used carelessly, it could create all manner of destruction—including unwanted pregnancies, sexually transmitted diseases, and psychological hurt. It wasn't just about calling things "sin" for the sake of it. God had created sex, He understood its power, and He had good reasons for giving us boundaries.

Homosexuality was outside of those boundaries. That didn't mean that God *hated* gay people; on the contrary, I was sure that God loved them! I was also sure, however, that God didn't want them to be gay. If homosexuality was a sin, why would God *make* people homosexuals? It didn't make any sense. I was pretty sure that meant people weren't "born gay."

This is why I, like many Christians, was concerned about the growing acceptance of homosexuality in our culture. Adolescence is a confusing time; I knew that well as a sixteen-year-old. Suppose other teenagers like me—teens who didn't have a strong faith like I did—heard people say that being gay was normal and acceptable; I worried that might lead them to declare themselves gay just because of a momentary same-sex thought or some other insecurity, and then the rest of their lives would go down a sinful path that could have been easily avoided. I saw it as my responsibility to speak up and warn people that the pro-gay messages they were hearing on TV were wrong, that no one was born gay, and that God had something better in store for them.

I knew some people would call this view homophobic. But I didn't hate or fear gay people; my whole point was wanting to love them the way God loved them. Loving people doesn't always mean agreeing with them. Sometimes you show your love for people by telling them what they need to hear instead of what they want to hear.

I considered how to apply this understanding to the situation at hand.

I hadn't seen the "Call to Arms" poster, but based on the descriptions I had heard from other students, I was disgusted by it. As a Christian, I have always opposed bullying and hate speech in any form. It's simply wrong. Yes, I had moral objections to homosexuality, but I would never, ever support calling people nasty names or threatening them. I was proud of the six students for standing up against that kind of hate speech.

But I had mixed feelings about the pamphlet they were distributing. I worried about the impact of their message, which was that it was okay and normal to be gay. I didn't believe that either.

I answered Sean with what I thought was the perfect Christian response: loving, compassionate, nuanced, and, above all, biblical.

"I think the words on that poster were wrong," I said. "God loves everyone, gay people included. There's no need for nasty language like that. But—"

"Here it comes," Sean interrupted.

"*But* it's still a sin," I said. "The Bible's clear on that. It's not God's best for us. But even though it's a sin, that doesn't mean God hates gay people. God loves us, and that's why He gives us rules to live by—so that we can have the abundant lives He's called us to."

"So basically, love the sinner, hate the sin?"

"Exactly!" I said. I smiled.

He didn't.

◆

At the time, I thought that conversation had gone exceptionally well. I felt good about defending the truths of Scripture in a way that was loving, not hateful. I was proud of myself for taking an unpopular stand in the face of a culture that was becoming more and more accepting of homosexuality. In short, I was sure that this was just how God wanted me to respond to a question like this. I imagined that even Jesus, though surely more eloquent than I, would have responded in a similar fashion. It was the only reasonable Christian approach.

Today, I'm embarrassed when I look back on that conversation. I recognize that my motives were good, and I still approach the issue as a Bible-believing Christian. But after everything I've been through, I now see many things about that situation that I didn't see at the time.

I'm ashamed to realize how my youth and pride blinded me to so much: The complexities of the question. The motives of the questioner. The unintentional callousness of my response. I thought I was sharing the gospel that day, when in fact I was probably only confirming Sean's negative views of Christians. A wiser Christian would have responded much differently.

Neither of us knew I was about to have a crash course in just how wrong I'd gotten things, a series of experiences that would transform me into a nationally recognized authority on this very subject, with a mission to forever alter the way Christians think about gay people.

God Boy's life was about to be turned upside down.

CHAPTER 3

◆

THE STRUGGLE

For all my confidence on the issue, there was one thing I couldn't tell Sean that day.

God Boy had a secret.

It was, I thought, the worst secret in the world. It was the deepest, darkest secret I could ever imagine having, one that I could never tell anyone, not even my parents or best friends. It was the secret I would take with me to my grave.

Years earlier, when I had first hit puberty and all my male friends were starting to "notice" girls, I was having the opposite experience: I was starting to "notice" other guys.

I wasn't a late bloomer; my young sex drive was kicking in right along with theirs, bringing with it all the mysterious feelings of attraction to classmates who had previously been only friends on the playground. But in my case, it was guys, not girls, who triggered this strange reaction.

At first I had simply ignored the feelings. With all the new sensations of puberty, I'd assumed these attractions to guys were just some sort of weird phase I had to pass through as I matured. I'd heard Christian authorities such as radio host Dr. James Dobson say that young teenagers sometimes went through a period of sexual confusion, and this seemed to be the proof. All of this only reinforced my view about the importance of opposing the normalization of homosexuality. What if someone else experienced feelings like these? They might think they were gay! Thank goodness I knew better.

I waited patiently to grow out of this phase. In the meantime, all I had to do was stay focused on the important things: my relationship with God, my schoolwork, my church, and my family. In time, this would pass. Of that I had no doubt.

But as I got older, I began to notice that none of my guy friends seemed to be going through the same sort of phase. More and more, their attentions turned toward girls, and a note of sexual tension was evident in their voices when they talked about them.

As kids, we had joked about who "liked" whom, but it had all been full of childish innocence. As teenagers, my guy friends had become interested in girls in a different way, and they talked eagerly about their eyes and lips and breasts and legs. I avoided these conversations, telling myself that the reason I didn't lust after women was that I was a good Christian boy. Lust was a sin, so I convinced myself I just didn't objectify women the way some of my friends did. That wouldn't have been Christlike, after all.

The truth, however, was that I didn't feel any of the things they did. I wasn't overcoming some great moral struggle to avoid lusting after women; in actuality, I didn't have any sexual feelings toward women at all. My sex drive was in full swing, but it was directed at guys, not girls, and I didn't know how to change it.

I was just beginning to recognize all of this when my best friend asked me about it one day on the way to class. "You never talk about girls, Justin. What's up with that?"

I panicked, terrified he would discover my secret. "I just want to be a gentleman, so I don't talk about them like that." It was true, but not the whole truth.

"Well, yeah," he persisted, "but isn't there any girl you like?"

My mind raced. I thought about all the girls we knew. One in particular popped into my head, a girl I considered a good friend. "Suzanne," I said. "But don't tell anybody."

"Ah!" He seemed thrilled to be my confidant. "What do you like about Suzanne?"

What did I like about her? I didn't know. I had just picked her so I'd have someone to name. "I dunno," I said. "She's nice."

Apparently this was the wrong answer. "Well, sure, but what about physically? Don't you think she's pretty?"

Pretty? The thought had never occurred to me.

It was an awkward conversation, but it was also a relief to finally have a girl I "liked." I began to talk about Suzanne more and more with my friends, secretly hoping that if I talked and thought about girls more, my natural attractions for them would eventually develop and I'd begin to feel what all the other guys felt.

My dad and I had a close relationship, and I had always felt like I could tell him anything. So one evening, during some private father-son time over a game of pool, I decided to broach the subject of Suzanne. I mentioned that there was a girl at school I was interested in.

"Tell me all about her!"

"Well, she's really nice…," I began, but then realized I didn't know what else to say about her.

"What does she look like?" he asked.

I didn't know how to describe her. I really hadn't thought much about her looks.

"For instance, what color hair does she have?" he offered helpfully.

"Blond," I said.

"Ooh, a blonde!" he said with a sly grin. "Blondes do have a certain allure, don't they?"

It was just the sort of conversation a father and son are supposed to have. And yet, for the first time in my life, I felt something I couldn't say to my dad. How could I tell him what I was really feeling, that I didn't care that she was blond, or what she looked like at all, that I never thought about any girls like that, but that there *was* a blond boy I couldn't get out of my head—a classmate with a shy smile and cute dimples and bright green eyes? Argh! How could I even think such things about a boy?

Still, I was convinced this was just a phase. It was going to be my deep, dark secret until I grew out of this period of sexual confusion, and then I'd fall in love with a beautiful girl, and we'd get married and have kids and I'd live my life in service to God. I just knew that was how things would go.

◆

I dated girls in high school, and even though I wasn't physically attracted to them, I was sure that those feelings would develop in time.

What concerned me more was that my feelings for guys weren't going away. They were just getting stronger and stronger as I matured. I found myself struggling to concentrate on my schoolwork and my faith, trying my best to avoid thinking about attractive guys. Even if I could keep my mind off of guys during the day, though, I'd go to sleep at night and have dreams about guys. I'd wake up in the morning feeling sick and disgusted with myself. Something was really wrong with me, but I couldn't tell anyone. I was too ashamed of my own feelings.

Night after night, I cried myself to sleep, begging and pleading with God to take away my sexual attractions to other guys. "Please don't let me feel this anymore," I'd pray over and over, sure that God would take the feelings away eventually, but wanting it to be soon. I hated myself for what I felt, and I was desperate to be rid of it.

On the outside, I was the kid every parent wanted their kid to be: a good student, active in the church, trustworthy, independent, and a smiling friend to anyone who needed one. Inside, I was falling apart.

My senior year of high school, I met a girl named Liz, and we became fast friends. She was a committed Christian, a gymnast, and an overall fun person to be around. We would go to church youth events, hang out at the mall, and go for walks in the park. The more we did together, the more I realized that she was everything I wanted in a girl. She was funny, spontaneous, cheerful, honest, and, above all, a Christian. We spent so much time together that our friends started to joke that we were going out "by default," since I had never actually asked her out.

Wanting to be romantic, I asked her out for the first time on Valentine's Day, but our making ourselves officially "a couple" didn't really change our relationship at all. I enjoyed the innocent friendship-based relationship we had, and I was in no hurry to move on to anything physical. I did the things a boyfriend was supposed to do—holding doors for her, paying for meals, putting my arm around her at the movies—but there was never any physical aspect to the relationship. I just didn't think of her in that way. My friends told me she was "hot," and one in particular was drooling over her, but to me she was just someone I enjoyed hanging out with. I didn't see her as physically attractive, but I was sure that I would...someday.

I felt kind of awkward cuddling with her, but I did it happily because I cared about her and I wanted to be a good boyfriend to her. Still, the romantic part of me wanted to save our first kiss for a time when I really felt the urge to kiss her. After months of dating, including the prom, I still hadn't done any more than kiss her on the cheek.

Things seemed to be going well, until the night I took Liz to see a concert by two of my favorite Christian artists, Michael W. Smith and Jars of Clay.

The evening was beautiful and the music was powerful. We sat there entranced, holding hands and swaying to the melodies. For a moment, my life seemed perfect.

Then, out of the blue, I noticed a face in the crowd. He was another young guy, there to see the concert, walking past us to rejoin his group. I only saw him for an instant, but I couldn't help noticing his attractive features, and suddenly I found my thoughts and emotions rushing toward him. I wanted to know everything about him. Who was he? Who had he come with? Where was he going? Where did he go to school? I wanted to meet him, to talk to him, to get to know him, to spend time with him. I think I would have been content just to sit near him and stare at him for the rest of the night.

I knew nothing about this guy, but just seeing him gave me feelings unlike anything I had ever felt around a girl. He intrigued me, tempted me, attracted me. For an instant, my head was filled with thoughts of him.

And then I suddenly caught myself. Here I was, holding hands with the most wonderful girl in the world—a girl whom I loved dearly and who loved me, my girlfriend, whom I even would have been willing to marry someday—and yet all I could think about was some guy I happened to glimpse in a crowd. What was wrong with me? Why did I still have these feelings after so many years of trying to be rid of them? Wasn't God hearing the urgent prayers I had cried for so long, asking not to have these horrible, perverted, unwanted feelings for other guys?

The song playing was an emotional one, so no one noticed the tears trickling down my cheeks.

The rest of the concert was a blur for me. All I could think was, *What's wrong with me?* Liz noticed my mood on the way home, but I couldn't tell her the truth. I was too scared to let my secret out, and too worried that it would hurt her if she knew.

The experience disturbed me, but all I knew to do was to keep doing what I always did: praying about it and focusing on my schoolwork.

Then, one night, everything changed.

I was online, chatting with some of my friends and other local students. One of them, Brian, was a friend of a friend at another school. We didn't know each other well, but there was something about him that made him different from the other boys I knew. Something about him seemed familiar—something I could connect with. But I couldn't put my finger on exactly what it was or why I found our connection so compelling.

On this particular occasion, Brian and I chatted late into the night. I needed to go to bed, but I couldn't tear myself away from the conversation. Something about this guy made sense to me in a way I couldn't explain. And the longer we chatted, the more keenly aware I became of just how similar he and I really were. Even though we hadn't broached the topic at all, I suddenly knew he was different in the same way I was different. And I needed to know what that was.

Brian seemed to feel it too. "There's something I should probably tell you," he finally admitted.

He paused. I caught my breath. This was it. He was going to tell me the thing that I had never been able to tell anyone.

"I'm bisexual," he typed.

And I burst into tears.

I cried more that night than I ever had in my life. For years, I had thought I was the only one in the world tormented by these feelings of attraction to other guys. Now here was someone else with the same feelings, and he had a word for them: *bisexual*. Finally, I wasn't the only one in the world. I wasn't alone. Someone else was like me.

I was...bisexual.

The word brought equal parts horror and comfort. It was like having suffered for years with strange medical symptoms no doctor could explain, only to finally be diagnosed with some rare illness. Even if the prognosis for the illness isn't good, there's something comforting about finally having a name for what you feel. Knowing that you're not the only one to have experienced the symptoms, that there's an explanation and a diagnosis for what is happening to you, is a powerful thing.

That's what the word *bisexual* was for me. It was a diagnosis. It was the word to describe what was wrong with me. Realizing that I was "bisexual" didn't mean I was establishing it as a core part of my being; that place belonged only to my faith. *Bisexual* was, in my eyes, just the name for the disease I had, and identifying it was the first step to finding a cure. Finally having that diagnosis, I felt hopeful about my sexuality for the first time in a long time.

There was only one problem with this. The word *bisexual* refers to people who experience significant attraction to both males and females. The truth was that I *wasn't* attracted to both males and females. Even though I was dating a girl and wanted desperately to be attracted to her, I had still never experienced even a moment of attraction for a woman, ever, in my life. All of my attractions were for other guys.

I didn't want to admit to myself that there was a different word for guys who are only attracted to other guys. That word was not *bisexual*, but it was a word I was nowhere near ready to use for myself.

I confided my deep, dark secret to Brian that night. It was the first time I had ever admitted to anyone that I was attracted to other guys. I told him how confused I was and how I didn't know what to do about it. He told me that he had found a boyfriend at school and that he was very happy. I cried more, because I knew a same-sex relationship was something I could never accept. Unlike him, I had to be rid of these feelings. My faith required it.

CHAPTER 4

◆

THE TRUTH COMES OUT

At the time, I had no idea where these feelings came from or why I had them. In chapter 5, I'll share some of the things I've learned since then that may shed some light on that question. Back then, it was still a complete mystery to me.

What I did know was that I was a Christian. Somehow I had to find a way to deal with this as a Christian. Encouraged by my discovery that I wasn't alone, but still terrified to tell anyone in my life what I was feeling, I turned to the internet for answers.

My first search brought only websites discussing why Christians should oppose homosexuality. I already knew that, but what were you supposed to do when the "it" you were opposing was inside yourself? Another search brought more of the same, and a third search led me to the website of a church that claimed you could be a committed Christian in a same-sex relationship and that God would be okay with that. *Ludicrous*, I thought. *Clearly they haven't read their Bibles.*

Finally, I stumbled upon the website I was hoping for: a Christian ministry offering support to "Christians struggling with homosexuality." It was a simple website with precious few details, but I read them over and over. The site didn't offer any specifics about what sort of support they offered, nor did it give any physical address or phone number. I didn't care. Here was evidence that someone out there could help me.

The only contact information the site offered was an email address to write to for more information. With trembling hands, I slowly typed out my confession, that I was a Christian teenage male who was attracted to other guys and that I didn't want to be. I took my time, chewing over each word, worrying the whole time about whether someone I knew might somehow see this message and trace it back to me. I reassured myself that this couldn't happen and sent the email. Now I just had to wait.

I went to bed that night happy. My troubles would soon be over.

At school the next day, I could barely concentrate. All I could think about was hearing back from the anonymous web ministry. When I got home, I raced to my computer, booted it up, and checked my email.

No response.

The next day was much the same. I doodled and daydreamed my way through class, able to focus on only one thing—hearing back from someone who would understand my situation. Alas, I returned to my computer that evening only to find an empty virtual mailbox.

This continued, day after day, for the next couple of weeks. With time, my hope of hearing from them vanished, and my hope of finding support vanished along with it.

I never did hear back from them.

With or without these strangers on the internet, I knew I couldn't continue to keep my struggles a secret. I was going to need the support of other Christians in my life to deal with this, and that meant I would have to tell the truth about what I was going through.

The idea terrified me. How could I tell others I wasn't straight when I could barely even admit it to myself? And yet, now that I *had* faced it myself, the need to talk to someone about it was growing every day. Plus, I thought, if having the support of other Christians meant that I could become straight faster, then I was willing to do it. To finally be rid of this burden, I was ready to do almost anything, however difficult it might be.

Just like that, my mind was made up. My deepest, darkest secret in the world, the secret I was sure I would take to my grave, was about to be a secret no longer. I was going to have to risk my reputation, the respect people had for me, and the relationships I had with friends and family, for the sake of being honest and finding a solution to the predicament I was in.

And I knew what that meant: I had to tell my girlfriend.

Liz already knew something was wrong. After the night at the concert, she hadn't pressed me for details, but she knew I was struggling with something stressful, and she wanted to help. I just didn't know how to tell the girl I'd been dating for months that I dreamed about guys instead of girls.

It had taken me years of dealing with my own feelings before I could admit them to myself, so I had no idea how anyone else would respond to the news without that time to process it. Telling Liz right away seemed too risky, so I needed to test the news out on someone else first. But who?

The answer came during a conversation with Brittany, a member of my church and a mutual friend of mine and Liz's. Brittany was a committed Christian and someone I trusted. Since she was a girl, I thought she might respond better than my guy friends.

Over the course of another tearful late-night internet chat, I confessed everything to Brittany. After swearing her to secrecy, I started typing and everything just spilled out: my years of struggle, my internet friendship with Brian, my desire to serve God, my fear about telling Liz. Brittany was shocked, but she offered to pray for me, and she encouraged me to tell Liz the truth. "I think she'll understand," she advised.

I broke the news to Liz while sitting on the curb outside my church after a youth event. It was the first time I had ever said the words out loud, and it proved to be much harder than typing them on a computer screen. With my voice constantly threatening to give out on me, I tried several times to work up to the revelation. In the end, the most I could get out was, "I'm not…straight." And then I was crying again.

She said it was okay. She told me she loved me. She said that no matter what, she'd always be there for me.

I didn't ask how she was doing. I was so caught up in my own pain and fear, it never occurred to me that my girlfriend was trying her best to mask her own sadness in order to support me.

I told her that I still wanted to keep dating if she wanted to, and that I just needed her prayers right now to help me overcome this temporary setback. I wasn't going to be "this way" forever; I just needed to get support and therapy and keep trusting God, and soon everything would be normal and I'd be rid of these horrible feelings.

I was sure of it.

BYE-BYE, BI

Once I'd told Liz, I felt better—for a little while. But the burden of this secret continued to weigh on me. So far, only three people knew: a guy from the internet I'd never met, a girl from church I rarely saw, and *my girlfriend*. I needed to be able to talk about this with someone in person. Someone I could open up to and trust— who *wasn't* my girlfriend.

Hesitantly, I settled on the idea of sharing my struggle with a couple of close friends from school. Over a period of weeks, I worked up the courage to drop some hints with various friends and see how they responded. I'd gently bring up the topic of same-sex attractions in a vague, theoretical sense, and if a friend reacted negatively, I'd quickly change the subject and never bring it up again. But when a couple of my friends seemed understanding, I gradually moved the conversation from theory to reality: "What if someone you *knew* was like that? Could you still be friends with them?"

My friends promised to keep my secret, even though the subject seemed to make them uncomfortable.

Then one night, one of them asked the question I didn't want to face.

"How do you know you're bi?" he asked me.

"What do you mean?" I said. "I'm attracted to guys."

"What I mean is...how do you know you're not *gay*?"

"I'm not gay," I said indignantly. "I'm not anything like that. I love Liz. We're dating. I'm going to get married someday. I'm not gay."

"So you're telling me that you are equally attracted to both men *and* women?" he persisted.

"Yes," I lied.

"You have sexual feelings and fantasies toward women?"

"Well, I mean...I don't think that way."

"Okay, so when you see an attractive woman, is there a part of you that wants to imagine her with her clothes off?"

"No, but..."

"And you don't think that's odd?"

"But I'm a Christian, and I don't think about women that way. I *respect* them. I think that's how this whole trouble started. Maybe I just respect them so much that I didn't allow myself to think about them sexually, and my sex drive got a little confused or something."

He laughed.

"That's not funny!" I protested.

"I don't know, but I don't think it works that way. I respect women too, you know. But I have a daily struggle to keep from lusting after them, because that's what my sex drive naturally wants to do if I don't keep a rein on it. Do you have a daily struggle?"

"No," I admitted. I *did* have a daily struggle to keep from lusting after guys, though.

"Do you dream about women at night?"

"No. Not really."

"Respecting women doesn't turn off your sex drive, Justin. I don't think you're really bi."

"You can't see in my head," I countered, and changed the subject.

I didn't want to admit it, but he was right. I had never had a sexual thought or attraction for a woman in my life. The real reason I called myself bi was that it didn't sound so scary. If I was bi, all I had to do was get rid of my same-sex attractions and keep the opposite-sex ones. But if I was gay, things were going to be a whole lot harder than I had imagined.

That night, I put it out of my mind, but as time passed I began to realize the truth in what my friend had said. As scary as the label was, the truth was that I wasn't bi. I was gay.

Gay.

The word seemed to hold the weight of eternity within its single syllable.

As strange as it may seem, in all the years I had struggled with my sexuality, the idea that I could be gay had simply never crossed my mind. I was a Christian! That was my whole life! And Christians weren't gay.

I already had an image of what gay people were like. They were sinners who had turned from God and had an "agenda" to mainstream their perverse lifestyles. I didn't actually know any gay people, but I had seen them in video footage of Pride parades, where they were dressed in outrageous outfits or wearing next to nothing at all, and I knew that they engaged in all kinds of deviant sexual practices. I had nothing in common with people like that, so how could I be gay?

Even after realizing it was true, it was a long time before I could bring myself to breathe the word aloud.

I sat up late at night, after everyone else had gone to bed, trying to come to grips with what this word meant for my life. In my softest whisper, paranoid about being overheard by anyone, I tried to muster up enough courage to say to myself those two words: "I'm gay."

"I'm…" A pause. A deep breath.

"I'm…"

But the *g* word would never come. It was dark and frightening. I knew it was true, but I couldn't bring myself to say it, not even in a barely audible whisper alone in my room at night.

◇

It's funny how our brains work. Once you become aware of something for the first time—a new vocabulary word, for instance—you begin to see it everywhere, and you wonder how you never noticed it before.

I had been feeling for a while that something was different about me, but I hadn't really understood what it was. Now that I knew, everything around me seemed to reinforce that I was a freak. Suddenly, it seemed that every guy I knew was talking non-stop about hot girls, with me only pretending to agree. *Fag* and *gay* had become ubiquitous insults overnight; I was sure they hadn't been before. Every TV show featured punch lines about a straight guy being mistaken for gay, resulting in raucous laughter from the audience. Every sermon at church was about either the goodness of marriage or the sinfulness of homosexuality.

Though none of them knew it, they were talking about *me*. Laughing at *me*. Condemning *me*. And it was getting to me.

I couldn't stay like this. I had to become straight. But how long would it take? Was it really fair for me to ask Liz to keep waiting indefinitely for me to feel something, someday, that I still didn't feel?

For her part, Liz had been doing her own research. The next time I saw her, she had a book in her hand.

"I checked this out for you," she said. "I don't know what the answers are, but I thought this might help." She passed the book to me.

I stared down at it, horrified. She had given me a book about gay Christians who had accepted themselves as gay, a book that seemed to suggest that God would be okay with same-sex partnerships.

Outwardly, I tried to be gracious. I knew she was only trying to help and that this whole subject was as new to her as it was to me. Inwardly, I was fuming. How could she give me something like this? Didn't she know that homosexuality was contrary to God's will? Wasn't she supposed to be praying for God to heal me? Had she already given up hope? Was she really willing to violate God's Word, or encourage me to do so? What kind of Christian was she? Perhaps, I thought, I had been wrong to date her—not because of my lack of attraction to her, but because anyone who could possibly accept homosexuality couldn't be a serious Christian. I only dated *serious* Christians.

All of these thoughts ran through my head as I accepted the book. I took it home with me and debated whether I should even open it. I wanted to be informed on the subject, but I feared that it might just be temptation from the devil. Reluctantly and with much prayer, I finally decided to see what it had to say and began leafing through its pages. Just as I had expected, it was wholly unconvincing. The writing was poor and unprofessional. The biblical arguments it made for accepting gay couples were flimsy. The book did nothing to convince me that gay couples were okay in God's eyes. On the contrary, it convinced me even more that I needed to become straight.

In the meantime, I gradually realized, I couldn't keep dating a girl I had no attraction to when I didn't even know how long it would take me to become attracted to women. She deserved better. She deserved to have someone long for her the way other guys longed for their girlfriends. For now, I couldn't give her that.

She also deserved to have me tell her the truth about my feelings. I'm sorry to say, though, that I took the coward's way out, letting our relationship gradually fade away as I prepared to move away to college. I can only imagine how difficult it must have been for her. All I could think about was how scared I was—of what I had discovered about myself and of what she would say if she knew that I had never truly been attracted to her in all the months we had been dating.

If I could live that time in my life over again, I would be up-front with her from the beginning about my feelings, confessing that I'd realized I was gay, not bi, and opening up about all I was going through. In reality, I was too ashamed to tell her the truth. Our relationship fizzled out, no doubt leaving her wondering what exactly had happened and leaving me feeling more alone than ever. All over one little word I couldn't bring myself to even speak aloud.

PASTOR RICK AND THE SECRET SOCIETY

I wasn't going to let that word define me. I couldn't. Instead, I continued to focus on my one primary goal: becoming straight. Whatever might have caused my attractions to guys, I was sure being gay wasn't what God wanted for me. It definitely wasn't what I wanted for myself.

For one thing, I wanted to have a family someday. I had imagined it many times: wife, kids, and a house in the suburbs. I couldn't have that if I was gay. I wasn't willing to marry a woman to whom I had no attraction, and I wasn't willing to enter into a sinful relationship with a man. The way I saw it, the only thing standing between me and my perfect future was my complete lack of attraction to women.

There was also another matter: As simplistic as it sounds, I wanted to fit in. I didn't mind distinguishing myself by being at the top of my class or standing up for what I believed in as a Christian; I was happy to be known for those things. Those were good things. But I was the good kid, not the rebel. I was "God Boy." And in my book, being gay was a bad thing. Everyone I looked up to viewed homosexuality as a sin and gay people as sinners. Never in a million years would I want to be known for something sinful.

Ultimately, it came down to one thing. My life had a single purpose: to serve God. I wasn't going to jeopardize that for anything. If God had created people male and female, designed for each other, and if the Bible condemned homosexuality, as I was pretty sure it did, then God clearly did not intend for me to be gay. Whatever might have gone wrong to make this happen, I knew God had the power to fix it. To fix *me*. I just needed willingness and faith.

I was willing. I had faith. Now what was I supposed to do? Was it just a matter of praying and trusting God, or was there more to the equation?

Once again, the internet was my resource. I began searching for information on orientation change, going from gay to straight. This time, I found exactly what I was looking for: groups known as "ex-gay ministries," Christian organizations that offered to help gay people become straight. I eagerly began reading everything I could about these groups. On their websites, they promised "freedom from homosexuality" for all who wanted it. One site had a list of people who had lived gay lives in the past but who had overcome their homosexuality through Jesus. Now they were heterosexually married, and many of them had kids.

That could be me! I thought.

I stayed up late that night, reading and rereading. This was exactly what I had hoped to find. This proved that I could be straight. Most of these men had lived sexually promiscuous lives with other men before turning their lives around. If even they could become straight, then surely I could! All I had were feelings; I hadn't acted on those feelings at all. That had to be a point in my favor. There was hope for me. I could be normal.

Eager for support, I nervously confided my struggle in my Sunday school teacher, a man I strongly admired. He put me in touch with Rick, an assistant pastor at my church who, he said, had experience working with the issue. That summer, following my high school graduation, Rick and I had conversations about my situation. He didn't seem surprised by my story, and he told me there were many others like me, committed Christians who had same-sex attractions through no fault or choice of their own. He assured me that it was often possible to undo the damage of whatever might have flipped this switch in my brain. In his opinion, I could ultimately be rid of this burden and married to a woman.

"I'd like to introduce you to some people," he said. He explained that there was already a secret group at my church for "men struggling with unwanted same-sex attractions." It was called Homosexuals Anonymous.

Although a number of other support groups in the church met openly and had posted schedules, the very existence of this group was kept hidden from almost everyone in the congregation. As Pastor Rick explained the need for secrecy around the group and its members, my already profound sense of shame grew even deeper. The secrecy wasn't only to honor our privacy. It was also to protect us from the judgment of others in the congregation.

Even though we as Christians knew that everyone was sinful, issues like mine were still viewed and treated differently. Being attracted to the same sex was just too shameful. Other Christians wouldn't know how to handle someone like me.

Following Rick's instructions, I drove around to the back of the church at the appointed day and time for our supersecret meeting of anonymous homosexuals.

I didn't like the word "homosexual." Something about it felt dirty. It made me sound like I was more sexual than everybody else, and in some weird way, I wasn't any more sexual than any of my friends were; it was just that, for some reason, my attractions went in the opposite direction, and I didn't know why.

Rick escorted me into a room where several tired-looking middle-aged men smiled up at me from around a table. These were the anonymous homosexuals of our church. And no one knew they existed. Well, almost no one.

I sat down in a chair a short distance away from everyone else. I felt awkward and uncomfortable. Did these men represent who I was to become? I wondered about their stories and how long they had struggled with the feelings I also had.

I observed silently for most of the meeting. The men talked a bit about the program and how glad they were to be part of it. They explained to me their theories about why they had gay feelings, mostly connected to faulty upbringings and other childhood traumas I couldn't relate to. And they shared their latest progress in trying to become straight.

At one point in the meeting, a man with a wedding ring on his finger said that he had some exciting news to share. Everyone leaned forward.

"This weekend," he said, "my wife and kids and I took a trip to the beach. While we were there, a woman walked by in a small bikini. And I *noticed* her."

He sat back with a satisfied smile. The small group erupted in cheers and congratulations. Clearly, for him this was a milestone achievement—noticing a woman on a beach.

I sat transfixed and horrified. Was this to be my destiny? Was I going to end up someday in a room like this one, middle-aged, married to a woman I wasn't attracted to, trying to act the part as well as possible for my wife and kids, and getting excited because after years of therapy, one day I noticed *one* woman walking by me in a bikini on a beach for a few seconds?

What kind of future was that? What kind of life would that be?

And what did it mean to "notice" a woman on the beach? Even a straight woman might notice another woman walking by with large breasts and a small bikini. She might envy her figure, or simply notice her lack of covering. We all tend to notice other people of either sex who are wearing very little, but that doesn't mean we're sexually attracted to them. Sometimes we wish they would cover up more!

I wanted more than that for my life. If I was going to marry a woman someday, I wanted to be able to do more than just notice one woman once in a blue moon, an event so out of the ordinary that I would go back to my support group and tell them all about it. I wanted to feel the way straight guys felt: attracted to women, desiring women, looking at my girlfriend or my wife and wanting her, wanting her body. I wanted to have to struggle to avoid lusting after women, the way my straight friends did. It shouldn't have to be an effort to see my wife as pretty. I should desire her in the innermost depths of my being.

I left the meeting feeling confused and discouraged. These weren't the success stories I had hoped for. Yes, these men were married to women, but they were struggling every day to try to feel some level of sexual attraction to their wives, or to any woman. Meanwhile, their passions, like mine, continued to be oriented toward men, something they perpetually fought against without change.

Though the people who knew them would have considered them heterosexual, these were clearly not straight men. A straight man doesn't have to fight to try to find women attractive, nor does he have to fight to keep from lusting after other men. These men were living in constant turmoil. They were trying their best to live as they believed God wanted them to, but they weren't happy.

This wasn't the kind of future I wanted. I wanted to *change* my feelings, not just get married in spite of them. I wasn't going to be like these guys. I was going to be completely straight.

Right?

For the first time, I began to feel a twinge of doubt.

GOD BOY SNEAKS OUT

I didn't go back to Rick's ex-gay group. I still wanted to change, but those men weren't experiencing the kind of change I wanted. I was going to have to look elsewhere for answers.

In the meantime, I told him, I had one more thing I needed to do. I was about to leave for college, and my parents still didn't know what I was going through. I didn't want to keep this a secret from them, but I was scared to tell them. Would he help me tell them the truth before I left home? He said he would.

Together, Pastor Rick and I formulated a plan. He would call my parents and set up a meeting in his office at church. Both of them were very active in the congregation, so they wouldn't think anything of it. When they arrived at the appointed day and time, I'd already be there, and, together, he and I would tell them the secret I had been keeping for so long.

Plotting something like this felt weird to me. I'd never gone behind my parents' backs before. But I was too nervous to try to tell them my secret alone, and if they knew what the meeting was about in advance, they'd either ask me about it or be worrying about it, so this seemed like the best way to do it. At least this way I was the only one worrying.

Pastor Rick called my parents and set up the meeting for an afternoon only a week before I would leave home to start college. As predicted, they assumed it was just about routine church business and put it on the calendar without worrying about it.

The day of the meeting, I could hardly focus on anything. I tried to keep myself busy around the house to take my mind off the inevitable, but it was of only limited use. All I could think about was what I would say to my parents, and what they would think when they learned the truth about their firstborn son.

Afternoon came, and the time of the meeting approached. Then something happened that I hadn't planned on. My dad stopped by my room, mentioned that he and my mom were leaving for a meeting soon, and asked me to get some chores done while he was gone. Had I been faster on my feet, I could have thought up some excuse for needing to leave the house instead of doing chores at that moment. But I was caught off guard, and I didn't want to lie to my dad. So, like a fool, I just stood there and said, "Sure."

My dad left my room, and I glanced at the clock. I was going to have to leave soon if I wanted to get to the church before my parents. That meant I'd have to sneak out of the house.

Sneak out of the house? I had never sneaked out of the house before, and now I was about to do it for the first time in my life— so I could secretly meet with a pastor. Even then it struck me as funny. Only God Boy would sneak out of the house to go to church. I tried to laugh, but the laughter stuck in my throat.

As soon as the coast was clear, I crept downstairs and made it out the front door without being seen. I was halfway to my car when my dad spotted me. He was outside, walking the dog.

Oops.

I didn't have time to stop and explain, and I was too nervous anyway. I quickened my pace, making a beeline for my car.

"Hey," my dad called, "I thought—"

"I have to, um...I'll be back soon!" I yelled over my shoulder as I jumped into the car, turned the ignition key, and sped out of the driveway, leaving my dad standing in the yard blinking.

I was finally away. My heart was racing. I wondered what Dad was thinking. He was probably perplexed; rushing off with no explanation was very unlike me. I hated leaving things that way. I wanted to go back and explain, but I couldn't. Soon, of course, he would understand.

The drive to the church was a blur, and suddenly I was there. I met Pastor Rick in the lobby, and he escorted me up to his office.

"Your parents should be here in a few minutes," he said. "You can sit here while I wait for them downstairs. Then when I bring them up and they see that you're here, I'll let them know that you have something to tell them. At that point it's up to you to actually tell them, but I'll be here to support you and answer their questions. Okay?"

"Okay," I said, trying unsuccessfully to sound okay.

"Okay, I'll go wait for them in the lobby, then," he said.

"Okay," I repeated.

And with that, I was alone in his office. The room was painfully quiet. I thought about what my parents would say when they saw me sitting there. Would they be surprised? Would he have given them a clue before they made it upstairs? I imagined their faces, and I tried to remember exactly how I'd planned to tell them my secret. I couldn't put the words together in my head. My whole body was trembling. I twisted my hands around each other, trying to focus. I felt queasy.

Telling my parents had been on my mind since I had first realized I was gay. It was the only major secret I had ever kept from them. But it was *because* I was so close to them that telling them the truth was so frightening. If anyone else reacted badly or their opinion of me changed, I could handle it. But my parents were the most important people in my life; if this news changed my relationship with them, my world would never be the same.

I wasn't afraid of my parents' wrath; I knew they would love me no matter what happened. I was just afraid of disappointing them. I had always been their pride and joy, and now I was about to shatter their image of me. I was ashamed too. Having to discuss my sexuality with my parents was embarrassing enough, but having to admit to them that I had sexual thoughts about other boys? It was shameful and humiliating.

As the minutes dragged by, I wondered what my parents would say when they knew. How would they feel? Shocked? Angry? Confused? Hurt? Would they blame me for these feelings, or would they understand that I hadn't chosen them? Would we argue? Or would they just be sad and disappointed? I tried to predict their reaction, but I couldn't. I didn't know how they would feel. I didn't know how I would have felt.

With every noise in the hallway, I started, thinking it was them. I took deep breaths to try to calm myself down. I just wanted this to be over. Soon it would be. And their impression of me would be forever changed. That wasn't a comforting thought.

Then I heard their voices in the hallway. I straightened up and tried my best not to look nervous. They sounded like they were having a pleasant conversation, just chatting and laughing like normal.

They came around the doorframe, and everyone looked at me. "Oh! Well, hello," my mom said. I couldn't quite read the expression on her face. She was surprised to see me, of course, but was there anything else? Did she know that this would be bad news? Could she tell how nervous I was? My dad looked slightly confused, but not upset.

Rick motioned for them to take a seat, and they did. "I invited you here today," he said, "because Justin has something he'd like to share with you. Justin?"

This was it. I had to speak. I had hoped his introduction would be longer. I cleared my throat and tried to find the words. He looked at me. They looked at me. I didn't know what to say. I wasn't ready. I needed more time. I stammered out a few words of apology for the way I had rushed off earlier.

"Don't worry about it," my dad said.

Then we were silent again.

I started talking about Liz. My parents knew her; we'd been dating for quite some time, and they loved her. I rambled on for a minute before finally getting to the point. "We...we broke up," I said slowly. I swallowed. "We broke up because..." My voice was failing me. The knot in my stomach felt immense. "We broke up because..." I looked at their faces. For a moment, I wondered if they knew what I was about to say. I looked down at my shoes for courage. "...Because...I'm"—I couldn't say the *g* word—"not attracted to...to girls."

The words were out. I stared at my feet, a million thoughts running through my head. I wanted to stop, but I knew I needed to say one more thing just to make it clear.

"I'm attracted to...to..."

Come on, Justin, say it.

"...to...guys."

And that was it. That was as much as I could say.

Silence engulfed the room. I kept staring at my feet.

My mom, who was sitting next to me, reached over and put her hand on mine.

Her voice was surprised and confused. She sounded like she was about to cry. But she said the words I needed to hear. "We'll always love you," she said. "No matter what."

My dad nodded his assent. His face was grim. He looked as if he didn't know what to say.

Pastor Rick began filling in the details, explaining how I'd come to him and asked him to hold the meeting. He used the *g* word for the first time—*gay*—and told my parents that there was hope for change, but that nothing was a sure thing. My parents listened intently, asking him a lot of questions: Why had this happened? Was it their fault? Was there anything they could do?

My mom eventually did start crying. This wasn't the life she had envisioned for her son. Even so, she and my dad continued to affirm their love for me and their desire to help me live the way God wanted. In all of our minds, of course, that meant I needed to become straight.

The conversation continued into the night. All I could do was sit there, silent.

My parents knew. My deepest secret had been exposed. And like Adam and Eve in the garden, I felt naked and ashamed.

THINGS PARENTS SAY

I was very fortunate in the way my parents responded. Neither of them had much knowledge about gay people, and both of them had always believed that being gay was a sinful choice. They'd never suspected that I was gay, and they certainly didn't want me to be. But they loved me, and they recognized that this was difficult for me to talk about. Rather than berating or disowning me, they listened and tried to understand. And they reminded me constantly that they loved me and always would, even if I made decisions they disapproved of.

Not everyone is as lucky as I was. Even my parents and I had many difficult, heated arguments over the years on the subject, and I know many other kids who had it much worse. Some parents have kicked their kids out, disowned them, and written them out of their wills. Some have even told their kids they wished they were dead. Imagine hearing that from your own mother or father! Such responses are by no means limited to Christian parents, but it makes me especially sad to hear Christian parents say things like this. I don't believe that Christ would ever approve of parents treating their children that way.

In one of Jesus' best-known parables, a son demands his inheritance early, leaves home, and wastes all he has on a foolish, extravagant lifestyle. Finally, with nothing left and nowhere to turn, he comes home with his tail between his legs, only to find his father running toward him with arms open wide, ready to embrace him and welcome him home with a celebration.[1]

Jesus uses the story as an illustration of God's unending love for us even when we make countless mistakes (and a reminder to us not to feel bitter or jealous when God shows that grace to others who have made more mistakes than we have). But there's surely an important message here for parents too. Even in the midst of his son's most heinous mistakes, the father never disowns his son or makes him feel unwelcome at home. When the son hits rock bottom, the father doesn't say, "I told you so." Instead, he simply demonstrates to his son that he will always love him, no matter what, even when the rest of the world has no more use for him.

I pray that Christian parents will heed the message of this parable and treat their children with that kind of love, even when they disagree on issues like homosexuality. If we can't get this right within our own families, how are we supposed to get it right on a larger scale? A loving response must start at home.

Most Christians I know would never dream of disowning their gay kids. Still, they may struggle with how to balance a desire to love and support their kids with a responsibility to raise their kids to live moral lives. If their gay son or daughter is going down a path that they believe to be sinful and destructive, how can they lovingly respond without appearing to condone something they believe to be wrong?

Here are some things many parents tell me they said and later regretted:

"DON'T TELL ANYONE."

My parents said this, and so have many other Christian parents I know. My parents were focused (as I was) on finding a way to help me become straight, and they were worried that if people found out in the meantime that I was gay, it would destroy my future chances of being a leader in the church. With that in mind, they asked me not to tell anyone I was gay.

As well intentioned as this advice is, it places a terrible burden on the child. A secret this big can produce a tremendous amount of shame and guilt, especially for kids from Christian families. Gay kids are already at increased risk for depression and self-harm, and adding to their feelings of isolation by asking them not to talk about what they're going through only makes matters worse.

Moreover, while people in past generations may have been content to "leave well enough alone" and not comment on others' sexual orientation, in today's culture, people will come right out and ask whether someone is gay or straight. That's particularly true among younger people, for whom learning this kind of information is a typical part of getting to know someone. Asking children to keep such a thing a secret isn't just asking them not to reveal information; it is often asking them to deliberately lie or otherwise deceive people in order to prevent the truth from being uncovered. That kind of behavior tends to wear at one's moral fiber over time.

Understandably, parents worry that if their kids confide in others or come out publicly, they'll end up spending time around other gay people and ultimately making decisions their parents don't approve of. In fact, every parent worries about their kids' decisions, especially romantic and sexual ones, whether the kids are gay or straight. But the way to combat bad decisions isn't by asking kids to keep secrets. The Bible reminds us that sin thrives in darkness.[2] Instead, the best way to cultivate healthy and responsible attitudes is by encouraging open communication—with parents, peers, and Christian leaders. A healthy level of openness can enable a child to develop their own identity and make wise choices rather than living under a burden of secret shame and guilt.

"You're not like those people."

Before he found out about me, my dad's only impression of gay people was negative. (Actually, so was mine!) He told me several stories of gay men he had encountered who were doing grossly inappropriate things, including one man who was caught spying on men using the urinals and another man who made inappropriate advances toward teenage boys. These were the representations of gay men in my dad's mind, so when I told him I was gay, it disgusted him to think of his own son in that light. "You're not like them," he told me.

He was right; I'm not like the men in the stories he shared, and neither are most gay people. A soft-spoken minister and a scandal-driven celebrity might both be *straight*, but they live very different lifestyles.[3] In the same way, I know gay people who are as different from one another as can be imagined. Some are as God-fearing as any straight person I know. Others are far from it. And yes, there are gay sex offenders out there, just as there are straight sex offenders. They don't represent everyone.

When parents tell their kids that they must not be gay because they're not like the negative images in the parents' heads, it doesn't change their kids' understanding of themselves as gay. Instead, it convinces the kids that their parents now associate those negative images with *them*, and that the only way they can avoid that association is to pretend not to feel what they feel.

"How could you hurt us like this?"

I'm very happy to say that my parents never said this, or anything like it, to me. Unfortunately, I know many parents who have.

If you are the parent of a gay child, it's important to remember that your child was likely struggling with this for a very long time before you became aware of it. He or she did not choose to be gay and was probably very worried about disappointing or upsetting you. When gay children don't tell their parents what they are going through, it is often because they are hoping to figure things out on their own and avoid hurting their parents. When they do make the decision to tell them, it is a sign of trust and of a desire for honesty and a closer relationship. Regardless, this can be a difficult and emotional journey for both parent and child.

The most important thing parents can do is listen to their children and seek to understand their experiences so far. If the child wants to talk about it, that's a good sign; parents should embrace the opportunity to find out what they've been missing in their child's life. Even if your child makes significant mistakes, this is still your child, whom you love and who is opening up to you about what may be the hardest thing to tell you, something that has dramatically affected their experience of the world. Resist the temptation to make it about you. Focus on being there for your child.

"What did we do wrong?"

While some parents blame their child, other parents blame themselves. Many Christian parents have heard that homosexuality is caused by poor parent-child relationships, so it's especially common for them to wonder if they did something wrong to cause their child to be gay.

In the next chapter, I'll review some of the theories about why people are gay, but in general, I don't believe there's anything parents can do to prevent their children from being gay. I had strong, warm relationships with both of my parents, felt fully and completely loved, was given healthy amounts of discipline and independence, and had everything else I've heard recommended to parents. If I turned out gay, any kid can turn out gay. Meanwhile, my three siblings turned out straight, and we were all raised by the same parents.

Having a gay child doesn't mean parents necessarily did anything "wrong." Instead of blaming themselves, parents should focus on showing their child all the love they can and keeping their relationship strong as the family works together through the moral and theological questions they face.

"THIS IS THE DEVIL'S WAY OF TRYING TO STOP YOU FROM DOING WHAT GOD WANTS."

This is another common response from Christian parents. They worry that their children's orientation will prevent them from fully living up to the potential God has given them.

My parents knew I wanted to do some kind of ministry work in the future, and they worried that this gay thing was going to prevent me from doing that. Instead, this journey—though sometimes turbulent—ended up giving me a unique understanding of an important issue for the church, resulting in the book you are holding in your hands today. The very thing my parents were so worried might destroy my future turned out to be something God used in my life to reach a lot of hurting people.

In the Bible, the obstacles that seem the most daunting often turn out to be things God uses for an unexpected purpose. When Joseph's brothers sold him into slavery (Genesis 37), none of them knew this act would ultimately enable him to save many lives.

Likewise, the crucifixion of Jesus must have felt to his followers like the worst possible act of the devil, yet Christians today celebrate it as the most powerful evidence of God's love. I encourage Christian parents not to jump to any conclusions about how God will use a situation like this in their child's life. Denying it won't make it go away, but if we respond as Christians, with open hearts to what God will do, we can be surprised at what happens.

When I first told my parents, one of the questions they had for Pastor Rick was what might cause something like this. I had the same question, and he didn't have an answer. In the next chapter, we'll look at the evidence.

CHAPTER 5

◆

WHY ARE PEOPLE GAY?

Over the years, I've shared my journey with many kinds of people in many different circumstances. Their responses depend a lot on their own experiences with the issue.

I've had hundreds of Christians tell me that my story reads like a page out of the book of their own life story. For some, hearing my story marked the first time they knew they weren't alone, just as hearing Brian's story did for me. I've had people break down in tears while trying to tell me what it meant to them to hear about another Christian who had gone through the same things. No one else seemed to understand them.

Others tell me how puzzling my story is to them, because they grew up in homes where being gay was, or would have been, perfectly acceptable. It's hard for them to fathom what would make a teenage boy so afraid to embrace what, in their mind, would be his obviously natural sexuality.

On many occasions, I've had the privilege of sharing my story with straight Christians who don't know many gay people and who have never really considered what going through all this would be like. Some of them were taught, as I was, that gay people *choose* to be that way, so hearing about my experiences raises all sorts of new questions for them. That's why so many people stop me at some point in the story to ask for my opinion on one of the oldest questions about homosexuality: Why are some people gay?

First, Let's Define What We Mean by *Gay*

It amazes me how long people can argue about a question like "Is being gay a choice?" without ever stopping to define what they mean by *gay*. If one person believes that *gay* refers to being *attracted* to members of the same sex and another person believes that it refers to *having sex with* members of the same sex, then it shouldn't surprise us when they come to two very different conclusions about whether "being gay" is a choice!

Of course, a century ago, *gay* didn't mean either of those things. It had meanings like "happy" or "brightly colorful," as in the classic Christmas carol line, "Don we now our *gay* apparel," or the *West Side Story* lyric, "I feel pretty and witty and *gay*." (In recent times, those lines have been the cause of many grade school giggle fits.)

But if we're going to talk about what causes some people to be attracted to the same sex and not the opposite sex, it's helpful to have a word for that. And in 1892, a German psychiatrist named Richard von Krafft-Ebing introduced the word *homosexual* into English, using it to describe both men and women who, for some reason, only experienced attraction to the same sex. It's important to note that von Krafft-Ebing specifically used the term to describe *attractions*, not sexual *behaviors*. Some of the homosexuals he wrote about had never acted on their feelings, and some had even married members of the opposite sex, but this had not cured them of their homosexuality; they were still attracted to the same sex and not to their own spouses.[1]

Following von Krafft-Ebing, *homosexual* became the standard term among psychologists to describe people attracted to the same sex. But in the mid-1900s, the word *gay* began to be used in some communities as slang for *homosexual*, and that use gradually caught on and became mainstream; *gay* was much easier to say than *homosexual* and sounded less clinical and less overtly sexual. By the end of the century, *gay* had almost entirely replaced *homosexual* as the common word. (Today *homosexual* is widely seen as outdated, and it can even be offensive in some contexts.)

So today, when we say someone is gay, we typically mean that he or she is *attracted to the same sex*. By contrast, someone who is straight is attracted to the *opposite* sex, and someone who is bisexual is attracted to *both*.[2] These words don't tell us anything about a person's behaviors, beliefs, or plans for the future; they only tell us to whom the person is generally attracted. A teenage girl might be straight (attracted to boys), but that doesn't mean she's ever had sex with a boy, kissed a boy, or been on a date with a boy. Even if she committed her entire life to celibacy, we would still say that she's straight, because she's attracted to the opposite sex.

Similarly, when I called myself gay, I wasn't referring to any kind of behavior in my life. I had never had a sexual or romantic relationship with a guy, and I didn't ever plan to. But even if I never acted on my feelings and never allowed my mind to turn to lust, there was no denying that I was different from other guys in one major way: Where they were attracted to and tempted by girls, I was attracted to and tempted by guys. I was *gay*. They were *straight*.

Some people don't believe we should use the words *gay* and *straight*—or any labels at all—to describe people's attractions. For me, though, having a word to describe my situation was helpful, and I think it's important for everyone to be clear about what these words mean. Throughout this book, when I say "gay," you can mentally replace that with "generally attracted to members of the same sex, not members of the opposite sex."[3]

So when we ask, "Why are people gay?" what we're really asking is, "Why are some people attracted to the same sex?" Let's examine a few of the more popular theories out there.

THEORY 1: PEOPLE CHOOSE TO BE GAY

Growing up, I firmly believed that gay people chose to be gay, but I learned by experience that this isn't the case. I most certainly did *not* want to be attracted to the same sex, and I would have done just about anything not to be. As a conservative Southern Baptist kid, I never would have chosen to be gay. Not in a million years.

Usually, when someone says that being gay is a choice, it's because they're defining *gay* to mean something other than "attracted to the same sex." This is why definitions are so important. Most people can agree, though, that while we do choose our *behaviors*, we don't get to choose to whom we're *attracted*. In case you have doubts about that, let's briefly consider what it would mean if people could choose their attractions.

Whichever sex you're attracted to, you're not attracted to *all* people of that sex, are you? Some of them you find attractive, and others you don't. You don't get to choose which ones your brain sees as attractive.

If we could, we might all like to turn those attractions off sometimes! If you're married, for instance, you might choose to be attracted only to your spouse and never to anyone else. It would make married life a lot easier, wouldn't it? Unfortunately, you don't get to choose that. Those attractions come whether you like them or not, and then it's up to you how you'll respond to them.

Likewise, if you're single, there may be times when it would be nice to be able to turn *on* attractions to someone you just don't feel anything for, like that really nice person who likes you but whom you just don't find attractive. Unfortunately, while your attraction to someone might shift as you get to know them, it also might not. You can't make it happen by sheer force of will.

None of us can choose to whom we feel attracted. We just are.

Most people discover when they're young that they are involuntarily attracted to people of the other sex. A minority of people, however, discover instead that they are involuntarily attracted to the same sex, and another minority discover that they're involuntarily attracted to both sexes. None of these people *choose* their attractions; they can only choose how they will respond to them.

I know a lot of people who were horrified when they realized they were gay, either because of their moral beliefs or because of prejudice against gay people among their family and friends. Like me, they would never have chosen to be gay, but they were anyway.

So no, it's not something people choose.

THEORY 2: PEOPLE ARE SEDUCED OR TRICKED INTO IDENTIFYING AS GAY

Okay, so maybe people don't intentionally choose to be gay, but is it something they're tricked into? Is it possible they're convinced that they're gay by teasing in the schoolyard or are seduced by an older gay crowd that shows them attention?

I can only speak for myself here, but I certainly was never seduced by anyone. At the time I realized I was attracted to other guys, I didn't even know any other gay people. And while I *was* occasionally teased at school (and really, who *wasn't* teased at some point in grade school?), I didn't ever think I was gay because of teasing; I just thought the kids doing the teasing were bullies. The first time I ever considered that I might be gay was, as I described, a result of years of same-sex attraction, not because of anything I'd heard at school.

In a similar vein, I'm sometimes asked whether gay people have same-sex attractions due to sexual abuse in their past. My short answer to this is that I wasn't sexually abused, and studies show that the majority of gay people weren't either.

In situations where people *were* sexually abused and later discover that they are gay, either they or their loved ones may wonder whether the abuse altered their developing sexuality in some way. The impact of childhood abuse on an adult's relationship with his or her sexuality is complex, and because of the extremely sensitive nature of the subject and the uniqueness of each individual's experience, that question ultimately lies outside the scope of this book. In my case, though, it was an easy question to answer: I'd never experienced any kind of abuse, sexual or otherwise, so abuse couldn't have made me gay.

THEORY 3: PEOPLE ARE GAY BECAUSE OF THEIR PARENTS

One popular theory says that people are gay as a result of problems in their relationship with their parents. This is sometimes called the "reparative drive" model, for reasons I'll explain in a moment. The idea was first popularized in the early 1960s by a psychologist named Irving Bieber. Decades earlier, Sigmund Freud had suggested that children's sexual development depends on their relationship with their parents; he believed, for instance, that a normal heterosexual boy subconsciously wants to kill his father and marry his mother. Bieber—who focused exclusively on men—also believed this was true, and proposed that gay men were gay because poor parenting caused this process to fail.

Bieber argued that gay men came from families "characterized by disturbed and psychopathic interactions" and that gay men's parents "had severe emotional problems." Gay men's fathers, he said, were usually "explicitly detached and hostile," while their mothers tended to be possessive, overprotective, and even "seductive" toward their sons. According to Bieber, male homosexuality was *always* the result of poor parenting. He blamed both mothers and fathers, but in his view, fathers got the lion's share of the blame. Every gay man, Bieber said, had a poor father, because "a constructive, supportive, warmly related father *precludes* the possibility of a homosexual son."[4]

Bieber's theories were extremely influential at a time when very little was known about the subject. Not surprisingly, they resonated especially well with gay men who'd had poor relationships with their fathers. However, there were a number of problems with his research from the beginning.

Bieber's theory had been developed by questioning gay men in the 1950s about their parents and then comparing their answers to those of straight men, but the men he interviewed were not at all representative of the general population. The interviewees were all already in therapy, many for psychological troubles unrelated to their sexuality. The straight "comparison" group was not a random sample, but was handpicked by the researchers, who had already decided the basics of their theory before doing the research. Not only that, but as many as a fourth of the supposedly "heterosexual" interviewees were identified by Bieber as having "evidence of severe homosexual problems" (that is, being attracted to other men). In spite of that, they were counted as *heterosexual* for the study because they hadn't acted on their feelings.

As it turns out, there are a number of people—both gay and straight—who grew up with detached, hostile fathers and/or possessive, overprotective mothers. There are also many people—both gay and straight—who didn't experience that dynamic at all. According to Bieber, it's impossible for a boy to turn out gay if he has a warm, loving relationship with his father. Yet that's exactly what many gay men had and continue to have to this day.

The psychological community eventually abandoned this theory, deciding that it didn't fit the evidence. However, Bieber's model remained popular in some Christian circles, largely due to the influence of Elizabeth Moberly, a Christian theologian and psychologist.

In the early 1980s, at a time when many Christians were condemning gays as intentionally wicked and sinful, Moberly pushed for understanding. She argued that gays hadn't *chosen* to be this way, but that something had *happened* to them in childhood and that they needed the church's compassion. In her book *Homosexuality: A New Christian Ethic*, Moberly outlined her theory of what made people gay. Picking up where Bieber left off, she agreed that parental relationships were the cause, but she altered the theory to include both men and women and added her own ideas about how it might work, focusing on an idea she called the "reparative drive."

Moberly theorized that if a child had a distant same-sex parent, he or she was left with an emotional deficit. The child needed same-sex bonding that was never met by the parent, and so as he or she grew, a subconscious drive would kick in to try to repair that hole. This *reparative drive*, Moberly thought, was the underlying cause of homosexual attractions. According to her theory, a man was attracted to other men because his father never met his emotional needs, and a woman was attracted to other women because her mother didn't meet her emotional needs. If those needs could be met in healthy (nonsexual) ways, Moberly believed, then those same-sex attractions would go away and opposite-sex attractions would develop.

Dr. Moberly's book didn't offer any compelling new research or evidence for this theory. Nevertheless, her theory was a huge hit with gay Christians who didn't want to be gay. Those who had had poor relationships with their parents saw themselves right away in her theory. Those who hadn't had poor parental relationships simply assumed that it must have all happened on a subconscious level. For both groups, the appeal was easy to see. It gave them a *reason* for their feelings, and it offered a simple *solution*. The answer to their gay dilemma, it said, was to meet their need for same-sex bonding through therapy and strong friendships with other Christians of the same sex.

The theory was also a hit with compassionate straight Christians. It said that the church needed to embrace and love gay people, because forming those connections with them was the key to healing them from their homosexuality.

The theory probably would have been a hit with me too, except for one thing. My upbringing was nothing like what Moberly or Bieber described.

For starters, I grew up in a loving, two-parent, Christian home. I had the sort of family you might see profiled in Christian media as part of a feature story on "How to Raise a Christian Family."

My dad wasn't absent, distant, or abusive. Far from it. I was his firstborn son, the "miracle baby" born after years of fertility doctors telling my parents they would never have any kids. Realizing he'd been given an extraordinary gift, my dad was determined to be the best possible father to me. From the moment he got home from work each evening, he always made time for me, no matter how exhausted he might have been. I can't think of any time in my childhood that my dad ever turned me down when I asked for his time. Whether it was helping me with homework, shooting hoops with me in the driveway, or just listening to me talk about my day, he was always there. Only many years later did I realize how truly uncommon that experience was.

Dad was a stockbroker who was passionate about the need for integrity in his line of work. From the time I was very young, he taught me the importance of Christian moral living. "Justin," he said once, in the midst of a difficult moral quandary of his own, "sometimes you'll be in a situation where everyone else is doing the wrong thing, and you have to stand up for what's right. It's not always easy, but it's important. You never know who might be watching, and God is watching even if no one else is." Those lessons, and his reminders that my name means "full of justice," had a profound influence on my developing sense of self. I wanted to be like my dad, someone who did the right thing even when it was difficult. I wanted to serve God.

My mom was also nothing like the overbearing "smother mother" Bieber described. A brilliant, effervescent woman, she had been a teacher and an assistant principal before leaving the work-force to become a stay-at-home mom when I was born. She never had a dull moment: After me, there were three more miracle babies, and she somehow managed to juggle all four of us, keep an impeccably clean house, and have a well-balanced, home-cooked meal for six on the table every night. Donna Reed's 1950s sitcom character couldn't have done it better.

As with my dad, what made Mom so special was her integrity. I don't think I've ever met anyone as profoundly admired by those around them as she was. She was deeply religious, but not in the annoying self-righteous way that so many people unfortunately associate with American Christianity. Her faith was the rock she built her life on, not a show to impress others. She had a real love for people and genuinely cared about how others were doing, and that shone brightly through everything she did. She was outgoing, friendly, and always willing to lend a hand. And yet, despite her seemingly impossible schedule, she always found time to retreat to her room each day for quiet Bible study and prayer.

Mom taught a hugely popular Christian parenting class at the large Southern Baptist church my family attended each Sunday, where Dad served as a deacon. Young parents throughout the church flocked to her class week after week, eager for her advice. Not only was she a mom to four children, but she also truly understood the delicate balance between providing discipline and guidance on the one hand and allowing kids the freedom to grow on the other. Ten years of childless marriage had given her and my dad a chance to mature into the right kind of parents, and that was what made her advice so sought after.

So yes, there were times when my childhood felt like a wholesome *Leave It to Beaver*–style classic sitcom, only with more modern furnishings. I don't mean to suggest that every day was scripted and flawless, but my parents raised me well, they gave me plenty of love, and I was a happy kid.

Were my parents perfect? Of course not. No parents are. Did we sometimes argue? Yes. But never—never for a moment—did I doubt my parents' love for me. Never did I wish for different parents. Even at the height of my own teenage angst and all the feelings of being misunderstood that come with that time in life, I felt loved and supported by my parents. They never smothered me and never felt distant. My relationship with my parents may be one in a million, but there it is.

As you can imagine, then, from the first time I heard about this "bad parenting" theory, I knew it couldn't be the whole story. It definitely wasn't *my* story.

To this day, many Christian counselors still teach a modified version of Bieber's 1962 theory alongside Moberly's "reparative drive" language. Since Bieber's depiction of a "hostile" father and "seductive" mother with "severe emotional problems" sounds so harsh, its proponents today describe the theory with softer terms like "distant or absent father" and "overbearing or overprotective mother" instead. Distant fathers and overprotective mothers are extremely common in American society, so this allows a larger percentage of gay people to say, "Hey, that sounds like me!" But these same dynamics are very widespread among straight Americans as well, and they are not at all present for many gay Americans. If distant fathers and overbearing mothers made people gay, there should be far more gay people in American society than there are. Meanwhile, I should have been the straightest guy in the world.

Elizabeth Moberly gradually withdrew from the public spotlight to study cancer instead, but a psychotherapist named Joseph

Nicolosi picked up her torch, building his reputation on the "reparative drive" concept and trademarking the term "reparative therapy." Rather than modifying the theory to account for the many stories that don't fit, however, Nicolosi took the theory to an even greater extreme, speaking frequently in generalizations that glossed over the real complexities of the issue and the experiences of many. "You will hear a shallowness in the voice of any homosexual who claims to love and respect his father," Nicolosi told a reporter in 1996. "On the other hand, when the straight man talks lovingly about his father, you will hear a richness in his voice."[5] Elsewhere he put it more bluntly, claiming, "I have never met a homosexual male with a loving, respectful relationship with his father."[6]

But Nicolosi's assertions are simply not accurate. I know many gay men who truly love and respect their fathers, and many straight men who don't. Meanwhile, scientific research does not support Nicolosi's claim that the fathers of gay sons are typically "immature," "narcissistic," or "inadequate."[7] In reality, both good and bad fathers have gay sons, and both good and bad fathers have straight sons. Despite Nicolosi's claims, there is no credible evidence that parents determine their children's sexual orientation.

THEORY 4: PEOPLE ARE GAY BECAUSE OF THEIR BIOLOGY

Ask gay people why they think they're gay, and a lot of them will respond that they feel like they were *born* gay—that for some reason, their brains are wired differently from straight people's and have been since birth.

Historically, a number of Christians have objected to this idea. They've argued that if gay sex is a sin, then God wouldn't allow people to be born with a biological attraction to the same sex. But that doesn't seem like a very good argument to me. Just because an attraction or drive is biological doesn't mean it's okay to act on, so whether behavior is sinful or not doesn't tell us anything about whether the related attraction has biological roots.

For example, suppose a man is just "wired" to be attracted to women. His hormones and brain structures work together to give him feelings of attraction when a pretty woman walks by, and that doesn't stop just because he gets married. Does that make it okay for him to cheat on his wife? Of course not. His attractions may be rooted in his biology, but acting on them is still sinful.

We all have inborn tendencies to sin in any number of ways. If gay people's same-sex attractions were inborn, that wouldn't necessarily make it okay to act on them, and if we all agreed that gay sex is sinful, that wouldn't necessarily mean that same-sex attractions aren't inborn. "Is it a sin?" and "Does it have biological roots?" are two completely separate questions.

But *is* biology involved or not? For an answer to that question, we have to look at scientific research.

It's amazing how much research has been done on this topic. Scientists have examined genes, hormones, and brain structures. They've studied humans, rats, monkeys, rams, and fruit flies. They've explored everything from fingerprint patterns to family birth order. And the results they've found are as complex as they are fascinating. At the risk of oversimplifying the issue, here are a few of the things researchers have discovered.

PHYSICAL BRAIN DIFFERENCES

Men's and women's brains are different, on the average, in a number of measurable ways. Several studies have shown that certain structures in gay people's brains more closely resemble the corresponding structures in average brains of the opposite sex than the corresponding structures in average brains of the same sex. In other words, some parts of gay men's brains look more like those parts in straight women than like those parts in straight men; and in lesbian women, those brain regions look more like those of straight men than like those of straight women. This doesn't mean that gay men have women's brains or that lesbian women have men's brains; it means that *specific structures* in their brains seem to have developed in ways that are more typical for the opposite sex. This may be due to differing hormone levels in the womb.

Our brains continue to change while we're alive, so it's possible these differences could be the *result* of being gay rather than the *cause*, but most scientists think that's unlikely. Many researchers now believe that these different brain structures help explain why some people are attracted to the same sex instead of the opposite sex—their brains may truly be different from birth.

BODY DIFFERENCES

Men's and women's bodies are different too, and not just in the obvious ways. Subtle differences like those in finger-length ratios and eyeblink responses tend to exist between men and women, and some of these are thought to be due to the different hormones they are exposed to in the womb. Research has shown differences between gay people and straight people regarding these kinds of measurements as well, suggesting again that gay people might have been exposed to different hormone levels than their straight counterparts at a critical period of prenatal development.

OTHER DIFFERENCES

Differences between men and women show up in nonphysical ways as well. Women, for instance, tend to perform better on tasks requiring verbal skills, and men tend to perform better on tasks requiring spatial skills. Once again, in these and other cases, gay people, on the average, perform more like people of the opposite sex. Gay men average better than straight men on verbal skills and worse than straight men on spatial skills. Lesbians average better than straight women on spatial skills but worse than straight women (closer to straight men) on verbal skills. This adds to the evidence that gay people's brains are built differently from straight people's of the same sex.

STUDIES ON ANIMALS

Scientists have also found similar brain differences in animals that corroborate the human results. For instance, 6 to 10 percent of rams mate only with other males, and their brains show the same kinds of structural differences that have been found in gay humans. Meanwhile, researchers have been able to change which sex rats try to mate with by changing the hormones they're exposed to in the womb. Rats, rams, and other animals are not humans, but experiments have conclusively proven that at least some animals' "sexual orientation" can be determined by hormones during their fetal development.

THE OLDER BROTHER EFFECT

Some studies have shown that gay men, on the average, have more older brothers than straight men. Of course, having older brothers by itself doesn't make people gay; plenty of gay men have no older brothers, and plenty of straight men have lots of older brothers. Statistically, though, gay men are more likely to have more older brothers. Is this due to social reasons (like being picked on in childhood) or biological reasons (like being exposed to different hormones in the womb)? Well, according to some research, the older brother effect only works if the brothers are biologically related through the same mother, not if they were half brothers with the same father or adoptive brothers raised in the same home. Interestingly, the effect still shows up when men have older brothers who were born to the same mother but not raised in the same home with them, so if further research continues to find that trend, it can't be due to social factors. This strongly suggests that something biological is involved.

Based on the evidence so far, then, many scientists now believe that sexual orientation is related to the hormone levels a baby experiences during its development in the womb. According to the theory, these hormones help distinguish boys' brains from girls' brains, but if the hormone levels are different from the usual amount at a certain time in fetal development, parts of the baby's brain (including parts responsible for sexuality) develop in a way closer to what is typical for the other gender.

In his book *Gay, Straight, and the Reason Why*, esteemed researcher Simon LeVay reviews the many different theories and studies on the subject, concluding that:

> Sexual orientation…emerges from the prenatal sexual differentiation of the brain. Whether a person ends up gay, straight, or bisexual depends in large part on how this process of biological differentiation goes forward, the lead actors being genes, sex hormones, and the brain systems that they influence.[8]

If this is true, it would explain why some people feel like their brains are "wired" to respond to the same sex instead of the opposite sex. It may be that this part of their brain really is wired that way. There could be a number of reasons for the differing hormone levels, and the tendency of women's bodies to respond differently to a baby after several male pregnancies might be one of them.

Despite the amount of evidence, there are still many unanswered questions. Researchers haven't definitively *proven* that hormones are the cause, and if they are, a lot is still unknown about why. Some scientists have searched for a single gene or set of genes that might be responsible, but the results have been inconsistent, and no "gay gene" has yet been found. Sometimes studies have shown evidence that seems to contradict the latest theories, meaning more research is needed to determine whether those studies had flaws or whether the theories need to be changed.

At this point, the evidence makes it look very likely that biology has something to do with sexual orientation, but scientists are still learning, and nothing is set in stone. Some research suggests that men's and women's sexuality may be influenced by different factors, and bisexual attraction (which is barely explored in the research) seems to be much more common among women than among men. Twenty years from now, the theories might look very different from the theories we have today, or we might have more concrete information to confirm the theories of today. For now, we can only make educated guesses and realize that there's still a lot we don't know.

CONCLUSION: WE DON'T KNOW!

So what's the answer? Why are some people attracted to the same sex? The truth is, we don't know for sure. The biological theories have the most evidence to support them right now, but even they have lots of questions, and at this point, we can't prove anything definitively. We can only make educated guesses.

In light of all the unknowns, it can be very tempting just to choose a theory that feels right, regardless of the evidence. For a gay person who had a troubled childhood, a history of sexual abuse, or poor parental relationships, it can feel obvious that these things caused him or her to be gay, even if it's actually coinciden-tal. For others, it can feel just as obvious that they were "born that way," making genetic or other biological theories more appealing. For everyone, it can be especially tempting to try to choose a the-ory that seems to fit better with our political or moral views on same-sex relationships.

But I believe our goal should be to know the truth, not just to confirm what we want to believe. That means we must be humble and admit that we still don't have all the answers. The current research gives us promising leads, and based on what I've seen and experienced, my own personal guess is that biology plays at least a significant role in all this. It doesn't really matter, though.

In the future, we may have definitive evidence to tell us what causes differences in sexual orientation. For now, the important thing is to keep an open mind and listen compassionately to peo-ple's stories.

CHAPTER 6

◇

JUSTIN IN EXGAYLAND

As a teenager, I didn't know anything about what had caused me to be gay. Sure, I was curious about it, but what I cared about more was finding a way to be rid of it and become straight. In the meantime, I had college to deal with.

I moved into a university dorm, where I went back to hiding in the closet. Once more, I was on my own with my secret, now even without the few friends I had confided in. Here I didn't know anyone, and no one knew I was gay.

My college roommate was a nice guy, also from the South. Unlike me, he wasn't from a conservative evangelical background, so I hoped he wouldn't judge me if I came out to him. I tried broaching the topic, searching for a way to casually ask how he might react to meeting gay people on campus.

"I don't know," he admitted. "I've never met any."

That wasn't exactly confidence inspiring. I decided not to tell him right away.

I poured myself into making new friends and taking hard classes. Even so, I was continually haunted by questions about my faith, my sexuality, and my future. I prayed for guidance, but I still had far more questions than answers. I looked for Christians who could help me, but I was far too scared to come out to anyone on campus. Even phone calls to my parents back home were more stressful than helpful; I felt ashamed of my sexuality, and they were still grappling with what it all meant.

The ex-gay path still seemed like the most logical way forward. The men at Homosexuals Anonymous hadn't been the success stories I had been hoping for, but, I reminded myself, they were still in therapy. They weren't done yet. Perhaps the real success stories were the ones I had heard about on Christian radio and read about in Christian magazines, the ones who were now *leading* ex-gay groups instead of attending them. I had to find out.

I discovered another local ex-gay ministry and gave them a call. A kind-sounding man on the other end of the phone listened to my story before apologetically informing me that no, there wasn't anything they could do for a nineteen-year-old with no sexual experience. Everyone in their group was much older and struggling with a lifetime of sexual addiction. Their focus was on changing those *behaviors*. They weren't set up to help a teenage virgin who just didn't want to be gay.

They did, however, send me a manila envelope stuffed with brochures for ex-gay conferences and crooked photocopies of ex-gay testimonies.

It should have been encouraging—a chance to read the stories of others like me and learn what God had done in their lives. Instead, the more I read, the more alone I felt. These testimonies were dramatic and powerful in many ways, but none of them sounded anything at all like my experience.

Most of the men's stories followed a certain pattern. Like me, they had developed attractions to other guys at puberty, but that was where our similarities ended. Unlike me, they almost all described childhoods of abuse and/or neglect, leading them to adulthoods where they tried to escape their pain through substance abuse, partying, and promiscuous, anonymous sex—something they often referred to as "the gay lifestyle."

"I slid right into the gay lifestyle," wrote one. "I shed about 40 pounds within a few months, literally dancing the nights away with glee, alcohol, drugs, and men."

"I gave myself over to the gay lifestyle," wrote another. "I began to abuse myself with alcohol and recreational drugs—anything to add to what I thought was a good time."

"Booze became my friend and comforter," wrote a third. "I continued to drink and go from one sexual encounter to another seeking some sort of hope."

In a lot of ways, these were the testimonies of recovering addicts. But it wasn't only drugs and alcohol they'd been addicted to; many of them also described their sexual behavior as a compulsion out of control. The headline on one man's testimony described how he "had a wonderful wife, two lovely daughters and held a responsible position in his church. But his frequent trips to the parks, porn shops and gay bars nearly ruined his marriage and his life."

Testimony after testimony went like this, telling stories of drug overdoses, alcoholism, STD scares, physical assaults, and unfaithful partners. In the minds of these men, that pattern of addictive and self-destructive behavior—much of it lived out in the sketchy gay club scene of the 1960s and 1970s—represented what it meant to be gay. As one man put it, "My [then-]current homosexual relationship was crumbling, and even the drink in my hand couldn't numb the ache inside....Homosexuality had caused the dark, smothering depression and loneliness in my life."

It was a scary picture of the gay world—and about as far from my experience as anything I could imagine. The stories usually ended with a description of how someone had ultimately brought these men to Jesus and the ex-gay ministries, where God had shown them a way out of their harmful behavior patterns.

The women's stories, like the men's, often began with abuse and tragedy. But where the men's stories tended to focus on sexual promiscuity, the women's tended to focus on emotional codependency. Many of them suggested that women in need of supportive friendship had fallen into lesbian relationships not because of any internal attraction to the same sex, but rather as a response to trauma. As one typical story put it, "My struggles with emotional dependency centered on two factors: A deep longing to be protected, and having no sense of personal boundaries, the latter stemming from my alcoholic family and the sexual abuse of my youth." I didn't know what to think of that. It was somehow even further from my experience than the men's scary stories.

I read slowly through the pages, unsure what to make of it all, pausing occasionally to look at the grainy black-and-white photographs accompanying some of the stories.

This wasn't what I had expected. I had imagined that ex-gay groups would be filled with people like me—ordinarily happy, well-adjusted Christians who simply wanted to be rid of their same-sex attractions. But these stories were heavy and heartbreaking—often depressing. And nothing about them was even a little bit relatable to me.

I hadn't experienced abuse or trauma, I had never been tempted by alcohol or drugs, and I had never had any desire to live the kind of hypersexual lifestyles the men described. All I wanted was to be attracted to girls instead of guys. Where were the testimonies from people like me? Was I the only one?

But of all the unexpected things about these testimonies, the thing that surprised me most was what they *didn't* say.

None of these people said they had actually become *straight*—that their *attractions* had changed.

They talked about how God had brought them out of their sinful lifestyles—but I already wasn't living a sinful lifestyle. They talked about how they had found their sense of identity in Christ—but my identity was already in Christ. They talked about how God had taught them self-control and how not to be mastered by their sex drives. But I was already practicing self-control, and I already wasn't a slave to my sex drive. It felt in many ways like my story was *starting* where theirs had *ended*.

Some of them were now married to someone of the opposite sex—but a number of them had been married all along anyway. Were they now truly attracted to their spouses, or were they like the men I'd met at Homosexuals Anonymous, still praying for those attractions to come? Most of them didn't say. A few who did talk about it said that their attractions *hadn't* yet changed; they were still waiting for that miracle from God.

I tried contacting ministries in other parts of the country, but they just sent me variations of the exact same testimonies—powerful evidence of God at work in people's lives, but still no stories of *attraction* change, just *behavior* change.

I knew I couldn't be the only one wanting more than that. Maybe these testimonies were just the most famous ones because they were so dramatic. Surely there were people out there somewhere—people like me, maybe, with less dramatic stories—who had simply gone from same-sex attracted to opposite-sex attracted. There must be!

Over the lonely months that followed, I took every opportunity to research ex-gays through the internet and in books, all while continuing to hide my true feelings from my friends and classmates. My parents, too, were willing to do whatever it took to get me answers to my questions. They made phone calls, wrote letters, and read even more books. They helped set up meetings for me with high-profile leaders in the ex-gay movement, and they offered to spare no expense to send me to any ex-gay conference I wanted to go to. One way or another, we were going to get this fixed and put it behind us.

Or so we thought.

MEET THE PARENTS

My parents went with me to my first ex-gay conference.

I was anxious. Spending a weekend discussing sexuality— particularly *my* sexuality—with my parents was not my idea of a good time! Even so, I knew it was important for me to go.

This particular conference was advertised as being for ex-gays and their parents. As it turned out, most of the attendees I met there were parents whose children were living openly gay lives. Their children hadn't come with them, but the parents were there to learn what they could do to help bring their children back to the Lord.

The conference opened with a praise and worship session. Here, in the midst of so many Christians singing their songs of praise to God together, I felt much more at ease. As we sang, our differences melted away. Even though I knew most of the people around me were straight, I no longer felt like the odd one out, hiding my secret for fear of rejection. In that room, we were all just broken, hurting, imperfect people, united in love and gratitude to God. We'd all been shown immeasurable grace. Nothing else mattered by comparison.

This—*this*—was what it was to be a Christian. I could have worshipped forever in that room. I felt peace.

Alas, it was not to last. The keynote address was more about controversial political issues of the day than about how to support Christians wrestling with their sexuality. The speaker charged his audience to fight against the "gay agenda," painting the world in simplistic us-vs.-them terms: *We* were the Christians. *They* were the gays. *They* had to be stopped at all costs.

"I think," he said with a broad grin, "that ultimately *our* values are going to prevail."

His mostly straight audience cheered. I felt uneasy. I couldn't help but wonder if the gay people out there were really so different from me. I was still a Christian, and I still stood for Christian values, but I was gay too. This polarizing language didn't sit well with me. It didn't seem very much like Jesus.

"Ultimately, *our* values are going to prevail." I thought about that. I imagined a gay conference meeting at the same time, with a speaker saying those exact same words. If this was to be a battle—*gays vs. Christians*—where did I fit in?

Other speakers followed, many of them self-professed ex-gays. The ex-gays spoke often about the childhood traumas they believed had caused them to become gay—nearly always sexual abuse, poor parenting, or some combination of both. Being gay, they insisted, was not something you were born with; it was something that happened to you as a child.

This theme permeated the conference. After one of the sessions, I picked up one of the ministry's brochures. Inside was a question and answer section. Among the questions, I saw this:

Q: Is homosexuality preventable in my child?

A: Absolutely. Show unconditional love for your child and ensure that he or she has positive and healthy doses of love from both parents.

In other words, if your child is gay, then you must not have done your job right as a parent.

I wondered if that was really a healthy message to be sending at a conference full of parents who were already worried about their gay kids. I hadn't been sexually abused. I didn't have any trauma. I had wonderful parents. What would these people say if they heard *my* story?

When the time came for breakout sessions, my parents chose one geared toward parents, while I went to the intriguingly titled session "The Root Causes of Male Homosexuality." This session was being taught by two friendly, clean-cut young gentlemen. As the session started, one of them held up two books. In one hand, he held a Bible. In the other, he held Elizabeth Moberly's *Homosexuality: A New Christian Ethic*, the "reparative drive" book I discussed in the previous chapter.

"Everything we're going to tell you in this session is based on these two books," he said.

I hadn't yet read Moberly's book, but I had read about it on the internet, and I knew it didn't fit me. It made me uneasy that the speaker came across as equating that one unproven theory with the *Bible*.

Each of the men told his story. Both had distant fathers. Both had overbearing mothers. For forty-five minutes, they explained the classic reparative drive theory in great detail, insisting that this distant father/overbearing mother paradigm explained every gay man in the world.

I squirmed in my seat, frustrated with the generalizations. Clearly, many ex-gay leaders had traumatic pasts, but that didn't mean *all* gay people did. I didn't have a distant father or an overbearing mother. I had wonderful, loving parents. How could they make claims about *everyone* based on their own limited experiences?

"Homosexuality," one of them said, "is an inability to relate to the same sex." He explained that gay men are gay because they're unable to properly relate to other men, leading them to "sexualize their emotional needs for male companionship."

Unable to properly relate to other men? I had always had plenty of close, healthy male friendships. I had more male friends than female friends, though I had plenty of each. I'd never felt unable to relate to my guy friends. Once again, nothing about this sounded like me at all.

The fact that their theory didn't fit me was one thing, but what really bothered me was watching how this talk was affecting the parents in the room. A large percentage of the attendees were straight parents of gay sons, and according to these guys, it was *their* fault that their sons were gay. Judging from their faces, many of them were taking it pretty hard. As I looked around, the parents' expressions seemed to be registering a mixture of hope and concern. On one hand, these men were offering them hope that their gay sons could still become straight with the right therapy. On the other hand, they were hearing that it was their own fault—and especially the fault of the fathers—that their sons were gay. One single mom had shared with me earlier that her gay son now had AIDS and was in poor health. I wondered how she was feeling right now, thinking that her only son's untimely death might be her fault because she hadn't provided a male role model.

I had to say something. I couldn't watch these parents struggle with needless guilt. If I didn't reassure them, who would?

The presenters opened the floor for questions. I nervously raised my hand, and they called on me. I stood up and introduced myself. "The model you've described doesn't sound like my childhood at all," I said. "I'm attracted to the same sex, and I don't know why. But I do know that I always had a good relationship with both of my parents, and I always felt fully loved and accepted by them. And it just really bothers me to see all of these parents here, feeling guilty and thinking that they didn't show their kids enough love, and that it's their fault that their kids are gay. I mean, what if it's not that? What if it's something else? I don't know what, but something else. I just think we should consider that possibility. I hate for all these parents to blame themselves."

I suddenly realized that I was giving a speech more than asking a question. My face got hot and I sat down. The presenters seemed perturbed, but I had said what I needed to say. They dismissively agreed that parents shouldn't focus on self-blame, then quickly moved to another question.

I wondered if I had done the right thing. I hadn't meant to be confrontational or argumentative.

As if in answer to my silent question, a man in front of me turned around and spoke to me as the session ended. "I'm so glad you said what you did," he said. "If you hadn't, I was going to." He leaned in to tell me his story. "The stuff these guys were talking about, that fits my childhood to a T. My father was cold and distant. He was never there for me. I never felt loved by him. I didn't have a good male role model in my life. My mother was bossy and overprotective. Every little thing those guys talked about sounded exactly like how I grew up."

His eyes lit up as he arrived at the twist in his story. "I'm heterosexual," he said. "Never had a gay thought or feeling in my life. When I got married and had a son, I didn't want him to have the kind of childhood I did, so I made sure I was always there for him. Everything my father wasn't. My son and I have a terrific relationship. He says so, and I know so. A few years ago, I found out that he's gay. According to these guys, I should have been gay, not him!" He chuckled wistfully.

People were getting up to leave the room. A college-age girl walked over and shook my hand. "Thank you," she said to me. "My brother is gay, and our parents aren't anything like those guys said. It's very good to know that there are other gay people who didn't have that kind of family either. I thought I was crazy, listening to them describe something that sounds nothing at all like my family." She introduced me to her mother, and the three of us had lunch together.

Later that day I ran into Jesse, one of the presenters of the "Root Causes" workshop. He recognized me and walked over, glancing at my name tag.

"Justin," he said, the slight edge to his voice belying his gentle smile, "I know you have your own beliefs, but during this weekend I think it would be helpful if you would just listen to what *we* teach."

His tone caught me off guard. I tried to be conciliatory. "Oh, gosh, I honestly didn't mean to sound confrontational this morning," I said. "I just didn't want all those parents to feel guilty, you know?"

"Well, the people you've been talking to may have told you things that are different from what we teach, but you're only here for three days, and I think it would be most worthwhile to you to just listen for the time you have left here."

The people I'd been talking to? "Wait a second," I said. "I didn't say that stuff because of anyone I've been talking to. This is coming from me. I don't fit the Moberly theory. That's just my life. I didn't have a distant father or any of that stuff."

"I didn't think I did either," he replied coolly, *"until I got into therapy and started looking harder."*

I didn't know what to say to that.

What kind of ministry takes a person who thinks he has a wonderful relationship with his father and convinces him that he actually has a bad one? This was feeling less and less like the work of God to me.

As I met more people at this conference and others, I discovered that I was far from alone. Many people told me similar stories of growing up happily, having healthy relationships with their parents, and then being pressured by ex-gay groups to find fault with their upbringing. But even as the evidence piled up that there were plenty of gay people *without* distant fathers and overbearing mothers, that dynamic remained far and away the most common explanation these ministries had for our gay feelings. The people I kept meeting who didn't fit that pattern were largely ignored or shoehorned in, forced to revisit their childhood memories over and over until they found some sort of problem to blame everything on.

By the time I rejoined my parents that evening, I was feeling thoroughly out of place. It wasn't just the workshop or the conversation with Jesse, though that had shaken me up some. It was the whole atmosphere. In novels, I had read the cliché "tension so thick you could cut it with a knife," but I had never truly experienced it until now. Outside of those glorious worship times, the air at this conference actually felt heavy, as if everyone were carrying some invisible weight that threatened to crush them at any moment. It was the polar opposite of the joyous experience I was used to in Christian spaces.

THE EX-GAY LEADER

My parents, meanwhile, had been spending some of their conference time connecting with ex-gay leaders, searching for someone whose testimony might help inspire me and give us all hope for my future. One of them, a man named Charles, had offered to sit down with us privately and answer some questions. So the next day, Charles, my parents, and I found a quiet room and settled in to talk.

Charles had a friendly, folksy demeanor, and he clearly wanted very much to ease my growing concerns about the ex-gay movement. After initial introductions, he told me a bit of his story. He was one of the ex-gay successes, he said. He'd lived "in the gay lifestyle" for a number of years before God transformed his heart and helped him to leave those promiscuous days behind. Now he was married to a woman, and they had a child together.

My parents seemed really encouraged by this story, and I could understand why. Here was someone who had apparently gone from gay to straight. As he jokingly put it, he'd "come out...

of homosexuality." (This, it turned out, was a common line in ex-gay circles.) If God had done it for him, surely God would do it for me too.

But as I listened, one question kept churning inside me. After all the other testimonies I'd read, I couldn't help but notice that he, too, hadn't said whether his *attractions* had changed from gay to straight. He'd only talked about his behaviors. Yes, he had a wife now, but so did those men at Homosexuals Anonymous. Even I'd had a girlfriend, but I'd never been attracted to her.

Charles noticed my expression. "You look like you have something to say," he said. Apparently I wasn't as good at hiding my emotions as I thought.

"Well...," I said, and then hesitated.

"Go ahead."

"Well, I was just wondering...have your *attractions* changed?"

"Oh, yes!" he said enthusiastically.

"Really?" I said, actually kind of surprised. I'd been starting to wonder if maybe people's attractions *weren't* changing after all.

"Yes, it's been a big change," he said. "I used to be a *slave* to my same-sex attractions. I thought they defined me. But Christ set me free from that bondage. I'm a new man. And now I'm married to a wonderful woman." He grinned at me, then at my parents.

There was something weird about this answer. On the surface, he was saying all the right things—using biblical language to talk about being set free from bondage and made a new man in Christ. And he had said that his attractions "changed." From the looks on my parents' faces, it seemed clear that they thought he had answered my question.

But he hadn't quite answered what I was asking. When I asked if his attractions had changed, I wanted to know if they had changed from gay to straight. He hadn't answered that. The only change he'd talked about was no longer being a slave to them, like the other testimonies I'd read. That was great, but, again, it wasn't the problem I was facing. I *already* wasn't a slave to my sex drive. Was he dodging my question on purpose? Or was I just nitpicking?

"So...would you say you're *straight* now?" I asked, trying to clarify.

"I don't use terms like *gay* or *straight*," he said. "My identity is in Christ."

Again, a very Christian-sounding response. But it still didn't answer my question—and it stung a bit too. Did he really mean that my identity wasn't in Christ if I didn't use the same words he did? I glanced over at my parents, wondering if *they* thought my identity wasn't in Christ.

We must have talked for at least an hour, maybe two. And I liked Charles a lot. He struck me as a genuinely nice man. But our conversation was frustrating. Every time I tried to ask if his attractions had changed from same-sex to opposite-sex, he would just talk about how he was married now and very happy with his wife. Eventually, I stopped asking because I felt like I was being rude.

The thing is, Charles didn't *seem* happy to me. His eyes had the same tired look I'd seen in the eyes of the men at Homosexuals Anonymous. He seemed to be carrying that heaviness I felt everywhere at this conference, like life had worn him down and it was all he could do to put on a smile and keep going. Years later, I was sadly unsurprised to learn that Charles and his wife had gotten a divorce.

The most frustrating part of the meeting, though, was the effect it had on my relationship with my parents. When we discussed it afterward, it was as if we'd sat through two completely different meetings. To them, it seemed that Charles had answered my questions very directly, and my reluctance to accept his story at face value had them concerned. Here was someone offering us hope; why wasn't I accepting it? I could tell they were worried for me, afraid that I was beginning to doubt the ex-gay path.

"Don't give up on God!" they urged.

"Don't worry," I reassured them, "I'm not giving up on God." It's true; I was still fully committed to following Jesus wherever he might lead.

Deep down, though, I was scared. Because I was becoming less and less sure where that was going to take me.

DOWN THE RABBIT HOLE

It was becoming clear to me that something wasn't right in the ex-gay world—or at least the parts of it I'd seen so far. But what other choice did I have? I wasn't willing to abandon my faith, and in churches like mine, ex-gay groups weren't *an* option for Christians attracted to the same sex; they were *the* option. Either I had to find an ex-gay group to connect with—one with integrity and actual stories of attraction change—or I was going to be left totally on my own.

But were there really any true stories of gay-to-straight attraction change? I needed to know the truth. I had to be sure. And that meant there was one more place I had to go: the annual Exodus International conference.

Exodus International was a Christian umbrella organization that referred people to hundreds of affiliated ex-gay ministries around the world. Exodus essentially functioned as the central hub for the Christian ex-gay movement as a whole. According to an ad campaign, "more than 850 former homosexuals" had attended the previous year's Exodus conference, making it by far the largest event of its kind. With that many people, I thought, surely I could find at least *one* person whose attractions had changed—if they actually existed. I went online and booked my ticket.

The weeklong conference was far nicer—and more expensive— than any of the events I'd attended so far, and the list of speakers and workshop presenters was a veritable who's who of all the ex-gay leaders I'd ever heard of. I went to their workshops, listened to their talks, and connected with as many people as I could between sessions.

I met people there who'd been in ex-gay counseling for years—some for their entire adult lives. I met people who'd willingly undergone exorcisms, thinking perhaps demons were causing their attractions. I met people who'd gone through every form of psychological treatment I could imagine, including shock therapy. These people came from all walks of life, and they had incredible levels of faith in Jesus and an overwhelming commitment to becoming whoever God wanted them to be. They had made drastic changes in their behaviors since coming to Christ. But when I asked them in private about their attractions, *none of them* could tell me that they had actually become straight. Not even the famous ex-gay leaders.

And that was strange. Because everyone seemed sure that it really was possible. Everyone had stories of how it had happened for someone else—someone whose testimony they'd read in a book or heard in a talk somewhere. Exodus materials loudly proclaimed that "change is possible" and "you don't have to be gay!" But when I asked people about their own personal testimonies, none of them could honestly tell me that they *themselves* had experienced that kind of change.

With each story I heard, my heart ached more. These people were putting everything on the line in the belief that God was going to make them straight. If that really was God's plan, I didn't want to do anything to get in the way of it, so I largely kept my concerns to myself. But I worried about what would happen to these people if, after so many years of trying, they didn't experience the change they all assumed would come. Most of them didn't seem to have any kind of backup plan.

Meanwhile, I couldn't help but wonder: If there really had been "more than 850 former homosexuals" at the previous year's conference, where were they now? So far, I hadn't found a single one.

TERRY'S STORY

As I wrestled with what I was learning about the ex-gay movement, I had no idea that someone I knew was also wrestling with these very same questions.

Terry was a family friend. He and his wife knew my parents and went to our church. I didn't know him well, but he struck me as a nice guy in a happy marriage.

I didn't know Terry was gay. His wife was his best friend, and he had married her as a "step of faith" toward becoming straight. They had adopted children, and he did his best to love his wife in every way he could, but the truth was that he had never been physically attracted to her, and marriage hadn't changed that. What they had was a friendship, not a romance.

Terry agonized over the situation. He was trying to follow God by being a faithful husband and good father, but a friendship is not a substitute for a marriage, and after years of trying, nothing had made him straight.

When Terry's wife was killed in a tragic car accident, he was devastated. He had lost his best friend, and it only made his loneliness feel all the more unbearable. His wife was dead, and he had never been able to see her the way a straight man would have. The grief tore him apart.

As time passed and Terry's life returned to normal, he had to think about what to do next. He had married once thinking that he would become straight. Now he knew better, and he could avoid making the same mistake again. Still, the pressure of being single and having to hide his same-sex attractions made him lonelier than ever. Seeking advice, he confided his story in a Christian counselor recommended by the church.

The counselor encouraged Terry not to give up on his quest to become straight. He urged Terry to get to know women in the church and allow them to provide the solace he was craving. He warned Terry not to let his doubts get in the way of doing what God obviously wanted him to do: find the right woman and get remarried.

Trusting the guidance of his spiritual adviser and confidant, Terry did just that.

But this marriage didn't work either. On the outside, Terry continued to pretend everything was going well. In truth, as it became more apparent that he was gay and wasn't going to become straight, his marriage was crumbling. Eventually, everything fell apart, resulting in tremendous anger and pain on all sides. Everyone was devastated: Terry, Terry's wife, and Terry's kids.

I didn't know about any of this until I ran into Terry a few years ago and he told me the story. Today he is bitter and angry at the church. He feels lied to, cheated out of years of happiness by a promise of change that never materialized. There is tremendous pain in his eyes whenever he talks about his experiences. When I asked for his permission to tell his story, he quickly agreed.

"I just don't want anyone else to go through what I've been through," he said.

Terry's is one of so many stories I could tell you of people who gave their whole hearts to trying to change their orientation, only to have everything come crashing down around them. The experience has left many people feeling broken and betrayed, some feeling so wounded by the church that they can't bring themselves to set foot inside a worship service anymore.

These were some of the most dedicated and devout Christians you could ever meet. They were willing to sacrifice everything to please God. But years upon years of trying to change and being told it would happen didn't do anything to make them straight. Instead, it only damaged their faith and their feelings of self-worth. When they finally came to the point of telling the truth about what they were feeling, their ex-gay mentors accused them of "backsliding," and the churches they had so loved seemed to have no place for them.

How could something like this happen? How could ministries run and recommended by so many loving, well-meaning Christians end up doing such damage? These ministries were built to help people and give them space to be honest. So where did it all go so wrong?

CHAPTER 7

◆

HOW DID WE GET HERE?

In one of my favorite scenes in *Through the Looking-Glass*, the second of Lewis Carroll's two Alice books, Alice meets Humpty Dumpty, who tells her that "un-birthday" presents are better than birthday presents, because there are 364 days for "un-birthday" presents:

> "And only one for birthday presents, you know. There's glory for you!"
>
> "I don't know what you mean by 'glory,'" Alice said.
>
> Humpty Dumpty smiled contemptuously. "Of course you don't—till I tell you. I meant 'there's a nice knock-down argument for you!'"
>
> "But 'glory' doesn't mean 'a nice knock-down argument,'" Alice objected.
>
> "When I use a word," Humpty Dumpty said, in rather a scornful tone, "it means just what I choose it to mean—neither more nor less."

In Wonderland, the characters constantly change the meanings of words to suit their own needs, resulting in much confusion for poor Alice, who has no way of seeing into their heads.[1] In the real world, though, communication depends on a *shared understanding* of what a word means. If I suddenly start using a word to mean something different from what most people mean by that word, I'll only confuse people—or possibly even mislead them.

That, I finally realized, was what was happening in the ex-gay world.

As we saw in chapter 5, the word *gay* in our culture usually means "attracted to the same sex." When I said I wanted to stop being gay, I meant that I wanted to stop being *attracted to the same sex*. So when I first heard the testimonies of people who said they "used to be gay" but weren't anymore, I thought that meant they used to be *attracted to the same sex*, and now they were straight—attracted to the opposite sex.

That's also what my parents thought they meant.

It's what my Christian friends thought they meant.

And it's what Terry, his counselor, and many others like them thought too.

But it wasn't true.

What most of us didn't realize was that the ex-gay movement often used a *different* definition of *gay*.

The lightbulb went on for me as I sat in a workshop on the third day of the Exodus conference. The workshop presenter was a prominent and influential ex-gay leader—a minor celebrity in ex-gay circles. And in this workshop, he explained how he and many other ex-gay leaders used language.

There was a difference, he told us, between being *homosexual* and being *gay*. To be *homosexual* was involuntary. It simply meant that you had unchosen same-sex attractions—the attractions I had and that most of the other people in the room had. By this definition, we were all *homosexual*. But to be *gay*, he said, was voluntary. It was a chosen *identity*. If you didn't *identify* as gay, then you *weren't* gay; it was as simple as that.

This meant, according to him, that you could be a "non-gay homosexual." And it meant that all of us could go home and proudly tell people we were "no longer gay" by simply choosing not to identify that way—even if none of our attractions had changed.

For a minute, all I could do was sit there in shock, staring at the terms on the worksheet he'd given us. No one I knew outside of the ex-gay world used the phrase "non-gay homosexual." It seemed almost designed to create confusion.

But as I quickly realized, this weird language quirk explained a lot about why the optimistic ex-gay messaging didn't seem to match the reality. When Exodus said "you don't have to be gay" and Exodus leaders referred to themselves as "ex-gay" or "formerly gay," it gave the impression that they were talking about becoming straight. In fact, though, they were using this alternate definition. They had changed their *language*—and in some cases their *behavior*—but their *attractions* were still for the same sex.

For a moment, I thought this might explain all the confusion. As it turned out, it was only the tip of the iceberg. I gradually realized that other terms, too—*change, identity, homosexuality, heterosexuality*—were being used in unexpected ways, creating misleading impressions in those who heard them. Even more confusing: Different ex-gays often had different definitions for the same words, and even the same people often used them inconsistently.

The workshop leader had said that *gay* was an identity and *homosexual* was a condition. But an Exodus policy document said that *homosexual* was an identity and made no mention of *gay* at all. (This, perhaps, explained how the conference could be filled with "former homosexuals" even if none of them had become straight.)

That same policy document, confusingly, defined *homosexuality* as "attraction to members of one's own sex," which suggested that when someone like Charles said he "came out of homosexuality," that should mean he no longer had same-sex attractions. In practice, though, ex-gay speakers nearly always described "coming out of homosexuality" as a change in their behaviors rather than their attractions.

Elizabeth Moberly's popular book, meanwhile, said that being a homosexual wasn't a matter of choice, identity, or behavior at all: "To 'stop being a homosexual' means to stop being a person with same-sex psychological deficits....A non-practising homosexual is still a homosexual."[2] On the other hand, psychotherapist Joseph Nicolosi, another influential figure in the movement, said that *homosexuality* was a changeable orientation but that there was no such thing as a *homosexual*. "I believe that all people are heterosexual but that some have a homosexual problem," he told the *New York Times*.[3]

Depending on which ex-gay leader you asked, then, a celibate Christian in my shoes might be described as gay, or homosexual but *not* gay, or *heterosexual*, or none of the above. "Coming out of homosexuality" could refer to a change in behavior, in orientation, or simply in language, depending on who said it and what impression they wanted to give. Some used the abbreviation *SSA—same-sex attracted*—as a substitute for *gay*, arguing that *gay* was an identity word Christians should never use. Others insisted that to use *any* of these terms at all, including *SSA*, meant your identity wasn't truly in Christ.

It was enough to make your head spin!

But if "God is not the author of confusion" (1 Corinthians 14:33 KJV), how had this complicated, often contradictory language become so deeply ingrained in the ex-gay movement?

THE SEEDS OF CONFUSION

When the earliest ex-gay ministries were founded, in 1973, it was with good intentions. That same year, the American Psychiatric Association stopped classifying homosexuality as a disorder, and a lot of Christians who didn't want to be gay felt the psychological community was abandoning them.

As I'd learned from their testimonies, many of the founders of these ministries had spent years immersed in a lifestyle of anonymous sex, sketchy clubs, and substance abuse. That world was where they'd first learned the word *gay* before it had become mainstream, and that particular way of life was what they still associated with the word *gay*. So when they began to label themselves "ex-gay," they didn't mean that their attractions had changed; they meant that their *lifestyles* had changed. As Frank Worthen, the so-called father of the ex-gay movement, later explained, "We had left the gay lifestyle, and so we would say, 'We're not gay anymore,' but we couldn't honestly say we were heterosexual."[4]

At first, these "ex-gays" were just happy to find each other as they left their past way of life and pursued Christ together. But it soon became apparent that they didn't agree on what was next.

Some thought that ex-gay ministries should promote *behavior change*. They believed it was important to be realistic and admit that they were unlikely to ever become straight. So instead of making that the goal, they wanted to focus on helping Christians with a homosexual orientation live celibate lives and resist the temptations posed by their same-sex attractions. After all, they reasoned, God had never promised that the Christian life would be easy or free of temptation.

Others, though, wanted the movement to continue promoting *orientation change*—fully convinced that God was going to take their same-sex attractions away entirely and replace them with opposite-sex attractions. In their minds, settling for celibacy represented a lack of faith and wasn't the complete change they were praying for. And it was this second group—the "God will make us straight" group—that ultimately set Exodus policy and determined the future of the ex-gay movement.

There was just one problem. As convinced as they were that they would eventually become straight, it wasn't actually happening.

THE WHITE LIE

Christians really are a compassionate bunch, even though the cultural reputation we have right now doesn't reflect that. Because so many Christians—especially evangelical Christians like me—believed that gay relationships were sinful, they also wanted to believe that there was some way that gay people could become straight so that they could legitimately enjoy all the benefits of romance and marriage. The ex-gays, too, wanted to believe this and to provide hope to others. Sadly, that desire for hope ultimately got in the way of being completely honest.

I wasn't immune to this. In 1996, shortly after realizing I was gay, I read a column by advice columnist Ann Landers in which parents of a gay son asked about counseling to help him become straight. "A 20-year-old male who has romantic fantasies about other males is unquestionably homosexual," Landers wrote in response. "Counseling will not 'straighten him around.' Nor is there any medication that will perform that magic."

At the time, I was convinced Landers was wrong. I worried about all the struggling teens out there like me, and I knew I needed to set the record straight (so to speak) and tell them that change *was* possible. I wrote a letter identifying myself as a gay teen who was becoming straight, urging others to trust God and have hope that they, too, could become straight like me. My life was proof.

The letter sat on my desk for days. I couldn't quite bring myself to mail it. At the time, I believed with all my heart that I was going to become straight and that I was in the process already. But in the letter, I had exaggerated the amount of "change" I was actually experiencing. I hadn't lied, but I hadn't been completely honest either. The trouble was, if I was honest about the lack of attraction change I had experienced so far, I knew no one would take my story seriously. They would write me off as deceiving myself. If I waited until after my feelings had changed before writing, I'd be too late to respond to this column. I had to respond right away, and I was so certain that I was in the process of becoming straight that it didn't feel like a lie to *lead people to believe* that I was further along in the process than I actually was.

In the end, I couldn't send the letter. It felt too much like deception, and as a Christian I believed it was wrong to lie, even for what I was sure was a good cause.

I thought back to that letter when I later noticed the differences between so many ex-gay men's public testimonies and the real-life struggles they shared in private. I'm convinced that many of them, like me, didn't really want to be deceptive; they just wanted to provide hope, and sometimes that meant not quite telling people *everything*. They'd minimize the amount of same-sex attraction they still felt, for instance, and focus on their commitment to their wives without mentioning their lack of sexual attraction to the female form or the impact that had on their marriages. It seemed justified; who would expect them to reveal such intimate struggles?

And I suspect many of those early ex-gay ministry founders had similar thoughts as they waited for their attractions to change. But little white lies have a way of snowballing into something much bigger. The more they talked about being "no longer gay" and called themselves "former homosexuals," the more they began to believe it. Soon, leaders began to emerge with powerful stories of how God had changed them—and those stories inspired churches around the world to believe that gay people could become straight.

But those powerful stories weren't what they claimed to be. They were really a combination of wishful thinking and confusing language. And sadly, the result of that has been a long history of pain and broken promises.

If only we'd seen the signs. They were there from the very beginning.

What a tangled web we weave

Homosexuals Anonymous began its life as a part of Quest Learning Center, an institution founded by Colin Cook promising "freedom from homosexuality." Cook, the married-with-children ex-gay "success story" who developed the Homosexuals Anonymous program, wrote in 1982 that "a change in orientation is [not] a requirement for acceptance with God or entrance into the fellowship in the church," but that "the orientation may be healed," that "freedom from homosexual drive...is a real possibility," and that "all who desire it may realize their inborn...heterosexuality."[5]

Four years later, Cook was forced to resign when a number of his male clients came forward to charge that Cook had been sexually molesting them in the course of therapy, telling them it was to help desensitize them to male stimuli. Cook finally confessed to inappropriate behavior, but told a reporter the next year that he had managed to overcome that impulse, and that "99.9%" of his same-sex fantasies were now gone.[6]

Eight years later, the *Denver Post* reported that Cook was still engaging in sexual contact and phone sex with his male counselees.[7] Cook's theories on orientation change have remained influential to this day.

◆

Michael Bussee and Gary Cooper were two of the original cofounders of Exodus International.[8] Both were married with kids. Early on in the ex-gay movement, Bussee helped coin the term *ex-gay*, and he and Cooper gained a reputation as two of the movement's most famous success stories. Together, they traveled across the country, speaking to excited Christian audiences and telling them that yes, it was possible for gay people to become straight.

In 1978, when psychological researchers contacted their ministry for an opportunity to interview some ex-gays and see whether orientation change was really possible, Bussee and Cooper combed through the files of about three hundred members, compiling a list of thirty who, in their opinion, had changed. Of those thirty, the researchers found eleven who agreed to talk to them and whom they identified as having successfully "changed to heterosexuality" based on their self-descriptions. Only five of the eleven claimed to have gone from exclusively homosexual to exclusively heterosexual, however; the others all admitted to continuing homosexuality in some form.[9] Michael Bussee and Gary Cooper were two of the five successes.

It was shortly after that study, on a plane on the way to another speaking engagement, that Bussee and Cooper broke down and confessed to each other that they were both still gay and had fallen in love with each other. Not surprisingly, their marriages did not survive. The movement they'd helped to start, however, did.

◆

By the time I came along with my own hopes for change twenty years later, people like Colin Cook, Michael Bussee, and Gary

Cooper were no longer household names of the movement. Instead, someone new had emerged as the ex-gay poster boy and most famous success story. When I asked people for an example of someone whose orientation really had changed from gay to straight, he was the one man they pointed to who didn't tell me otherwise.

His name was John Paulk.

Paulk had written a book called *Not Afraid to Change: The Remarkable Story of How One Man Overcame Homosexuality.* In it, he told how he had changed from a promiscuous drag queen to a heterosexual family man with a wife and son. Together with his wife, Anne, John appeared on national talk shows and news programs as "living proof" that orientation change really was possible for anyone who wanted it.

John Paulk's powerful story made him an important figure in ex-gay circles and beyond. He was named chairman of the board of Exodus International and head of the Homosexuality and Gender Division of Focus on the Family, an influential Christian nonprofit with a massive media empire. These roles allowed him to reach millions of Christian homes with his personal testimony, while his appearances on programs like *The Oprah Winfrey Show* and *Good Morning America* helped the ex-gay movement become a topic of mainstream discussion.

All of this meant that just as I was coming to the conclusion that ex-gay therapy didn't work, my friends and family members were hearing for the first time about the man whose "remarkable story" seemed to prove me wrong.

"Change *is* possible," they insisted. "Just read John Paulk's testimony. He overcame homosexuality."

I did read John's testimony. And to be honest, I wasn't sure what to make of it.

Like most other ex-gay leaders, Paulk stopped short of explicitly saying that his same-sex attractions were gone, but he strongly implied that they were. He referred to himself as a "heterosexual" who was "formerly gay," someone who had "changed [his] sexual orientation" and "come out of homosexuality."[10]

To most people, that meant he was straight, but I was skeptical. It didn't match what I had seen in other ex-gays. I suspected he was still living with same-sex attractions just like me, even though he was married to a woman. But there was no way for me to see inside his head or prove to anyone else what he did or didn't feel. All I knew was that if he really had gone from gay to straight, his experience was extremely rare.

That wasn't good enough for my Christian friends, though. In their eyes, if John Paulk had become straight, *anyone* could become straight. If it hadn't happened for me, that only meant I didn't have enough faith. Nothing I said could convince them otherwise.

But then, in September of 2000, Paulk wound up in the middle of a scandal when he was recognized at a gay bar while on a business trip in Washington, D.C. When confronted later about the incident, Paulk claimed he hadn't known it was a gay bar and that he had only gone in to use the restroom. He later confessed that this was a lie but claimed he hadn't had any inappropriate motives for going to the bar. After the incident, he was removed from his position at Exodus, but he continued to serve as the homosexuality specialist for Focus on the Family and to be cited as proof that anyone could become straight.

It wasn't until over a decade later that Paulk publicly confessed that he was still gay—that the testimony he'd used to convince millions of Christians that orientation change was possible had, in fact, only been what he *wanted* to be true, not what actually *was* true.

"At the time, I truly believed that it would happen," he wrote in a public apology letter. "[But] while many things in my life did change as a Christian, my sexual orientation did not. . . . I am truly, truly sorry for the pain I have caused."[11]

OPEN EYES, HEAVY HEARTS

For decades, many well-meaning Christians supported ex-gay ministries, believing, as I had, that they were God's solution for Christians with same-sex attractions. Maybe, like John Paulk, we believed what we wanted to believe, because believing that God would make people straight was easier than wrestling with difficult questions when we didn't have all the answers.

But once our eyes are opened to the truth—once we've seen the damage this approach has done in so many lives—we can't shut them again and pretend nothing has changed. We have to humble ourselves and find a way forward. That's not easy, especially when you've invested a lot of yourself in an idea that turned out to be wrong.

Several years after John Paulk's scandal, amid growing criticism of the ex-gay movement, Exodus president Alan Chambers assured an audience that there were still "tens of thousands of people who have successfully changed their orientation." He was one of them, he said.[12]

By 2013, however, with more and more ex-gay leaders publicly confessing that they were still gay, the truth had become impossible to ignore. Exodus International closed its doors, and Chambers also publicly apologized for the harm the ex-gay message had caused.

Today he admits that there aren't "tens of thousands" of ex-gay success stories. In fact, he says, in all his years running the largest ex-gay ministry in the world, he never actually saw any evidence that *anyone* had gone from gay to straight—including himself.

Even that wasn't the end of the ex-gay movement, though. In the aftermath of Exodus's closing, a new ex-gay network called Hope for Wholeness was formed by a man named McKrae Game. Game had led one of Exodus's affiliate ministries, and he thought Chambers had been wrong to give up on the ex-gay approach. He wanted to continue Exodus's work, convinced this new ex-gay network could help people finally find "freedom from homosexuality."

In 2019, Game became the latest ex-gay leader to publicly confess that he, too, was still gay, admitting to the *Post and Courier* that the ex-gay ideas he'd promoted for so many years were "not just a lie, but...very harmful."[13]

Hope for Wholeness closed in 2020.

◆

Today, terms like *ex-gay* are rarely heard anymore, and many people think of the ex-gay movement as a thing of the past. Having seen how many people were hurt by it, I wish that were true.

Unfortunately, while the term *ex-gay* has mostly disappeared, the teachings themselves haven't. Books of ex-gay testimonies continue to circulate in some churches, even though many of them were written by people who now admit their stories were lies or half-truths. And many well-meaning pastors and ministry leaders, having heard these stories in the past, continue to teach that God will make anyone straight if they want to be—suggesting that anyone who doesn't become straight must not have wanted it enough or had enough faith.

As long as that's the message Christians are hearing, there will continue to be heartbreaking stories like Terry's.

And James's.

James and I met several years after my involvement with the ex-gay ministries. He was about my age, celibate, and a Christian. He confessed to me that he, too, was struggling with his same-sex attractions. We became friends, and although we didn't live near each other, we kept in touch by phone over the years. We both enjoyed intellectual conversations—and sometimes friendly debates—about issues of the day, and we openly shared our struggles as gay Christians in a world where gays and Christians are at war.

But where I had become convinced that ex-gay ministries didn't work, James wasn't so sure. He was deeply uncomfortable with his orientation, and the claim that gays could become straight was very appealing to him.

Eventually, his discomfort with his sexuality proved too much for him to bear, and he told me he was going to pursue an ex-gay path. I honestly told him my concerns and my fears for him but promised that whatever he decided, I would always be his friend.

Time passed, and he told me he felt like he was becoming straight. Then he told me he had met a girl. They had become friends, and it was such a great friendship that he was sure it could turn into something more.

"Be careful," I cautioned. "This isn't just about you anymore. This is about her life as well."

He assured me that he knew what he was doing.

They started dating, and James enthusiastically talked about the relationship and his new girlfriend every time we spoke. I had grown to know James pretty well by this point, and I could tell by the way he talked about her that his feelings for her weren't the same kind of passionate feelings a straight guy would have for a girl, or that James still had for guys. He was, I thought, blinded by love—not romantic love for his girlfriend, but love for the idea of being in love—or, perhaps more accurately, love for the idea of being straight. I realized that it wasn't this girl he was so passionate about; it was the simple fact that she was a girl. She was a friend, but she had come to represent something much more important to him, and the thing she represented—the promise of heterosexuality—had become far more important than the actual human relationship they had.

James began talking about asking his girlfriend to marry him.

"Does she know about your attractions?" I asked him. "I mean, does she know that you're still attracted to guys?"

"She knows some of it," he said. "I didn't tell her everything because I didn't want her to worry too much."

"What did you tell her?" I asked.

"I told her that I used to have attractions to guys," he said.

"But you *still* have attractions to guys," I said.

"They're going away!" he said. "Anyway, it's in my past."

"Did you tell her you're also not attracted to girls?" I said.

"I'm attracted to *her*," he said defensively.

"You told me that you didn't feel the same things for her that you do for other guys," I reminded him.

"It's getting better," he said unconvincingly.

"Please be careful, James," I urged. "She deserves to know the truth."

He assured me again that he knew what he was doing.

James proposed, and soon the two were married. After the wedding, James told me how sure he was that he had made the right decision—how happy he was to finally be married. Also, he mentioned impishly, it was nice to finally be able to have sex.

Sex had been one of James's primary concerns. He had a reasonably strong sex drive, but he believed it would be wrong for him to be in a relationship with a guy, so getting married to a woman had felt like his only option to tame his feelings.

Thanks to that pent-up sexual frustration, James had no trouble performing sexually with his wife. But rather than tame his sex drive, the sexual contact seemed only to ignite it.

James began calling me more frequently now, and I noticed that he often tried to steer our conversations around to sex. He delighted in sharing graphic details of his and his wife's sex life. He confessed that he was still as attracted to guys as ever. He confessed that his fantasies were all still about men, not women. And he told me what I had suspected but hadn't wanted to ask: that his wife's body didn't really turn him on sexually, but that he was able to perform with her by fantasizing about men.

And then he said something that knocked the wind out of me.

"Sometimes," he said, lowering his voice to a seductive whisper, "*I think about you.*"

"Dude! That's not okay," I hissed back into the phone. "You're married! You can't say things like that."

I realized what was going on. James had feelings for me. He was trying to meet needs through our friendship that his wife couldn't meet because she was a woman. Telling me about his sex life had been his way of vicariously having a sexual connection with another guy without admitting to himself that this was what he was doing. It was, perhaps, the same thing that made ex-gay support groups so appealing to married men struggling with same-sex attractions.

Even though I thought it had been a mistake for James to get married, now that he was married, there was no way I could participate in undermining the vows he had made to his wife. Perhaps he wasn't being physically unfaithful, but he was being emotionally unfaithful, and I couldn't be part of it.

I stopped talking to James on the phone, though he still sent me occasional updates through email. James ended up making "friends" with a local guy, and in one of his emails, he confessed to me that the two of them had had sexual contact. I was horrified and wrote back to remind him that he was cheating on his wife.

He told me not to worry, that it was only "fooling around" and not full-blown sex.

From the outside, James's marriage looks happy. His wife still doesn't know the full extent of his same-sex attractions. She doesn't know that he knows me or that he tried to flirt with me while they were married. She doesn't know about his local friend, who has been putting increasing pressure on James to take their relationship in a more sexual direction—pressure James has so far resisted, but not entirely spurned. Deep down, though, I'm sure she must suspect that something isn't quite right in their marriage.

Those who know James would consider him an ex-gay success story. On the basis of his testimony, they would encourage their gay friends and family members to follow in his footsteps.

I hope and pray that no one does.

CHAPTER 8

◆

THAT THE MAN SHOULD BE ALONE

*D*id I do thaaaat?"

Say those four simple words—bonus points if you get the nasal tone just right—and I'm instantly transported back to my childhood. It was the catchphrase of Steve Urkel, the klutzy, nerdy, hilariously annoying neighbor on the popular TV sitcom *Family Matters*. Urkel, played by Jaleel White, provided the wacky comic relief on an otherwise sweet and thoughtful series about a family dealing with, well, family matters.

Family Matters was one of several shows I regularly watched with my parents and younger siblings, alongside other family-friendly fare from across the decades like *I Love Lucy*, *Little House on the Prairie*, and *Home Improvement*. My parents were careful not to let us watch *too much* TV, but there was something special about those times when we gathered after dinner to laugh or cry together, sharing in the adventures of these characters who somehow managed to solve all their problems by the end of each episode. To this day, I can still hear my mom mimicking Carol Brady from *The Brady Bunch* as she served us "pork chops and applesauce" for dinner, or my dad calling, "Goodnight, John-Boy!" in imitation of *The Waltons*.

Like many evangelical families, my family had always had a somewhat rocky relationship with Hollywood. We knew that not all "family-friendly" TV shows and movies would align with *our* family's values, and my parents taught us to be discerning about what we watched and the lessons we took from it. But there were a lot of good, wholesome messages we could support in these shows, and a key theme of all of them was right there in the title of one of our favorites. These were shows about family matters, but they were also shows about how family *matters*. Families are important. Friends may come and go, but families are supposed to stick together through thick and thin.

As kids, we trust our parents to be there for us even if we mess up, and when we get married and start our own families, we make a commitment "for better or for worse, for richer, for poorer, in sickness and in health." It's a formal way of saying, "This is deeper than friendship. This is *family*. You can count on me to stick around and support you even when no one else does." Real-life problems aren't always solved in thirty minutes, and we need to know that when things aren't going our way, there's someone we can count on to tough it out alongside us.

Of course, human beings don't always live up to those expectations, and as Christians, we believe that our ultimate support is found in God, who is there for us even when the most devoted human beings let us down. But God also knew from the beginning that we would need *human* companionship too—because God built us that way.

After creating Adam in the Garden of Eden, God observed that

"It is not good that the man should be alone," recognizing that Adam would be better off having someone like himself—another human—to share this life with. It was out of love, then, that God gave him Eve, a partner and life companion, not simply a good friend but a sexually attractive lover.

For the vast majority of us, that special, exclusive partnership is something totally irreplaceable. A spouse provides companionship, comfort, support, love, and so much more. Those who are single search eagerly for someone to date and ultimately to marry; those who are married often rely on their spouse far more than they realize. The apostle Paul saw marriage as a concession, not the ideal, but even he recognized that it is a concession many of us would be deeply unhappy without.

I've met people who seem to have what some Christians would call "the gift of celibacy." Whatever challenges they may find in singleness, it also seems to be the situation in which they most thrive. They don't particularly mind being alone; they may even prefer it. Ask them if they would like to have a significant other someday, and they have no hesitation in shaking their heads and saying, "Why? I'm perfectly content the way I am." They seem to be wired that way.

But the rest of us aren't wired that way. For most of us, our years of singlehood are a struggle, and though we may surround ourselves with friends and things to do and never complain about being alone, being single remains a burden rather than a blessing for us. We long for God to say to us, too, that it is not good for us to be alone, and to fashion someone out of the earth to be our companion.

Film critic Roger Ebert understood the importance of that companionship. Thyroid cancer robbed him of his TV career, his ability to speak, and portions of his face, leaving him severely deformed. Through it all, his wife, Chaz, gave him strength and support. In a 2010 entry in his blog, Ebert wrote about the importance of such connections:

> What do lonely people desire? Companionship. Love. Recognition. Entertainment. Camaraderie. Distraction. Encouragement. Change. Feedback. Someone once said the fundamental reason we get married is because we have a universal human need for a *witness*. All of these are possibilities. But what all lonely people share is a desire not to be—or at least not to feel—alone....
>
> Why do people marry with no prospects of children? Babies are not the only thing two people can create together. They can create a safe private world. They can create a reality that affirms their values. They can stand for something. They can find someone to laugh with, and confide in. Someone to hold them when they need to be held. A danger of the internet would be if we begin to meet those needs without feeling there has to be another person in the room....
>
> A few weeks ago, something happened. Chaz needed emergency surgery. There were two nights when I was alone and she was in the hospital, just as there were months when she was alone and I was in the hospital. And in the middle of the night a great fear enveloped me. If "anything happened" (as they say), I would be so terribly, terribly alone, and sad. I would miss her so much. This feeling came over me in a wave. I pulled the covers tighter around me. Then I would know what loneliness was.[1]

There are, of course, many single people in the world, and I'm not suggesting that one needs a spouse in order to have a happy, fulfilling life. But for those who have a spouse or don't particularly feel the need for one, it can be far too easy to offer trite platitudes about how God is sufficient, ignoring the realities of loneliness that so many single people face. After all, seeing that Adam was alone, God did not simply say, "I am sufficient for you"; nor did God expect Adam to meet all his needs with a *friend*.

As the truth about ex-gay ministries began to settle in and I considered the life ahead of me, I found myself experiencing the kind of loneliness Ebert describes. Was I destined to be alone? What sort of future would I have?

Growing up, I had always assumed certain things about how my life was supposed to go. I would date girls until I found the right one, and then we'd fall in love, get engaged, get married, and have kids. I would work in a job where I could serve God with my talents, and I'd be a loving husband and devoted father, just as my father had been.

Even after realizing I was gay, I'd thought I was still on that path, that with prayer, faith, time, and therapy, I could become straight and still live out my dream future. That was what I wanted, and more importantly, I'd been confident that was God's plan for my life.

Now, realizing that I might always be attracted to guys instead of girls, I had to face some harsh truths. I had to face the fact that I might never again be the golden boy, so respected in my church and Christian community, and that the stigma of being gay could follow me my entire life. And I had to face the realization that my future wasn't going to be what I had always assumed it would be.

But what would it be? If I couldn't become straight, I had basically three options.

One option was to hide the extent of my same-sex attractions, pretend to be straight, and marry a woman in spite of my lack of attraction for her. This would allow me to have all the perks of marriage, raise a family, and be respectable in the eyes of others, even though I wasn't really straight.

I only briefly considered that option before dismissing it outright. I not only lacked sexual attractions to women, I also lacked any kind of romantic feelings for them. I knew that without romantic or sexual attractions, such a marriage would be a sham at its core and would be completely unfair to my wife. She would deserve a relationship with someone who felt things for her that I could never feel. Beyond that, I knew I would never feel comfortable in my own home trying to "play marriage" with someone I felt nothing for.

A second option was to have a relationship with someone I *could* fall in love with: another guy. The romantic feelings I lacked for girls, I had for guys instead. When I became close friends with a guy I really cared about, I felt all kinds of happy, intoxicating, silly, tender, exciting feelings bubbling to the surface, feelings I had to suppress because I knew he could never return them. I was beginning to realize that these were the feelings that straight people felt in the presence of the opposite sex, the reason straight men and women went to such great lengths to impress one another and the reason they wanted to be in each other's presence whenever they could. It wasn't just about sex; it was about human connection and love.

Around the right guy, I felt as if I were walking through the clouds and radiating sunlight from within. I wouldn't have minded making a fool of myself or writing sappy love poems or reenacting a grand romantic gesture from his favorite movie, if only I thought it would make him happy. But when I met guys who made me feel this way, I always fought to keep any evidence of those feelings locked away inside. It was hopeless to feel that way for someone who wasn't attracted to people of your gender.

But what if I met someone who made me feel that way *and* who had the same feelings for me? That seemed almost unimaginable. I'd spent so many years suppressing my feelings that I had never considered that someone might someday return them. Just imagining this possibility made my heart leap for joy like almost nothing I had ever experienced. For a blissful moment, I allowed myself to dream about what it might be like to fall in love with someone who actually loved me back. What must that be like? Even just to share a simple meal together, or a quiet night watching TV side by side on the couch, knowing that we had each other—

But no. The image lasted only a moment before harsh reality crashed back in. Even if I did meet someone like that, could God really approve of such a relationship? If not, there was no use in wishing otherwise.

Suppose, I thought, I committed to abstain from sex entirely. In that case, could I at least have a sex-free romance? Or was it the very idea of romance between two men that God abhorred?

I looked to the Bible for guidance on this question, but the things I found didn't help. In Genesis, I read the story of Sodom, a city destroyed by God after a threat of male-male gang rape. In Leviticus, male-male sex was called an abomination, punishable by death. In Romans, homosexuality was linked with idol worship and rebellion against God. In 1 Corinthians, "homosexual offenders" were one of the sinful groups Paul said wouldn't inherit the kingdom of God. Taken together, these passages clearly seemed to say that God condemned gay sex, but none of them were any help to me in figuring out how a gay *person* should live or whether there might be a place for a nonsexual romantic relationship—some way I might still be able to fall in love as long as I maintained boundaries about sex.

As beautiful as the idea of falling in love seemed, I couldn't help but worry that it was splitting hairs. Would God really approve of romance in a situation where He condemned sex? If male-male sex was so offensive to God, I imagined that male-male romance would be as well, even if it wasn't explicitly mentioned. I was committed to God first and foremost, so if God didn't approve of it, I couldn't have it.

The third option, of course, was lifelong celibacy. No relationship, no sex, no romance. I didn't like the sound of that at all. Still, I knew that if I wanted to serve Christ with my life, and if He was calling me to celibacy, then I would have to be celibate.

I considered what this would mean. Obviously, it would mean no sex. Ever.

Imagine telling a typical teenage boy that he can never have sex, that he must go his entire life without being able to experience it even once. I suspect his response would be less than enthusiastic. Mine was likewise. When you're a teenager, abstaining from sex can be difficult enough when you're waiting for the right time. It's far more difficult when you know there will never be a right time, even if you find the right person.

It wasn't just the physical pleasure I wanted; I craved the intimacy of sex. I craved that experience of total vulnerability with another human being.

And yet, as difficult as I knew it would be to go without sex for the rest of my life, I felt I could handle that. It wasn't what I wanted, but if that was where God ultimately called me, I would do it, and I'd be fine.

Other parts of lifelong celibacy were harder for me to handle. To go without sex was one thing, but to go without romance and companionship was quite another. People don't marry for the right to have sex; they marry for love and the opportunity to build a life together with another human being. They marry because when everything goes wrong and life is at its most challenging, it's comforting to have a hand to hold. Because in the darkness of the night, a bed feels a lot less empty when you are lying next to someone who loves you.

I imagined what kind of future I would have as a celibate gay man. I thought of my grandfather, who developed Parkinson's disease and was cared for in his later years by his loving wife and children. When I got older, who would care for me if I couldn't care for myself? I would have no spouse to support me and no children to look after my well-being. When I got old, would anyone care? If I suffered from Alzheimer's or dementia as so many in my family had, who would notice and get me the help I needed? Who would make sure I wasn't taken advantage of or mistreated? Was I doomed to die alone and unwanted?

I thought about all the years leading up to that. I imagined coming home from work to an empty house, day after day. I would never have someone to cuddle with on the couch, never watch my child take his or her first steps, never love someone as my parents loved each other, and never have that special person I could lean on and serve Christ together with. I had dreamed about these things for years, but now they seemed impossible.

That future looked bleak indeed. Was that really what God wanted for me? More importantly, if that *was* what God wanted for me, was I willing to accept it?

I don't have the words to convey how much this question weighed on me. I knew I couldn't continue calling myself a Christian unless I was willing to accept whatever God had planned for me, even if it was a life of loneliness. I also knew I couldn't just lie to God, pretend I'd be okay with it, and then try to find some other solution. God knows your heart. You can't lie to God.

After agonizing over the decision I knew I had to make, I finally reached the inescapable conclusion: I had to follow God, whatever that might mean. I knelt down in my bedroom and I made a promise to God.

The story sounds ridiculously melodramatic in print, and I hesitated to tell it here. But that prayer was a turning point in my life, and that night still stands out to me as one of the most important nights of my life.

Dear God, I prayed, *I don't want to be celibate. I don't want to be alone. I want to fall in love with someone and spend my life with that person. But even more than that, I want to serve You. And if Your will is for me to be celibate my entire life, I will do it. Please show me what You want for my life, and help me to do Your will, whatever it is.*

I prayed and prayed that night. And God heard me.

It would be wonderful to say that God spoke to me in an audible voice that night and gave me a direct revelation about what to do. It would make a terrific story. However, that's not what happened. Instead, I felt a wave of peace rush over me. For the first time since beginning my journey, I knew things were going to be okay. Deep down in my spirit, something told me that I wasn't going to get the answers I wanted right away, but that they would come in time, as long as I kept trusting the Holy Spirit.

Whatever the future might hold, I was committed to endure whatever God called me to. And God was going to be with me.

The church, however, was another matter.

CHAPTER 9

◆

SOUTH PARK CHRISTIANS

In an episode from the first season of the controversial animated series *South Park*, young Stan discovers that his dog, Sparky, is gay and decides he just needs good training.

"Sit, Sparky," he commands. The dog sits.

"Good boy. Now shake." The dog lifts his paw, and Stan shakes it.

"Good boy. Now...don't be gay! Don't be gay, Spark; don't be gay!"

Sparky only cocks his head, confused.

"Did it work?" Stan's friend Kyle asks.

The punch line goes to wisecracking Cartman: "He still looks pretty gay to me."

As I opened up about my struggles to the Christians in my life, I started feeling a lot like Sparky. When many Christians found out I was gay, their only response was to shout uselessly, "Don't be gay! Don't be gay, Justin; don't be gay!"

Yes, but I am gay. So what do I do now?

"Don't be gay!"

But how? What if those programs don't work? What if God doesn't change me? What if I'm like this for a really long time, or forever? How do I live my life today, as a gay Christian who wants to follow Jesus?

"Don't be gay!"

Sure, the ex-gay world was like a bizarre Wonderland, but at least people there understood that I hadn't *chosen* to be attracted to guys. They knew what it was like because they had the same attractions I did, and they didn't blame me for what I felt. My experiences with the rest of the Christian world were very different. The Christians I knew typically assumed it was all a matter of choice, so admitting the truth about my feelings only subjected me to ostracism, misunderstandings, and the brand of "unrepentant sinner." And that was even while I was trying to become straight. I dared not admit to most Christians that I was thinking of giving up on ex-gay therapy.

I tried to break the news as gently as possible to my parents. They still had their hearts set on seeing me become straight. They were convinced that this *gay* thing was an obstacle that would keep me from ever having a normal, happy life, not to mention fulfilling my dream of doing Christian ministry work. They knew a lot of people wouldn't understand, especially in the church. And they were afraid for me.

When I told them I wasn't going to actively pursue an ex-gay path anymore, their concern for me morphed into a series of arguments about my future. They were afraid I was throwing away my life. I said I didn't *want* the life I saw in those groups. They said I was giving up on God, and that I needed to hold out hope. I countered that I was still open to what God wanted to do in my life, but that I wasn't going to spend my whole life waiting for something that might not even be God's plan for me.

For years I had been praying for God to change my feelings and make me straight. Now I had started praying for God's will to be done, whatever that was. Ever since, I had been feeling more and more strongly that the ex-gay path just wasn't it. God had something else in mind for me.

Now if I could just convince anyone else that I hadn't suddenly turned from God. Until then, I was back to feeling all alone, misunderstood by the very church I loved so much.

"Don't be gay, Justin! Don't be gay!"

Eager for the advice of a mature Christian leader, I set up a meeting with one of the pastors of my Southern Baptist church back home. This particular pastor was a longtime family friend and someone I deeply respected. If anyone would hear my story, I knew he would.

On the day of our meeting, he brought me into his office and listened intently as I poured out my frustrations. I told him how my self-discovery had rocked my world. I told him how I had tried for years to rid myself of these feelings, and that they weren't going away. I told him that I felt the word *gay* best described my situation, but that I was still celibate and seeking God's guidance on what to do next. I told him that the ex-gay thing didn't seem to work.

When I was done talking, he looked thoughtful. I asked him what advice he could offer me. He had been to seminary and counseled many people through difficult times in their lives. What should I do?

"Well, Justin," he responded, sitting back in his chair, "I want you to know that as long as you stay celibate and don't enter into a sexual relationship with another man, you are welcome to continue worshipping here as part of the congregation. So I don't want you to worry about that."

I looked back at him, stunned. It had never even crossed my mind to worry about that.

"Of course," he added, almost as an afterthought, "if you did enter a relationship, we'd have to ask you to leave. But that's the same way we would respond to, say, a heterosexual man in an adulterous relationship."

He said more things after that, but I didn't hear them. Suddenly, all I could think about was whether I might someday be kicked out of the church that had been my spiritual home for almost my entire life. Until that moment, I'd never thought of that. Why would I? I wasn't an unrepentant sinner. I was trying my best to live the way God wanted me to, and to be honest about feelings I didn't want or ask for.

In my pastor's defense, he was surely trying to be compassionate. He wasn't trying to threaten me; he was trying to explain church policy. His church, like many others, taught that people living in sexual sin should be asked to leave the church as a form of discipline. (More on this in chapter 18.) I'm sure his intent was to reassure me that he didn't view my feelings themselves as a sexual sin and that he thought I was doing the right thing by staying celibate.

But I hadn't come to him with concerns about being kicked out of the congregation. I had come to him for understanding, compassion, and advice about what to do. I was scared about the future, not knowing if this meant I'd have to be alone for the rest of my life, and I was worried about what my fellow Christians would think of me. And in that frame of mind, all I heard from him was, "We'll allow you to stay...for now. Just make sure you don't do anything that might change that."

That hurt.

Before I left, he encouraged me to reconsider the ex-gay ministries.

◆

Other Christians went further in their attempts to help, but the help they thought they were providing wasn't always the help I needed. One of my friends, after hearing I was gay, told her mom. Her mom contacted Focus on the Family. Focus then sent me a pack of resources promoting the same ex-gay groups I already knew didn't work, featuring testimonies from many of the same people I already knew weren't really straight.

Then there was another very well-intentioned Christian acquaintance of mine. When I told him I was gay, he grew concerned and promised to do all he could to help. Days later, he came to me with a brown paper bag and a serious look on his face.

"Listen," he said, "I would normally really frown on this, but I care about you, and desperate times call for desperate measures."

He handed me the bag, and I opened it up. Inside was a *Playboy* magazine.

"I thought maybe this would help awaken your natural desires," he said.

"It doesn't work like that," I said.

"Just promise me you'll try it," he urged.

Not wanting to argue with him, I relented and said I would. After he was gone, I leafed through the pictures of naked, buxom women. It was my first real exposure to pornography, and it made me feel dirty.

And for the women? Nothing. Not even the slightest bit of arousal or attraction. Only revulsion and self-loathing from the sleaziness of it all. The experience made me feel sick to my stomach.

◆

Not all Christians were so charitable. I tried sharing my story with a handful of close Christian friends, but most of them responded by condemning my feelings as sinful and telling me that if I would only give my life over to Jesus, I wouldn't feel that way anymore.

"But I have given my life to Jesus," I'd say. "And I recommit myself every day."

"If you really had faith and trusted Him," they'd counter, "God wouldn't allow you to be gay."

What could I possibly say to that?

"Don't be gay! Don't be gay, Justin; don't be gay!"

"Did it work?"

"He still looks pretty gay to me."

BANNED

I had only told a few people, but rumors about my sexuality were already spreading through my Christian circles on campus. Out of the blue, friends were asking me if the rumors were true and quoting the same Bible passages to me over and over. I tried to explain that I was celibate and that I wasn't violating the Leviticus prohibition of "lying with a man as with a woman," but it didn't make any difference. In their minds, gay was bad, and that was all there was to it.

Tired of being badgered and afraid that the rumors would follow me through any local Christian community, I turned to online Christian communities for fellowship.

In those days, before the existence of modern social networking apps, it was common to meet people in online chat rooms, virtual spaces for real-time text chat with people who shared your interests. People used screen names, not real names, so you could share as much or as little as you wanted about yourself.

In the chat rooms, no one had to know I was gay. Sometimes, when I needed to unwind, I would hop on my computer and spend hours chatting away with other young Christians in my favorite Christian chat room. It was nice. In this one space, I could be just me—not the gay guy, or the gay Christian guy; just me, a Christian who loved Jesus.

Over time, I made a few friends in the chat room. Occasionally, as I got comfortable enough with someone, I'd reveal a few details about my personal life, but for the most part I enjoyed my anonymity. My screen name had no connection at all to my real life, and that was the way I liked it. There was some irony, I thought, in the fact that to be known for myself, I had to hide part of myself and use a pseudonym.

One afternoon we were chatting away about some minor point of theology. I was just getting into the discussion when, without warning, the window closed and a message popped up on my screen: "YOU HAVE BEEN BANNED."

What? Surely that was a mistake. I tried to reenter the chat room, but, sure enough, I had been kicked out and banned by one of the room moderators.

I sent a private message to the guy in charge.

"What happened?" I asked. "I just got kicked out, and now I can't get back in."

His response was only three words: "Are you gay?"

I was dumbfounded. How did he know? Who could have told him?

"Who said I was gay?" I asked, not answering the question.

"It doesn't matter. Are you gay?"

I briefly considered lying, telling him that it wasn't true and that someone had given him bad information. It would have been easy, but I couldn't do it. I had to be honest.

"Yes," I typed back, "but I wasn't saying anything about gay stuff in your chat room. I really am a committed Christian, and I'm not sexually active or anything." Maybe he would understand.

"We don't allow gay people in the chat. It's a Christian chat," came the reply.

"I'm a Christian," I said.

"We don't allow gay people in the chat," he repeated. "That's the rule."

I knew he wasn't trying to be mean; he just didn't understand. If I could help him understand, I was sure that would make the difference.

"I know you're really busy," I said, "but can I tell you my story to explain? I think if you knew how I got to this place, it might help."

"Sure," he said. At least he was willing to listen.

I told him my story, typing as quickly as I could and hoping he wouldn't close the chat window before I was done. I explained how I had grown up a committed Christian, how I had struggled for years with my feelings of attraction to other guys, how I had prayed desperately for God to take them away, and how I had kept myself sexually pure, never having been with a guy or a girl. I told him how I would be straight if I could, and how I'd only admitted to being gay because it was the honest truth: I was attracted to the same sex. I explained it all, and he listened to it all, occasionally asking a question or offering a "wow."

Maybe I was getting through.

At the end of my story, I asked him, "So if you were in my shoes, would you have done things differently?"

"I don't know," he said after some thought. "Maybe not."

"Well, now that you know the rest of the story, and know that I'm not trying to 'recruit' anybody or start any debates in the chat room, and that I really am pursuing God with my whole heart, is it okay if I come back in the chat?"

"Sorry," he said. "We don't allow gay people in the chat."

That was the last time I was allowed in my favorite Christian chat room.

JOB DOES THE JOB

I began to take comfort in the book of Job. It's a fascinating book, and it's one of those stories everyone thinks they know, but few know it as well as they think they do.

The story most people know goes something like this: God and Satan have a conversation in which God brags about Job's righteousness. Satan argues that Job wouldn't be so righteous if he had to endure suffering, so God allows Satan to take away Job's wealth, health, and children. As Job suffers from painful sores, having lost everything, his wife encourages him to curse God, but he remains faithful. In the end, God rewards his righteousness by blessing him with even more than he had at the start.

That's the story most people know. But that story takes up only three chapters out of a forty-two-chapter book. The other thirty-nine chapters center on what I think is the most important part of the story: the responses of Job's friends.

Job's three friends appear to be good people who care about him. When they hear of his suffering, they come and sit with him for a week without saying a word. Unfortunately, then they open their mouths and screw it all up.

Over the course of thirty-nine chapters, they argue back and forth with Job, telling him that he needs to repent of his sin and turn to God, and that if he'll just do that, God will heal him and stop his suffering. The more Job insists that he *is* trusting God, the more they argue that this *can't* be the case, because God wouldn't let a righteous man suffer the way he's suffering. Clearly, they say, God must be punishing him for something, and it's only his own arrogance that's keeping him from acknowledging it. He insists that they're wrong, and they just use that as more evidence against him.

Some friends!

Obviously, these guys care about Job. They're not bad guys. They want to help. But their theology tells them that if God is just, then suffering must be evidence of God's discipline, because God wouldn't punish a good person for no reason. It seems like a logical argument. It's just that in this case, they happen to be completely wrong.

Job's friends make the mistake of putting their own theology ahead of the testimony of their friend. They get cocky about their religious beliefs (which seem to make perfect sense!) and fail to recognize that they—not Job—are the ones who need a lesson in humility. Instead of telling Job what God would or wouldn't allow to happen, they ought to simply take his word for what he's experiencing and offer him comfort and support, not lectures.

At the end of the story, Job is vindicated, and God rebukes Job's friends. If only things always worked out so neatly! But the story serves as an important reminder to all of us that sometimes, when people are hurting, they don't need our advice and theological theorizing as much as they need our understanding and comfort. As Proverbs 18:13 says, "To answer before listening—that is folly and shame."

When I had read the book of Job before, those thirty-nine chapters of dialogue with his friends had always seemed like a waste of space. Now they became powerfully relevant. I found myself resonating strongly with Job's lament, "A despairing man should have the devotion of his friends, even though he forsakes the fear of the Almighty. But my brothers are as undependable as intermittent streams. . . . Now you too have proved to be of no help; you see something dreadful and are afraid" (Job 6:14–15, 21).[1]

My Christian friends, too, had proved to be of no help. My homosexuality was "something dreadful" to them, something they were afraid of, and the only way they knew to handle it was to tell me it would go away if I just trusted God. Nothing I said could convince them otherwise.

Bit by bit, I was learning a painful lesson. In this gays-vs.-Christians culture, Christians weren't such great people to be around if you were gay. They might lecture you, talk down to you, or quote the Bible at you, but they weren't very likely to make you feel loved. Quite the opposite.

But all my close friends were Christians. I didn't have anyone else to talk to.

Campus Christians

I don't mean to suggest that every Christian was antagonistic. The trouble was, there were a lot who were, with the result that I always felt like I had to have my guard up in any Christian setting. I never knew when my very presence was going to turn into a controversial issue.

For a while, I was nervous about getting involved in any Christian group on campus for fear of being found out and becoming an object of scorn. Gradually, though, I ventured out, finally getting involved in a Bible study group meeting in my dorm.

The people in the group were nice, and they warmly welcomed me. They weren't connected to my usual social circles, so by the end of my first year in the group they still didn't know I was gay, and I still hadn't told them. Although the members of this group had become my friends, I had held them at arm's length emotionally. They had given me no reason not to trust them, but they were Christians, and unfortunately that was enough.

At the last meeting of the Bible study group, we had a time for sharing what God had been doing in our lives that year. As we went around the circle, I got tenser and tenser. *It's now or never,* I thought. After several silent prayers for courage, I took a deep breath and told them the truth—the real struggles I had been going through.

They all just sort of stared at me like they weren't quite sure what to say. A couple of the girls came over and hugged me, thanking me for sharing. The guys sort of nodded awkward affirmations but didn't say much.

No, it wasn't the enthusiastic support I wanted from the church, but it was something. One of the girls, Ronda, stayed afterward to encourage me. We became fast friends, and her Catholic boyfriend, Marc, ended up being my roommate the next year. They were my reminder that not all Christians were uncomfortable around gay people. Maybe it wasn't so simple as *gays vs. Christians* after all. I wasn't the only one on the middle ground.

Encouraged by this, the next year I decided to join one of the larger campus-wide Christian groups, a group I'll call Campus Christian Fellowship, or CCF for short.

Being around a large group of Christians still made me nervous, but I wasn't going to let my faith wither. I needed something like this, and the previous year's Bible study had proven to me that it was possible to spend time in a group of serious Christians without ever having to get into a discussion of my sexuality. I just wouldn't say anything, and it was all going to be fine.

I managed to (mostly) calm my nerves enough to make it to the orientation meeting. I did my best to watch myself to make sure I didn't seem too gay; I was starting to realize that some people could tell by things like vocal inflection or careless mannerisms, and that had me paranoid. With my most masculine mannerisms and in my most masculine voice, I introduced myself to some of the many new faces around me. They welcomed me warmly and handed me a copy of the schedule for the year.

I looked over the folded yellow page. The event titles were the sorts of things I'd expected:

"September 5—Drawing near to God."

"September 26—Spurring one another on in Christ."

And then I saw it. "October 17—Homosexuality: Combining Compassion and Truth."

Oh, great.

Listed under the title was the name of a speaker who was coming from a ministry in another state. I didn't have to read any further to know it was an ex-gay ministry.

I went back to my dorm and looked up the speaker online. His name was Derek; he was apparently what ex-gays sometimes called an "ever-straight"—someone who was involved in ex-gay ministry but had never identified as gay or had any kind of same-sex attraction. In other words, he was just a straight guy who wanted to help gay people become straight like him.

Well, *this* was going to get interesting.

I was curious about Derek and his message. If he was going to come to my campus to talk to Christians about gay people, I wanted to know what he was going to say. Would he really offer them a message of compassion? Or was he just going to make things worse for people like me who wanted to tell the truth?

I sent Derek an email asking for more information on his ministry. Since he was with an ex-gay ministry, I already assumed he believed that gay relationships were sinful and that some kind of change was possible. That much was a given. What I wanted to know was whether he could at least agree that there's a difference between *behavior* and *orientation*, and that I wasn't sinning by simply being *attracted* to guys—something I didn't choose and couldn't control.

I asked him this question point-blank. His response surprised me. In a verbose, unnecessarily convoluted email, he danced all around the subject at hand. "Bottom line," he said, "we'd say the whole behavior/orientation distinction is bogus and in real life actually detrimental to folks who buy into it."

Bogus? In what way? I wrote him back for clarification, explaining more of my situation and why it was so important to me for Christians to understand the difference. Even if they condemned gay sex, I didn't want them to condemn me for attractions I wasn't even acting on. After all, those attractions might be *temptations* to sin, but temptation isn't sin itself.

In his reply, he disagreed. Some kinds of attractions are inherently sinful, he said, even if we didn't choose to experience them and never give in to them. To say otherwise was a "biblically unsubstantiated assumption," he claimed, arguing that the primary reason people care about distinguishing behavior from orientation is for "self-justification." After all, he said, although "you would like to think that your attraction, because you didn't consciously or deliberately choose it...is not something that you have any responsibility for," it was really like being a chain-smoker: "Would the guy in the iron lung because he spent all his life smoking say he chose his emphysema?"

I was nothing short of astounded by this conversation. He wasn't just saying that I should try to become straight. He was saying it was *my fault* I was attracted to guys; that I had somehow made it happen; that even if I fought those temptations with every ounce of my being, never lusted in my heart, and never had any kind of sexual or romantic relationship for the rest of my life, I was still sinning just by admitting I was gay—something he acknowledged I might never be able to change.

What sort of messed-up theology was that? And if *that* was to be the church's message to gay people—"Hey, we know you didn't choose to feel this way, but since you do, you're now in perpetual sin regardless of how you live or what you do"—where was the motivation even to try to live holy lives at all?

And *this* was the guy who was about to come to campus to tell hundreds of Christians about gay people. This wasn't going to make anything better—not for those Christians, not for me, and not for any other gay people they encountered in their lives. It was only going to make things a whole lot worse.

I considered that the CCF leaders were probably unaware of the details of Derek's theology. I was sure they'd never intentionally invite someone who would condemn people just because of their temptations. Most likely, I thought, they had invited him because he represented an ex-gay ministry, and, like many Christians, they thought ex-gay ministries were the most loving form of ministry Christians could offer to gay people. I disagreed with them about that, but it was an understandable belief.

I envisioned the potential blowup on campus when the gay

community found out about this guy coming to speak. I knew it could do permanent damage to any future relationship between gays and Christians on campus, a relationship I was hoping, somehow, someday, to be part of building. I worried, too, about the impact a speaker like this might have on any other closeted gay Christians in CCF. I couldn't be the only one, and if there were others, some of them might be struggling even more than I had been. If they were feeling alone, having someone use the Bible to preach at them and blame them was the last thing they needed.

Maybe if I just talk to the CCF leaders, I thought, *I can help avert disaster.*

◆

The next week, I stayed late after the Campus Christian Fellowship meeting, watching for an opportunity to talk to Warren and Claire, a married couple who served as the paid staff leaders of the group. They seemed friendly, so I decided to take my concerns to them. After the meeting, I spotted Claire with a free moment, so I approached her.

"Hi, Claire!" I said, my hand outstretched. "I'm Justin Lee. I'm new, but I'm really excited to be involved."

"Nice to meet you, Justin," she said with a smile.

"Can we talk?" I asked.

"Sure," she said.

I glanced around at all the people. "Maybe someplace a little more private?" I ventured.

"Of course. How about over here?" She motioned to me, and we stepped into a quieter adjoining room.

I wasn't sure how to start. "Um, so I was looking at the schedule for this year—"

"Uh-huh..."

"And I noticed that there's an event coming up about homosexuality, with a speaker from out of town."

"Right..."

I realized I was sweating. "Well, I guess I should explain. I'm a committed Christian, but I'm also gay." Her brow furrowed at this, but I kept talking. "I'm celibate, but I'm attracted to the same sex. I didn't choose to be. I don't know why I am. But it's true."

She fidgeted uncomfortably but didn't say anything. I continued. "Anyway, I looked up this guy who is supposed to come speak, and I'm concerned about some of the things he says. He seems to believe that just being tempted like I am makes you a sinner, and I'm not sure that's the message you really want to send... is it?"

She was frowning now. She took a deep breath before responding. "You would have to talk to Mandy about that," she said flatly. "She's the one who recommended him."

"Mandy?" I asked.

Claire explained that Mandy was another leader in the group and a personal friend of Derek's. As she told me how to get in touch with Mandy, I became aware that her manner had changed noticeably. She was frowning at me with her arms folded in front of her. Her voice had become a low monotone. Suddenly, it seemed that she had a very pressing need to be somewhere else.

I contacted Mandy after the meeting, but she was out of town. She promised to meet with me at some point before the speaker came.

◆

After Claire's somewhat icy response to my question, I was nervous about going back to CCF the next week, but something pushed me to do it anyway.

It seemed divinely inspired when Warren, Claire's husband and coleader of CCF, made his way over to me during the meeting and invited me to have lunch with him the next day.

"I'd love a chance to sit down and chat with you," he said. "It would be great to just get to know you and talk a little over lunch."

And so the next day there we were, sitting in a quiet section of one of the campus dining rooms. As I ate, he peppered me with questions. "How's life?" "How are your classes going?" "What else is new?"

It was nice to have a leader of the Campus Christian Fellowship take an interest in me. I was sure his wife had told him by now that I was gay, so that made this the first time a Christian leader, knowing I was gay, had taken an interest in me for me and not as a pretense for preaching at me about my sexuality. It felt good.

Then, without warning, Warren pulled out a big, thick Bible and dropped it on the table with a thud. "Justin," he said, his tone suddenly serious, "I'd like to hear your thoughts on some Bible passages."

Ah. So this was it.

He had opened the Bible and was thumbing through the pages. "Here," he said, turning the Bible so I could see it. "Leviticus 18:22 says, 'Do not lie with a man as one lies with a woman.'[2] How do you respond to a passage like that?"

I didn't even need to look. By now I knew the passage by heart. "I'm not lying with anybody," I tried to explain. "When I say I'm gay, that's not a statement on my sexual behaviors; it's just being honest about what I feel. And besides—"

But he wasn't listening; he was already thumbing to the next page he had marked.

"First Corinthians 6:9," he said, interrupting. "It says homosexuals won't inherit the kingdom of God."

"It says 'homosexual *offenders*,'" I pointed out, noting the wording of his Bible translation. "Whoever they were, they were at least *doing* something. I'm not doing anything."

He didn't acknowledge the comment. "When God created humanity, he created Adam and Eve," he said, his voice growing in intensity. "The Bible says a man will leave his parents and cleave unto his *wife*. It doesn't say anything about homosexual partners. It's clear God designed men and women for each other. Men and men aren't designed to fit together the same way."

So much for Warren wanting to know my opinions. None of this was about me at all. It was about Warren preaching against the sin of homosexuality. By the end of lunch, I knew exactly where he stood. He still didn't know the first thing about me.

◇

Mandy contacted me shortly thereafter to let me know she was back in town and free to meet about the upcoming event. I shared my story and concerns with her, but while she was warmer than Warren and Claire had been, she ultimately agreed with Derek. She said that being gay was sinful even if I wasn't acting on my feelings, and she pushed me to go back to ex-gay therapy. She also gave me a small booklet about homosexuality. They were going to pass these out at the event when Derek came to speak, she said.

Back in my dorm, I looked over the booklet. I wasn't surprised to see that it argued that gays could become straight. But I was shocked to see that it also perpetuated a number of ugly stereotypes about gay people, suggesting that they were sex fiends and pedophiles, obsessed with kinky sex, and virtually incapable of monogamy. This wasn't the kind of message a Christian group should be sending during a talk billed as "combining compassion and truth." Real compassion would mean teaching people how to be more sensitive to the needs of the gay people they encounter and helping them understand our struggles better. This was just the same "Don't be gay!" message I had been hearing all along, supplemented by misleading and unfair characterizations. It was heartbreaking.

I took the booklet to Claire before Derek's talk. In my gentlest, most conciliatory tone, I pointed out my concerns and shared my worries with her about the impact of a Christian group's passing out a booklet like this. "Please," I said, "I'm begging you, don't pass this out. It would only make other people like me feel unwelcome."

She sighed. Reluctantly, she agreed not to pass them out—on one condition.

"Justin," she said, quietly and slowly in that same low monotone, "I don't want you to feel unwelcome here at CCF. We love you and we want you to be able to come and worship with us and explore God's Word with us. But," she said, placing a hand on my arm, "the one thing I need from you is for you to respect our views about homosexuality, and leave your own agenda at home."

I stared back at her, shocked and unsure what to say in response. She patted my arm, gave a faint smile, and walked away without another word.

Back in my dorm room that night, her comments burned themselves into my brain. My *agenda*? No one had ever accused me of having an "agenda" before. The only "agenda" I knew I had was my day planner, and although I was certainly happy to leave that at home, I was pretty sure that wasn't the one she was talking about.

I tried to make jokes about it to cheer myself up, but I felt only an overwhelming sadness.

It was official. God Boy was now the heretic.

CHAPTER 10

❖

THE POISONED YEAST

It's easy to sit in judgment of Warren and Claire.

Yes, they should have taken more time to listen before talking. But in some respects they and the many others like them are victims too. They are victims of decades of misinformation that has been perpetuated in certain Christian circles.

These Christians are not bad people. I knew from years of growing up in an evangelical church that Christians could be among the most giving, loving, compassionate people in the world. The Christians I knew were generous with their time and their money. They were quick to sacrifice of themselves to help anyone they knew in need. If they found out that a neighbor or friend had experienced a tragedy, they were the first to call and offer to bring food or babysit or simply be a shoulder to cry on. The Christians I knew were flawed, yes, as all of us are; but they truly did live their lives as evidence of their belief in a loving God who wants us all to love each other.

It was hard for me to square my experience of Christians *before* coming out with my experience of Christians *after* coming out. My interactions with Warren, Claire, and those like them felt anything but loving. If this had been my first exposure to Christianity, I would have wanted nothing to do with it.

So why the discrepancy?

Part of it, I believe, is simply that human beings are flawed, Christians included. Warren and Claire were uncomfortable about the subject of homosexuality, and it showed in their interactions with me. But I think the biggest factor is the amount of misinformation about gays that people like Warren and Claire have been exposed to.

Misinformation is a powerful force. In his book *The 7 Habits of Highly Effective People*, Stephen R. Covey illustrates the concept of paradigm shifts with a story about an experience he had on a New York subway:

> People were sitting quietly—some reading newspapers, some lost in thought, some resting with their eyes closed. It was a calm, peaceful scene.
>
> Then suddenly, a man and his children entered the subway car. The children were so loud and rambunctious that instantly the whole climate changed.
>
> The man sat down next to me and closed his eyes, apparently oblivious to the situation. The children were yelling back and forth, throwing things, even grabbing people's papers. It was very disturbing. And yet, the man sitting next to me did nothing.
>
> It was difficult not to feel irritated. I could not believe that he could be so insensitive as to let his children run wild like that and do nothing about it, taking no responsibility at all. It was easy to see that everyone else on the subway felt irritated, too. So finally, with what I felt was unusual patience and restraint, I turned to him and said, "Sir, your children

are really disturbing a lot of people. I wonder if you couldn't control them a little more?"

The man lifted his gaze as if to come to a consciousness of the situation for the first time and said softly, "Oh, you're right. I guess I should do something about it. We just came from the hospital where their mother died about an hour ago. I don't know what to think, and I guess they don't know how to handle it either."

Can you imagine what I felt at that moment? My paradigm shifted.[1]

Covey's story is a powerful example of how a little information can alter our entire understanding of a situation. Now imagine things from the other side. Suppose you knew, and assumed that Covey knew, this man's situation already. Wouldn't Covey's irritated request for the man to control his children, however restrained he might have intended to be, come across as incredibly insensitive and rude? I would be tempted to think of him as rather a jerk for saying something like that.

All of us have the potential to be jerks, or worse, if we are operating based on faulty information. If I see a thief getting away and I run out and tackle him, I'm a hero. If he turns out to be just an innocent man going for a jog, I'm not only a jerk, I'm guilty of assault! So it is that actions intended to be loving can be anything but loving if someone is acting on misinformation.

This is especially true in situations where one person sees danger and another person doesn't. Suppose I discover that the building is on fire but you don't believe me when I tell you. If I love you, I'd pull you out of the building kicking and screaming rather than let you burn to death. Sure, you might be ticked at me in the moment, but I'd be saving your life. Once you realized the real danger you had been in, you'd be grateful I ignored your protests, right?

Of course, if I was wrong about the fire, then I've just become the deranged nutcase who forcibly dragged you outside for no reason at all.

Warren and Claire were trying to save me, thinking they knew something I didn't. They thought, as I had thought years before, that they understood this subject and that they had answers I lacked. They had been taught, as my parents had and my Christian friends had, that being gay would only lead to misery and separation from God, and that I could avoid that fate by choosing to become straight.

THE ONLY GAY PERSON IN THE ROOM

Our Campus Christian Fellowship had an affiliation with a larger, national Christian organization that held regional conferences for Christian college students. I had already decided to attend the regional conference with my CCF friends before learning that the theme of this year's conference was sexuality.

Great.

Included in the weekend's events was a class promising the "truth" about homosexuality, taught by an ex-gay leader named Mark.

Speaking to a packed room of mostly straight evangelical Christian college students, Mark explained to us all that "there's hope for the homosexual." However, he warned, some homosexuals would claim that they couldn't change. "They'll tell you that they're 'born this way,' that it's biological," he said. "But that has never been proven."

Mark spent most of his workshop time trying to disprove any biological link to sexual orientation. He listed several famous studies that had suggested such a link, such as an early study that had shown brain differences between gay and straight men, and another that had suggested a possible genetic influence. He then picked each study apart for the audience, showing how each left unanswered questions.

By now, I had already read all of these studies and many others, and I knew he was right on most of his facts. But I also knew that in many cases, the study authors themselves had raised the questions that he was now using to discredit them, and that none of these researchers had claimed their studies proved anything about the cause of homosexuality, only that they provided more data to help other researchers get closer to the answer. A few times, Mark got something wrong or left out an important detail and I wanted to say something, but I held my tongue. This was his show, not mine.

Mark concluded his presentation with a brief explanation of the father/mother theory I had heard so many times by now. This, he insisted, was the true origin of homosexual feelings.

When Mark opened the floor for a Q & A session, I already knew what I wanted to ask.

"I have two questions," I said when he called on me.

"Sure, go right ahead," he said.

"Well, you said in your presentation that we should reject the biological theories, because there's no conclusive proof that there's a biological link."

"That's right."

"But then you told us that it's really because of distant fathers and overbearing mothers. Is there any conclusive proof of that?"

He looked at me like a deer caught in headlights. I suddenly felt bad for asking the question. He looked genuinely shocked, as if no one had ever asked him that before.

"No," he said simply.

I swallowed. I hadn't meant to embarrass him. I wanted to make a point, but I hadn't really expected him to concede it. I realized I'd caught him off guard, and I really didn't want to be a jerk. I just wanted the truth to come out. That was all.

I softened my tone as I asked my next question.

"Well, my other question was, Is there any other possible explanation for why someone might be gay? Because—" Suddenly, I was nervous. The room was full of conservative Christians, and every eye in the room was on me. I was about to come out to all of them. "Because I'm gay," I continued. "I didn't want to be, and I didn't choose to be, but my whole life I've only been attracted to guys, not girls. And I didn't have a distant father or an overbearing mother."

"Oh yes, there can be other reasons!" he exclaimed, seemingly happy for the question. Where other ex-gays had insisted on Bieber's theory as the only explanation, Mark didn't mind theorizing about other causes at all...as long as they weren't biological.

"Sometimes," he said pointedly, "it's a matter of sexual abuse, for instance."

"Well, I wasn't abused," I replied.

"Sometimes it's something else," he said, unfazed. "Like maybe you were separated from your parents as a child?" He looked at me expectantly.

"No, I'm pretty sure that never happened."

"Maybe you were in an incubator as a baby."

I shook my head.

"Or you could have been adopted."

I shook my head again.

He continued to rattle off suggestions until I stopped him.

"Here's what bothers me," I said. "I'm willing to bet that if we took a poll of this room right now, and asked anyone to raise their hand if they had a distant father, or an absent father, or an overprotective mother, or were adopted, or sexually abused, or were in an incubator, or any of these other things, almost every hand in here would be up for at least one of those—except mine! None of them applied to me, and as far as I know, *I'm the only gay person in the room!* At some point, it seems like you're just throwing everything at the wall to see what sticks, and you're not really explaining any-thing at all, because this stuff could apply to anyone."

Mark didn't seem to get my point. "Well, if I could sit down with you and talk to you for long enough, I could figure out what caused it for you!" he said.

"If you really want to, I'd be happy to," I replied, curious to see where this would go.

"Meet me after this session and I'll figure it out," he shot back. I had become his new challenge.

After the session was lunch. Mark invited me to sit at a private table with him. As we ate, he grilled me on every aspect of my childhood. Every detail was a potential cause of my gay feelings. At one point, he asked which denomination I'd grown up in.

"Southern Baptist," I told him.

"Well, that could be it, then," he said, "because a Baptist church probably didn't give you opportunities for artistic expression, and if you were an artistic child, that might have created a form of defensive detachment."

I tried not to laugh. I thought about how my Southern Baptist friends would respond to the suggestion that their entire denomi-nation was making people gay. Even Mark didn't seem to buy that one, in spite of the fact that he had come up with it.

He was most interested, though, in trying to find something that had made my childhood imperfect. I was a rarity, a happy kid raised in a two-parent Christian home by his biological mother and father, with no divorce, abuse, or trauma, having plenty of one-on-one time with his father, bonding well with both parents—I was a minority within a minority, having grown up in the kind of environment few children are privileged enough to experience. And that was driving him crazy.

Finally, after his long series of questions had failed to turn up anything he could blame, he asked in exasperation, "Wasn't there *anything* unusual in your childhood? Anything at all?"

I racked my brain to think of what might have been unusual. In many ways, the most unusual thing about my upbringing had been how wonderfully absent of dysfunctional elements it had been.

There was one thing that was out of the ordinary. I have a hereditary condition called alopecia areata, which causes unpredictable hair loss. Although many people know little about it, it's a surprisingly common disorder, affecting over four million people in the United States alone, most often developing in childhood. As a kid, I lost my hair a few times, though it always grew back. Today I just keep my head shaved.

I mentioned this to Mark as the only unusual thing I could think of.

"Aha!" he shouted, pointing an accusing finger. "You lied to me!"

I was perplexed. "Lied to you?"

"Yes, you told me that you had an idyllic childhood. And losing your hair was clearly a traumatic experience."

"Whoa. First of all," I corrected, "I never said my childhood was 'idyllic.' I said it was happy, and it was. I was happy. I'm sure my childhood wasn't perfect; nobody's childhood is perfect. But if we have to live perfect childhoods in order to come out straight, then how is anybody straight? The truth is, I was very happy. And secondly, as obvious as it might seem to you that losing my hair must have been traumatic, it honestly wasn't."

That was true. I was only four when I first lost my hair, too young to care about what my hair looked like. Have you ever seen a four-year-old boy look in the mirror and worry about his hair?

My parents had learned everything they could about alopecia before I even knew I was different from anybody, and they always had the right attitude about it. My dad used to say, "Everybody's got problems. Some kids lose their hair due to chemotherapy. Aren't you glad the worst thing in your life is that you've just lost your hair? And hey, you don't have to wash it, or comb it, or blow it dry..."

As a kid, I learned all about the condition and was happy to inform any curious classmates. It was never an issue for my friends. And sure, I got teased sometimes. So did the kids with glasses or freckles, and the ones who were too tall, or too thin, or too fat, or too short.

Alopecia is traumatic for many children, especially for girls. But it was never a big deal to me. And of all the people I've met over the years who have the same condition that I do, I know only one who's gay.

I told Mark all of this, but he wouldn't listen.

"You're being defensive," he told me. "You're not willing to admit it, but this was the traumatic event that sent you down the path of homosexuality."

"But it really wasn't traumatic!" I protested. "I think I would know."

"You're just not willing to face how traumatic it really was," he insisted.

What was I supposed to say to that?

"Justin," he said, leaning across the table, "if you want me to, I can help you. I've found freedom, and you can find it too. But you have to stop being so defensive."

I wondered what he considered "freedom." He had shared earlier that his continuing temptations were so strong, he couldn't trust himself to have the internet or cable TV in his home, for fear of "surfing for naked bodies." But I wasn't surfing for porn, and I wasn't sexually active. What exactly did he think I was going to gain by becoming more like him?

It didn't really matter to me what Mark thought of me. I would likely never see him again, and I was getting used to the realization that there would always be people looking down on me.

It was Mark's influence that bothered me. No matter what I said, Mark was going to keep going to groups like this one and telling thousands upon thousands of Christians that being gay was caused by faulty parenting, that it only led to misery, and that anyone who wanted to become straight could. They would believe him, because he said he'd been there. And they would pass those beliefs on to their children and other Christians, who would act upon that misinformation whenever they encountered gay people.

Jesus understood that one of the biggest threats to the church was the potential for this new movement he was starting to be derailed by false teachings and misinformation that could infect the church, harming its witness to the world.

"Be on your guard against the yeast of the Pharisees and Sadducees," he said (Matthew 16:6), referring to religious teachers of the day who claimed to serve God but whose legalism and false teachings had the potential to distort the good work God's people were doing.

Yeast is a common biblical symbol for an idea that permeates an entity or group and alters it, for good or for evil. As the apostle Paul points out, "A little yeast works through the whole batch of dough" (Galatians 5:9).

A little bit of misinformation, like yeast or poison, can work its way through the entire church, contaminating an important force for good in the world and turning it into something that does damage. With the church contaminated by misinformation, people feel that they have two choices: either accept the church and the misinformation along with it, or reject the whole thing.

The third option? Fight the misinformation.

In the words of author Bruce Bawer, "They [some gay people] think that their enemy is conscious oppression and that their salvation lies in the amassing of power, when in fact their enemy is ignorance and their salvation lies in increased understanding."[2]

Christianity isn't the problem. The problem is the yeast.

CHAPTER 11

◆

FAITH ASSASSINS

In Pixar's 2018 film *Incredibles 2*, the superpowered Incredibles family must stop a mysterious villain known as Screenslaver. But rather than fight the Incredibles directly, Screenslaver employs a mind-control device to turn them into their own worst enemies, causing them to use their powers to fight for evil and destroy their reputation in the process.

It's a popular strategy for fictional villains. Nearly every cartoon I watched as a kid had at least one episode in which the heroes were somehow hypnotized or brainwashed into doing their ene-mies' bidding. Often the plot involves something that removes the heroes' free will—Loki using a magic scepter to control Hawkeye in *The Avengers*, for instance, or *Star Trek*'s Captain Picard being turned into a robotic Borg drone.

Other times, the plot is craftier. In one action thriller, the hero races across town, dodging roadblocks and breaking laws, all in pursuit of a van he believes is carrying a bomb. Only after arriving at his destination does he realize in horror that he's been tricked. In the film's shocking conclusion, we learn that the van he was following was clean; the bomb was in *his* car, and he's just brought it to the villains' target.

A good twist ending, like a good magic trick, depends on misdirection. While you're watching one hand, the magician is doing something with the other hand. While you're focused on the van, the villains are planting the bomb in the car. And while so many of us in the church have been focused on the "threat" to our culture posed by homosexuality, we've missed the realization that the church in our culture is under attack—not by gays, but by Christians.

We Christians are the threat. The bomb is in *our* car. *We* have become the unwitting assassins of people's faith.

The Christians are killing Christianity.

◇

A once-popular bumper sticker read, "Lord, save us from Your followers." People laughed at it because they knew exactly what it meant without having to ask. The reputation of *Christianity* in our society is poor because the reputation of *Christians* in our society is poor.

This is especially—but not only—true of those of us called *evangelical* Christians, a term (from the Greek for "good news") for a subset of the church that emphasizes the idea of a personal relationship with Jesus and salvation through his death and resurrection. Evangelical Christian author Philip Yancey writes:

> Recently I have been asking a question of strangers—for example, seatmates on an airplane—when I strike up a conversation. "When I say the words 'evangelical Christian' what comes to mind?" In reply, mostly I hear political descriptions:

of strident pro-life activists, or gay-rights opponents, or proposals for censoring the Internet. I hear references to the Moral Majority, an organization disbanded years ago. Not once—*not once*—have I heard a description redolent of grace. Apparently that is not the aroma Christians give off in the world.[1]

Political issues matter, from war to abortion to poverty to same-sex marriage. As Christians, we ought to care about these issues, because they affect people's lives. But Jesus was known for his compassion, not for his politics. The messiah people were expecting was a political leader; the Messiah they got was a suffering servant. If his followers are now known more for our politics than for our grace, something is wrong.

Sadly, that's not the only thing wrong. Our bad reputation extends far beyond our political views.

As a young man, I took a job waiting tables at a local chain restaurant. I soon discovered something very curious: *No one* wanted to wait tables on Sundays, even though most of the staff wasn't religious and I was one of the few who went to church.

"Sundays are the worst," one of the servers explained to me. "That's when the church crowd goes out to eat."

"What's wrong with the church crowd?" I asked.

"Oh, honey," she said. "They're usually the most demanding, and they're always the worst tippers. I guarantee you, if you see your table praying before the meal, you can mentally subtract a third from your tip."

Standing nearby, the manager cracked a smile. "They already gave at church," he said. "They don't have any money left."

In North Carolina, as in most states, servers work almost exclusively for tips. We were paid just over two dollars an hour, including the time we spent setting up before the diners arrived and cleaning up after our shifts had ended. Waiting on tables where people sat for a long time and didn't leave much of a tip could mean that you didn't have enough money to pay your bills at the end of the week.

As much as I hated to admit it, it was true that the obviously Christian tables—the ones where people prayed before the meal or where church or God seemed to be a big part of the discussion— were often the stingiest with their tips. Even worse, some of them would leave fake "money" as part of their tip—pieces of paper designed to look like high-value bills until you picked them up and realized they were tracts telling you about giving your life to Jesus. Why would anyone think that tricking and disappointing a broke food service employee would be a good way of spreading the Christian good news? Not surprisingly, behavior like this only served to further convince my coworkers that they wanted nothing to do with Christianity. The devil himself couldn't have planned it any better.

Don't misunderstand me. I know that Christianity isn't about us at all. It's about Jesus. Our human failure to live up to what we believe doesn't make the gospel any less true. But as the old saying goes, we are the only "Jesus" most people will ever see. People inside *and* outside the church judge Christianity by what they see in its practitioners.

I don't know why the Sunday-morning churchgoers who ate at my restaurant were such poor tippers. There could be many reasons. People having drinks with friends on Friday or Saturday night were often the best tippers, and I'm sure alcohol played some part in loosening up their wallets. Statistics show that Christians as a group are actually incredibly generous with their money. But my restaurant coworkers weren't looking at statistics. They were looking at the people sitting in front of them, people who had no idea they were representing God in that moment, for better or worse. Experiences like these shape how Christianity is viewed by our culture far more than we realize. And if our reputation can be damaged by poor tipping, how much more can it be hurt by the perception that we are actively *hostile* to an entire group of people!

OUR OWN WORST ENEMY

Everyone makes mistakes, and there will always be times when Christians don't represent the faith well. That has been true throughout history. But it only takes one key ingredient to completely ruin the church's reputation: bad yeast.

As the yeast of misinformation about gay people has spread through the church, it has turned the church not only into the perceived enemy of gays, but into its own worst enemy as well.

Well-intentioned Christians, believing that being gay is a sinful choice or can be easily changed, speak and act accordingly, recommending ex-gay therapy and fighting against cultural acceptance of homosexuality. To those who know better, this comes across as hurtful and unkind. As the Christians fight harder for what they believe is the truth, following the van they mistakenly believe is a threat to us all, they honestly don't realize that *they're* the ones creating the conflict, dealing death blows to the church's image. From an outside perspective, our reputation just gets worse. Instead of Christians sometimes looking like jerks in spite of our faith, it now looks like we're jerks *because* of our faith. In the eyes of gay people and those who love them, Christianity itself has just become the threat.

Throughout history, one of the most compelling arguments for the truth of Christianity has always been the evidence of changed lives. We can't put God in a test tube. We don't hear a booming voice from the sky when we pray. We see God at work in the hearts and minds of believers whose lives have been changed by their encounter with Jesus Christ. That is what draws people to the church.

"A new command I give you," Jesus said to his followers. "Love one another. As I have loved you, so you must love one another. By this everyone will know that you are my disciples, if you love one another" (John 13:34–35).

Sadly, that's no longer what we're known for. In a world where Christians are known as the biggest jerks, the "changed lives" argument no longer holds any sway. As science continues to explain previously unexplainable natural phenomena, our behavior is taking away one of the strongest reasons people have to believe.

We Christians can say Jesus changed our hearts, but if our reputation is that of uncompassionate culture warriors, why should people believe us? We can say that God is loving and merciful, but if the church isn't loving and merciful, why would we be in any sort of position to know that God is?

At its best, the church is something amazing and beautiful, caring for our neighbors with no regard for ourselves, serving the poor and disenfranchised, offering hope and comfort in times of tragedy. We are a family to those who have none and an arrow pointing to the One who loves us unconditionally and who forgives us over and over. When the early Christians talked about being "not of this world" (John 15:19; Romans 12:2), it was because they knew how hard it was to love their enemies and continue being generous in the midst of oppression and persecution. Who could say that about the American church today?

In some ways, I think, Christendom is better off when it must function as an oppressed minority. Christians who live under the threat of persecution have to put their lives on the line for their faith, and it strengthens them. The early Christians suffered and died to share the gospel. They gave all they had. They didn't have time to get comfortable and stingy and self-involved. In today's America, Christians are ostensibly the majority. Without that oppression, it's much easier for a sort of "cultural Christianity" to develop—one where people call themselves Christians, use

Christian language, and so forth, but without really internalizing the gospel or actually having to put their lives on the line for what they say they believe. We as a church have become spiritually lazy, substituting aggressive culture-war tactics for the generous, self-sacrificing humility Jesus taught and modeled.

Cultural aggression is easier, and it allows us to think we're still "not of this world," even as we use worldly strategies to get our way.

As Jesus was being arrested, Peter drew his sword and cut off the high priest's servant's ear in an attempt to defend him. Jesus immediately rebuked him, saying, "Put your sword back in its place, for all who draw the sword will die by the sword" (Matthew 26:52). Jesus' way was never the way of aggression or the culture war, but sometimes we forget that, and the swords come out. We think we're defending the gospel. We don't realize we're actually attacking it.

A RECIPE FOR KILLING THE CHURCH

Our failure to live out the gospel doesn't only affect Christianity's reputation outside the church; the poisonous yeast is killing the church from within as well.

In the classical Greek myth of Jason and Medea, Jason is faced with the task of defeating an army of warriors much too strong for him. His clever strategy, suggested by Medea, is to throw a stone into the midst of the warriors without being seen. Not realizing that the stone came from outside their camp, the warriors angrily turn on each other, defeating themselves with minimal work on Jason's part.

It's a famous story with an important lesson. If you want to destroy a movement, sometimes the most effective way is by turning it against itself. Here's a simple recipe:

1. Pick two critically important elements of the movement.
2. Convince members of the movement that these two elements are actually in opposition to one another.
3. Watch as people pick sides and destroy each other.
4. Finally, watch as the movement's reputation goes down the drain as a result.

Nowhere is this strategy proving more effective than in the modern American church.

So far, I've been speaking about the church as if it were nearly unified in its approach to homosexuality. In fact, that is not the case. Many Christians have been working for a more welcoming and compassionate church for years. Unfortunately, what has resulted is a major schism—a rift through the church dividing one denomination from another, splitting churches within the same denomination from each other, and even tearing apart individual congregations.

It often seems that there are two distinct groups calling themselves Christians. Each group looks at the other and sees its flaws, and in an effort to avoid making the same mistakes, it moves further in the opposite direction. As a result, instead of learning from one another, the two groups just keep getting more and more polarized.

On one side are churches like the one I grew up in. They care deeply about following the Bible and teaching proper Christian doctrine. They emphasize the reality of their faith: For them, the Christian faith isn't just a set of moral ideas; it's a set of core teachings about Absolute Truth. It isn't just one of many paths to truth or peace; it *is* Truth. They emphasize that Jesus wasn't just a great moral teacher but was in fact the real, unique Son of God—the Creator of the universe in human form. For them, therefore, it matters what we believe about God, about Jesus, about heaven, about sin, about the Bible, and about every other major doctrinal point of the faith. Unfortunately, in their zeal for correct doctrine, many Christians on this side come across as preachy and condescending, putting legalistic adherence to certain Bible passages over listening to and loving people.

Only Christians on this side, for instance, would come up with a video game like *Spiritual Warfare*.

Spiritual Warfare was a video game I played as a kid. It was designed by a Christian video game company and was widely viewed as a rip-off of *The Legend of Zelda*, a popular game by Nintendo. The look and feel of the games were virtually identical, but *Spiritual Warfare* had Christian themes in place of its predecessor's fantasy themes. In *The Legend of Zelda*, you're on a quest to save a princess; along the way, you collect various weapons and battle monsters. In *Spiritual Warfare*, your quest is against the powers of darkness. Rather than weapons, you collect the fruits of the Spirit—only they're actual fruits: bananas, apples, pomegranates, and the like. (Yes, really.)

It gets worse. Rather than monsters, your enemies are *the unsaved*. When you encounter them, you *throw the fruits of the Spirit at them*—or blow them up with "vials of God's wrath." Then they convert, dropping to their knees and vanishing instantly.

I could write a book about all the things wrong with that game. As hilarious as it is, it's also tragically reflective of the worst elements of many churches, treating non-Christians as obstacles or enemies, throwing the fruit of the Spirit *at* them and expecting them to repent, convert, and disappear.

That's not the gospel. It never has been.

It is the horror at this extreme that sends so many people—Christian and non-Christian alike—heading as fast as they can in the opposite direction. But in so doing, some of them have thrown the baby out with the bathwater, abandoning the idea that the Bible is in any way trustworthy, or that the core elements of

Christianity—a personal God, the supernatural miracles of Jesus, the reality of an afterlife—are anything other than superstition. As these basic Christian concepts become linked in the popular mindset to ignorance and homophobia, even many churches are turning away from them, keeping the rituals of the faith but without any real belief that Jesus actually rose from the dead or that there's anything more for us after we die.

A while back, I was visiting a new church and heard a sermon about the feeding of the five thousand, the Bible story in which Jesus feeds over five thousand people with only a handful of loaves and fish. It is one of the most famous miracles of Jesus, used by the gospel writers as evidence that Jesus wasn't just a great teacher, but was indeed the supernatural Son of God.

The preacher read the passage and then, acknowledging that supernatural miracles are hard for modern Americans to swallow, suggested that the passage didn't have to refer to anything supernatural at all. Perhaps, he said, these five thousand people who claimed to have no food were actually hiding bits of food under their cloaks, afraid to bring it out in the midst of a hungry crowd. When Jesus began passing out the little bits of food he had, everyone else began bringing their food out too, so that there was enough for everyone with plenty left over. The real miracle, the pastor suggested, was that Jesus taught people to *share*.

But this is not at all what the gospel writers suggest. The texts make it clear that the incident was viewed as a supernatural event, not merely a lesson in generosity. If Jesus was able to rise from the dead, why would it be difficult for us to believe that he could multiply food? And if he was not able to rise from the dead—if that is simply a metaphor of some kind and not a real event—then what exactly is Christianity about, anyway?

The idea of Christianity without the supernatural—without the Resurrection—is not new. It was one of the earliest heresies of the church. In his first letter to the Corinthians, the apostle Paul says:

> But if it is preached that Christ has been raised from the dead, how can some of you say that there is no resurrection of the dead? If there is no resurrection of the dead, then not even Christ has been raised. And if Christ has not been raised, our preaching is useless and so is your faith. More than that, we are then found to be false witnesses about God, for we have testified about God that he raised Christ from the dead. But he did not raise him if in fact the dead are not raised. For if the dead are not raised, then Christ has not been raised either. And if Christ has not been raised, your faith is futile; you are still in your sins. Then those also who have fallen asleep in Christ are lost. If only for this life we have hope in Christ, we are of all people most to be pitied (1 Corinthians 15:12–19).

From the beginning, Christianity has made certain claims about Truth—about the nature of God and the universe, about life after death, about sin and repentance and grace. Unfortunately, some churches are now so worried about being arrogant and unbending like certain *other* Christians that they fail to stand for anything at all. They hang question marks over all the major doctrines of the faith or throw them out entirely. Bit by bit, they lose the things that set them apart as Christians.

The Canadian comedy troupe The Frantics has an old sketch about a church called Worshippers 'R' Us. The sketch opens with an energetic preacher who says, "Welcome, brothers and sisters, to Worshippers 'R' Us, the first church of *all* denominations! Please open your generic prayer books and pray along with me as you stand, sit, kneel, face Mecca, or dance."

The congregation dutifully chants along: "O large Person or Persons of whatever gender or branch of the animal kingdom, who did something great and is now someplace where we aren't, please forgive us for whatever You deem bad, and help us to do whatever strikes You as good, whether that be to work hard, eat no pork, or wage a holy war. Grant us whatever You tend to grant, unless You don't interfere with earthly concerns. Watch over us, or save us from evil, or let us find out for ourselves, or damn us randomly. Amen. Praise Allah. Have a nice day."

It's a comic exaggeration, but I've been to churches that felt not so different from this fictitious one. Fear of ever alienating anybody has nearly turned *doctrine* into a bad word for them. They put little to no faith in the Bible as a guide, implicitly conceding that it probably is a homophobic book after all.

These churches often have very good intentions. They want to emphasize God's unconditional love and include people who have felt excluded by other churches. In some communities, they may be the only churches where gay people know they'll be welcomed. Those are great things! But when the churches known for welcoming gay people are also departing from mainstream Christianity in so many ways, it sends a terrible message. To Christians and non-Christians alike, it now appears that supporting gay people requires becoming less definably Christian—and that "real" Christians must therefore be anti-gay.

Tastes great . . . less filling

In an old series of Miller Lite beer commercials, two beer drinkers (both Miller Lite fans, naturally) break out into an argument or even a fistfight over whether the beer's supposed superiority is because it "tastes great" or because it's "less filling."

"Tastes great!" one shouts.

"Less filling!" the other argues with equal enthusiasm.

The joke, of course, is that (according to Miller, at least) both of these things are true, and they don't have to be at odds with each other at all. The comedy is all in the absurdity of watching two people on the *same team*, both preferring the same brand, fight it out for reasons that make no sense.

Sometimes, when I look at the church today, I feel as if I'm living in those commercials.

"God's Truth!" one side shouts.

"More loving!" comes the response.

"God's Truth!"

"More loving!"

"God's Truth!"

"More loving!"

But there shouldn't be a clash between "God's Truth" and "more loving." In the Bible, Truth and Love are two sides of the same coin. You can't have one without the other. God's Truth is all about God's Love for us and the Love we ought to have for one another. We are being untrue to that Truth if we treat people unlovingly. And we are missing out on the full extent of that Love if we try to divorce it from Ultimate Truth.

We Christians must work to repair this schism in the church. If the church is to survive much longer in our culture, it must teach and model the Christianity of Jesus—a faith that combines Truth and Love in the person of Jesus Christ, revealed to us in the Bible and lived out in the everyday lives of his followers.

That is what we say we believe. It's time we start acting like it.

CHAPTER 12

◆

THE OTHER SIDE

You might think that the negative messages I heard from Christians would drive me away from Christianity. Indeed, many people I know walked away from the faith for that very reason. I couldn't do that. I had known God's presence in my life from a young age, and I couldn't turn my back on that.

Nor did those negative messages make me straight. I don't believe they've ever made anyone straight; all they've done is give people a reason to lie in order to fit in. I refused to lie.

What the messages did do was make me hate myself.

I had grown up in a sort of insulated bubble, with no exposure to openly gay people at all. In today's world, with admired openly gay celebrities and a wide range of gay characters in popular films and TV shows, it seems bizarre to imagine a world before "gay" was such a mainstream part of our culture. As a young person in the late 1990s, however, I had no concept of a happy, successful gay person. I had no gay role models. I didn't know anything about gay life.

The people I looked up to were my parents and various leaders in the church. Theirs was the life I wanted to imitate. Yet all of them were straight, and all of them looked down on homosexuality. It was hard for me to see my sexuality as anything other than an obstacle keeping me from getting where I wanted to go.

In his book *A Place at the Table*, gay author Bruce Bawer writes about being in a store and noticing a fifteen-year-old boy trying to work up the courage to reach for a gay newspaper:

> Standing there, he reached down to the foot-high counter, slipped out from under some other periodical a copy of a gay weekly called *New York Native*, and, trying to appear casual, opened it to the first inside page....
>
> As I stood there behind him, I looked over his shoulder at the pages of the *Native*. I don't remember the specific contents: there were, I suppose, the usual articles about AIDS research, gay bashings, and recent gay-rights advances and setbacks.... What leapt out at me, and stayed in my mind for some time afterward, were other things: a photograph, probably accompanying a review of some cabaret act, of a man in drag; photographs of black-clad men in bondage, presumably in advertisements for leather bars and S&M equipment; and photographs of hunky, bare-chested young men, no doubt promoting "massages" and "escort services" and X-rated videotapes.
>
> These pictures irked me. The narrow, sex-obsessed image of gay life that they presented bore little resemblance to my life or to the lives of my gay friends—or, for that matter, to the lives of the vast majority of gay Americans. Yet this was the image proffered by the *Native* and other such magazines.... That image had provided ammunition to gay-bashers, had helped to bolster the widely held view of gays as a mysteriously threatening Other, and had exacerbated

the confusion of generations of young men who, attempting to come to terms with their homosexuality, had stared bemusedly at the pictures in magazines like the *Native* and said to themselves: "But this isn't *me*."[1]

I first read those words while sitting in my college library, trying to find something to help me make sense of who I was. I felt like I was that kid, looking at the only images I'd seen of gay life and saying over and over, "But this isn't *me*!"

I'd tried looking for gay people on the internet, but most of what I'd come across was gay men looking for sex. I'd tried leafing through gay magazines, but they seemed full of the same-sex equivalent of the sleazy, near-pornographic imagery I had always diligently avoided in the straight world. As a Christian, I wanted to live a life focused on serving God and others, not egocentric carnality. The images I was seeing of gay people weren't me. And if that was what "gay" was, I didn't want to be it.

The trouble was, I already knew I was gay. This is what left me feeling so torn. In rejecting those images of gay life, I thought I had to become straight, which drove me toward the ex-gay ministries. But the ex-gay ministries clearly didn't work, so my honesty drove me back toward admitting I was gay. This is why, even while admitting I was gay, I felt the need to constantly apologize or explain myself: I didn't want to be associated with the kind of hedonistic, sex-obsessed lifestyle that was my only image of gay people. I didn't know where to find any other image.

Today, of course, there are plenty of other images of gay people. Does this mean, then, that stories like mine are a thing of the past? Not at all. In fact, it means that kids today are going through this process at a much younger age than I did. I've met many kids from Christian backgrounds like mine who realized they were gay by twelve or thirteen years old. These kids have advantages I didn't, but they also have frightening new challenges. By the time I was asking the tough questions, I was in college and on my own. Gay kids today are going through the same struggles at an age when they are much more vulnerable to predators and bullies. They're also still completely dependent on their parents, some of whom may react very badly to learning the truth about their children. For the sake of these young people, it's vital that the church get a better understanding of this issue.

◆

When Bawer's book came out, asserting that sex-laden images and stereotypes of gay culture were unfair and harmful to the millions of gay Americans who didn't fit the stereotypes, some took issue with his approach, arguing that he had gone to the opposite extreme and was demeaning gay people whose lives didn't fit within "mainstream society." Whatever the case, his words were exactly what I needed at that point in my life. Thanks to books like *A Place at the Table* and Mel White's *Stranger at the Gate: To Be Gay and Christian in America*, I realized that there was more to being gay than the images I had seen.

Bolstered by the knowledge that I wasn't alone, I set out to find other gay people I could relate to. I searched the internet for gay Christians, and after several fruitless attempts, I finally stumbled upon a gay Christian chat room. To my amazement, there were people in it. Real, live gay Christians.

Everyone in the chat room was significantly older than I was, but I didn't care. I nervously introduced myself, and a chorus of screen names happily welcomed me to the chat room. They seemed nice! Maybe they would have some answers for me.

I told these anonymous gay Christians my story, and they sympathized. Many of them had been rejected by their churches too. But here I discovered a major difference between them and me. While I was still wrestling with what my future would look like, they had already found their answer. They were all either in, or seeking, relationships with someone of the same sex.

This surprised and intrigued me. Everything I'd read in the Bible seemed to condemn homosexual relationships, so I was curious to know how this group of Christians had managed to reconcile their behavior with the Bible. If they had a good answer, it could change everything.

Unfortunately, they didn't have a good answer. They hardly had any answer at all. Years later, I would discover that there *were* gay Christians in relationships who had done a lot of deep thinking and study about what the Bible had to say and had thought-provoking biblical arguments to back up their conclusions. These, however, were not those Christians. When I asked them about the Bible passages that dealt with homosexuality, they largely dismissed my questions without real answers. Some of them chided me for even asking them, and a few of them accused me of being an ex-gay plant trying to disrupt their community. This environment felt just as anti-intellectual as that of the ex-gays, but on the other side.

I left the room feeling more discouraged and alone than ever. I had thought that if I could only meet other gay Christians, then we would have a lot in common and I would get the answers I so craved. As it turned out, it was going to take a lot more than that.

GAYS WHO COULDN'T SPELL

It didn't matter. I wanted more than internet support anyway. More and more, I found myself craving a real-world connection with others who knew what it was like to feel all of this. Chat rooms could be nice, but they were just words on a screen. I wanted to have friends in the flesh.

The campus directory listed a student group called GALBA.

According to its official charter, GALBA stood for Gay, Lesbian, and Bisexual Issues Awareness Group. I tried without success to figure out how to make the acronym fit. Apparently these gays couldn't spell.[2]

GALBA didn't seem to do much, from what I could tell. They had no website, and I'd never seen a meeting advertised. But at least they existed! After some hesitation, I decided to look up the student president of the group and see if he had any answers for me. I sent him an email, and he agreed to meet with me at lunch in the campus cafeteria the next day. His name was Jules.

Jules could hardly have been more different from me. He was loud, boisterous, and self-assured. Everyone knew he was gay, and he was just fine with that. If an attractive guy walked by, he would turn his head to look—and if they caught him, so what? He didn't care. Jules's philosophy was that he was going to be himself, and if anyone had a problem with it, that was their problem.

Not me. I was a people pleaser. I was shy. I was uncomfortable with my sexuality. And I was terrified to be seen sitting at the same table as the president of the campus gay student group. Not all of my friends knew I was gay yet, and I wasn't ready to tell them.

I furtively glanced over my shoulder as Jules happily chatted away about his plans for GALBA. Occasionally he would raise his voice enthusiastically or break into a good-natured guffaw, his laughter seeming to echo loudly off the walls and draw all eyes directly to our table. Over and over, I had to stifle the urge to beg him to quiet down.

Jules explained that the group had dwindled to almost nothing in recent years, and that at the moment, *he* was pretty much the entire group. He wanted to rebuild it, and he wanted my help in doing so. I wasn't sure I was ready for all that attention, but I told myself I couldn't be scared for the rest of my life. This was my chance to meet other gay kids on campus, and I intended to take it. I agreed to help—as long as I didn't have to be too publicly visible. He laughed.

The first GALBA meeting I attended consisted of only four people: Jules, a graduate student, the club's faculty adviser, and me. Even I knew we couldn't possibly be the only four gay people on the entire university campus. So where was everyone?

I asked Jules about this, and he explained that although there were many other gay students on campus, a lot of them lived in the metaphorical closet. The environment on campus was overwhelmingly conservative and overwhelmingly Christian, with strong Baptist roots. Not surprisingly, many students opted to keep quiet rather than risk ostracism. Jules told me stories of students he knew who were in secret same-sex relationships, publicly pretending to be just friends or roommates while privately carrying on a romance. He told me, too, about methods some were using to arrange sexual trysts with strangers—from internet postings to messages scribbled in bathroom stalls. They'd meet for secret sexual encounters, then return to their normal lives to pretend that they were straight.

This repulsed me. I couldn't imagine meeting anyone for a sexual encounter in a bathroom, and I was firmly against one-night stands. Once more I felt the cold stab of revulsion in the pit of my stomach. Was that all gay people were about? *But that isn't me!*

I had to remind myself that there were thousands of students on this campus. There had to be at least hundreds who were gay. Of those, Jules knew a few who were out and a few more who were secretly hooking up. So where was everyone else? At least a few of them, I thought, must be like me. If only they knew there was a place for them, whether for support or friendship or just solidarity.

"We've got to publicize this thing," I told Jules.

He agreed. Over the months that followed, Jules and I worked together to publicize GALBA. We put up signs, followed leads, and privately met with some of the low-profile gay students on campus.

"You know," Jules said to me one day as we discussed plans for the group, "next year I'm going to be a fifth-year senior, and I'm going to need help running the group. Would you like to be the vice president?"

I blinked at him for a moment. Vice president of the gay student group? But I was God Boy! What would people say? Even so, I knew he was right. If I wanted to see a support group for gay people, I was going to have to help build it myself. Right here, right now.

"Yes," I said. "Let's do it."

◆

And so we did, and GALBA grew by leaps and bounds. With the help of other new members, we turned GALBA into a support group, force for change, and social outlet all rolled into one. People turned out for meetings, and I met many of the gay, lesbian, and bisexual students on campus.

I began to feel as if I had two separate and incompatible identities: Christian Justin was a grown-up God Boy, active in CCF, well versed in Scripture, perhaps a future minister. Gay Justin was a leader in GALBA, working to change the campus environment, but persona non grata in the eyes of the church. As Christian Justin, I had my Christian friends, and as Gay Justin, I had my gay friends. I was the physical embodiment of the gays-vs.-Christians culture war—yet somehow I felt oddly out of place in both communities.

I had imagined that once GALBA had more members, I would meet others with stories like mine, gay Christians struggling to reconcile their faith and their sexuality, eager to work with me to help groups like CCF understand us. Instead, I discovered I had very little in common with the other GALBA members. As a group, they weren't particularly religious, and they didn't seem to have much interest in what CCF or any other Christian group on campus thought of them. Some had grown up in Christian homes, but most had either dropped Christianity altogether or relegated it to a relatively minor part of their lives.

At first, this puzzled me. We were in the Bible Belt, and a large percentage of the student body was Christian. My experiences with ex-gay groups had already taught me that Christians were just as likely as anyone else to discover themselves to be gay, so statistically, there should have been many gay Christians on campus—and at least a decent percentage of them should have been committed evangelicals like me, including quite a few members of CCF. So why weren't there more Christians at GALBA?

Whenever the topic of religion came up around my new gay friends, I listened carefully to what they had to say about it. Gradually, the sad truth dawned on me.

It was all about the culture war.

The one big thing the gays and the Christians had in common was that they both believed in a gays-vs.-Christians cultural dynamic. They might not all phrase it that way, and some might limit their antipathy to a particular subset of the other group—evangelicals, say, instead of all Christians—but at the end of the day, belief in this dichotomy was so strong on both sides that even those of us who should have known better, the gay Christians, had bought into it.

Yes, there were gay Christians on campus. They were all over. But they had grown up, like me, seeing *gays vs. Christians* as the only option. You had to pick one or the other, and whichever one you didn't pick had to be squelched or hidden or forgotten.

What a horrible choice: Would you be a good person, or be an honest person? Deny what you believed about God, or deny what you knew about yourself? Condemn yourself to a lifetime of faking it, or condemn yourself to an eternity in hell?

Given the choice, some people chose to serve God, living every day with their own private pain. They were the ones smiling and singing in CCF meetings as they secretly tried to change their feelings, desperately hoping no one would find out. Some of them were in ex-gay ministries, yearning for a day that would never come, a day when they'd be straight. Some wouldn't even be able to admit the truth to themselves, much less anyone else. They might marry someday and have families, and their spouses would always feel that something was wrong but never know exactly what it was.

Others would make the opposite choice, deciding to be honest about their feelings and live their lives in the here and now, casting aside the theology of their youth, something they would come to view as dangerous and harmful. Having seen how Christianity turned their families and other people against them, many of them would blame God, or organized religion, or Christianity, or certain brands of Christianity, for years of guilt and pain and abuse hurled at them and their gay friends. Whatever joy or peace they might have taken from their faith as children would be gone; they would come to view Christians with suspicion, and if they did manage to hold on to some aspect of Christianity, it wasn't likely to be a major focus of their lives anymore. "Spiritual but not religious," some of them might say to describe themselves, if they were even spiritual at all. And while some of them might not view the loss of their childhood faith as a tragedy, for many there would be an undeniable hole left behind, something that "spiritual but not religious" couldn't quite fill—nor could parties or drinking or sex or romance or money or any of the other things they might try.

It wasn't that there weren't any gay Christians to begin with. It was that in a gays-vs.-Christians culture, everyone had to pick a side. One side would never set foot in a GALBA meeting. The other would never set foot in a CCF meeting.

The effect of all this was a self-perpetuating cycle. A significant percentage of GALBA members were not only *not* Christian, they were actively *antagonistic* toward Christianity. CCF's history of bringing ex-gay speakers like Derek to campus only made things worse.

When I casually suggested that GALBA should reach out to CCF to offer to open a dialogue between the two groups and, I hoped, educate CCF members about gay issues, I already knew I'd encounter resistance from CCF. What I *didn't* expect was the strength of the hostility to the idea from within GALBA. Though a few members thought it would be a nice step, others were angry at the suggestion. "Why should we try to reach out to them when they've already made it perfectly clear how they feel about us?" was the general sentiment. "We don't need their approval."

And so, in this microcosm of society, as the Christians judged the gays and the gays shunned the Christians, the misunderstanding and resentment fed into itself, giving all the more reason for people to feel a need to pick a side.

I felt compelled to break the cycle. If I could help build a bridge between these two groups on a college campus, maybe I could do it in the real world too.

All this time, I had been thinking that if I could just help the Christians understand, then the gay community would eagerly embrace an attempt to reach out. Not so.

Yes, I was gay. But I couldn't have been more out of touch with the other gay people I knew.

THE OUTSIDER

The bigger GALBA got, the less connected I felt. It was an odd pattern. I would meet a closeted gay guy on campus, often from a background similar to mine, and introduce him to the people at GALBA—only to watch him come out, gain confidence, and then effortlessly fit into a gay world that still felt incredibly foreign to me.

What was keeping me from fitting in? Was it some kind of

internalized homophobia from years of feeling inferior because of my sexuality? Was it the fact that I insisted on keeping one foot in the CCF world, a world that so many GALBA-ites had branded the enemy? Was it my Southern Baptist upbringing and my goody-two-shoes persona?

One of my friends called me "the straightest gay guy I've ever met." One of the guys from GALBA said to me, "Justin, you've got a lot to learn about gay culture."

It was true. In spite of now being one of the most visible gay guys on campus, I didn't know very much about gay culture at all. What I knew was Christian culture—specifically, evangelical Christian culture in America. That was my world, and it always had been.

Part of me resented the implication that I had to change. Why should my sexual orientation force me to change my tastes in music, clothes, recreation, and so on? Why should I have to change my sexual ethics, such as the belief I had been raised with that you were supposed to wait for marriage before having sex? Why should I have to abandon my evangelical faith? Couldn't gay people be just as diverse as straight people? Not all straight people listen to the same music or believe the same things or go to the same places to hang out. Why couldn't I just be me? Did I really have to change everything that made me unique in order to fit in?

No, I didn't have to, and I wasn't going to. I was going to be myself, and I was going to keep standing up for the diversity of the gay community—diverse in religion, interests, tastes, backgrounds, body types, and every other aspect. I made up my mind never to abandon myself in the name of fitting in.

Still, if I was going to stand up for the gay community and try to build bridges on its behalf, I needed to break out of my childhood bubble.

◆

I didn't really hang out with the other GALBA leaders socially. They rarely invited me to go along when they did things, even though I counted several of them as friends.

So, hoping to improve our relationship, I privately asked one of them about it. Did the others not like me for some reason?

"Honestly?" he said.

I nodded.

"Well, you've gotten the reputation of being antisocial."

"Antisocial? Why?" I asked.

"Because you never go out to the club with us. If you always say no, then people don't have a reason to keep asking."

The club in question was a local gay bar, the favorite hangout spot for my gay friends and many of the other GALBA members.

"Yeah, but bars and clubs really aren't my scene," I said.

"You've never been. How do you know it's not your scene?"

"I just know."

The truth was that I was intimidated. Southern Baptists frown on alcohol, even in moderation. My parents had both been raised as teetotalers, and they raised me as one. My grandfather, a man whose memory I felt a strong emotional connection to, had refused to sell alcohol in his grocery store as a matter of conscience. When I was very young, he had been killed while working in the store—shot in the stomach by a would-be robber who was heavily intoxicated at the time. As a kid, I blamed alcohol for my grandfather's death, and all my life, I had never seen any positive, moderate use of alcohol to counteract that image. Yes, Jesus drank wine, but that was two thousand years ago. In my church, we drank grape juice, and my mom didn't even have a bottle of wine in the kitchen for cooking. The images of alcohol use I saw at college—loud frat boys binge drinking at parties and the like—certainly weren't helpful in changing my negative perception.

With all the emotional baggage I had regarding alcohol, the idea of going to a bar was intimidating enough. Add to that the fact that this was a *gay* bar. The only image I had of gay bars came from a scene in the British film *Beautiful Thing* in which two teenage boys venture to a seedy little gay bar. Inside, they find gay couples talking and making out all around them as a drag queen hits on them both. It makes me laugh now, but for a kid with no knowledge of the gay world, it was an unsettling depiction of gay life.

Karen and Erika were the ones who finally convinced me.

Karen and Erika were two of my straight female friends. They had gotten to know some of the guys from GALBA, and when they found out the guys were going out to the gay club one weekend, they decided to join them and ask me to come along.

"No thanks," I said, as I always did.

"Oh, come on!" they insisted. "We'll stay with you, and if you don't have fun, we can come home."

I was hesitant. Me? At a club? I gave them every reason I could think of why I shouldn't go, and they gave me every reason they could think of why I should.

"Okay," I said reluctantly.

◇

The club was in an old, unattractive building. As a good Christian kid from the suburbs, I knew I was out of my element before we even stepped inside. We paid our entrance fees at the door and I followed my friends in.

A low bass line and pulsing beat filled the room. A couple dozen men, ranging from my age to middle age, were moving about on the dance floor while dozens more men stood nearby, sipping their drinks and watching. A crowd of others milled about the room, going to and from the bar, talking and laughing loudly.

I stood just inside the doorway to take it all in.

"I like the music," I said, looking toward the dance floor. "But does it have to be so loud? That can't be good for your hearing."

"Quit being such an old man," one of my friends teased.

"What?" I shouted back.

They dragged me toward the dance floor. "Come on, dance with us!"

"I don't know how to dance," I protested.

"Just move to the music. That's all anyone does."

For the next half hour, I stood with my friends on the dance floor, self-consciously trying to "move to the music." The lights and beat were intoxicating in a way; it was easy to see how this could be a welcome place of relaxation and escape. But I was still too uptight and nervous to have any fun.

It wasn't the dancing per se that bothered me. Although many Southern Baptists in the past had frowned upon dancing and some still did, my church had never had a problem with it. In another context, I likely would have gotten over my initial fears and discovered how much fun it can be. But at this time, in this context, I couldn't get myself to relax. It was hot, my ears were buzzing, and I couldn't shake the feeling that my parents would disapprove.

"I'm going to take a break!" I shouted to Karen, who was dancing next to me.

"Do you want me to come with you?" she shouted back.

"No, I'm okay. I'll be back!"

I left the dance floor, pushed my way through the crowd, and began to explore the room. The club actually consisted of several rooms, I discovered, and as I got farther from the loud techno dance floor, the relative silence was welcoming.

There were men—and a smaller number of women—everywhere, of all ages, shapes, and sizes. Some were deeply engaged in conversation with each other; others were quietly surveying the room. Most, though, seemed to be just enjoying themselves without taking much notice of anyone else.

I had imagined that my first trip to a gay bar would involve being leered at and hit on by sleazy-looking older gay men. Much to my surprise, no one even seemed to notice I was there. At first I was relieved to be able to pass by unnoticed. But then I started to wonder: Was there some reason no one paid attention to me? Was I unattractive? I had to laugh at myself. The stress of this whole gay Christian thing was starting to make me neurotic! Deep down, I realized, in the midst of my loneliness and depression, I was secretly wanting someone to notice me just so I could turn them down!

God, I've discovered, has a sense of humor. As I was thinking about being ignored, a young woman near my age approached me. She was pretty obviously drunk.

"Hi," she said with a smile.

"Um, hi," I stammered back, not having *actually* expected anyone to talk to me.

"You here with someone?" she asked.

"Just my friends. They're back there." I pointed toward the dance floor.

"You have a boyfriend?"

I silently shook my head.

"You have a girlfriend?"

I shook my head again, laughing to myself. Had she expected to find a straight man in here?

"Wanna dance?" she asked.

"Oh, I, uh, um, no...thank you," I said. And then, by way of explanation, I added, "I just needed a break from the music."

"Oh, okay," she said, and walked away.

I felt bad. I hadn't meant to make her feel rejected, but I really didn't want to dance with anyone. For the moment, I just wanted to be alone with my thoughts.

The more I walked around the club, the more I didn't like it. Everything about it felt sleazy, and away from the dance floor, the air was thick with cigarette smoke—another vice my Southern Baptist parents would have been upset about. Even though there weren't any sleazy men hitting on *me*, there was definitely a vibe of lust in the place, and it made me uncomfortable. Years later, my gay friends would tell me that I had picked a really bad club to be my first experience, but at the time it was all I knew. To me, this club represented all gay clubs, and it wasn't where I wanted to be.

As I made my way through the crowd, looking for an escape from the smoke and noise, I saw someone go through a door a few yards ahead of me, and I thought I felt a breeze. Was that a door to the outside? I walked over to it, but it was shut now and I hesitated to open it without knowing where it led.

A tall man was standing next to the door, chatting with some others. "Um, excuse me," I said, "but where does this door go?"

He grinned down at me. "You've got to pay to go through there," he said with a wink.

I looked back at him, confused. Was he kidding? Was this a doorway to some kind of seedy back room? If so, I wanted no part of it. Or was he just trying to take advantage of my naivete? I waited a moment, hoping he would explain further or give me some clue that he was joking, but he looked serious. My face was hot, so I turned around and walked away, feeling like a fool.

It was, I later discovered, the door to the patio. No admission fee required.

THINGS FALL APART

I had hoped that the outing to the club would help me feel connected to the other gay guys. But instead, it had the opposite effect. I felt more alienated than ever. It seemed like everyone in the gay world spoke the same language, and no one had ever taught me. Worse, their language felt fundamentally at odds with everything I had been taught in the church, everything that made me God

Boy, everything that made me *me*. I wasn't like the other gay people I had met. I wasn't having sex. I didn't want a hookup. I didn't drink. I didn't smoke. I didn't like to dance. I was just a sheltered Southern Baptist boy who wanted to serve God and couldn't help being attracted to other guys.

I was a freak.

Back at the Christian fellowship, rumors were circulating that I was gay, and people were beginning to treat me differently. I kept having to defend myself over and over from well-meaning Christians who'd begin with the words, "I think you should see this Bible passage…" And I was getting tired of having to explain how I could be gay and Christian.

For a while, I stopped taking calls from my parents, because I was tired of arguing with them about it all. My dad wrote a letter expressing his deep disappointment and begging me not to let Satan keep me from doing God's work—which is what would happen, he said, if I accepted myself as gay. I read and reread the Bible passages on homosexuality, trying to make sense of them and figure out what to do. My choices, it seemed, were to be branded a sinner and live my life alone; to abandon my faith, the one thing I held most dear in the entire world; or to lie to everyone, pretend I was straight, and forget about it all.

I prayed more fervently than ever for God's help. And I fell into a deep depression.

I had originally been admitted to the university on a prestigious, full-tuition, merit-based scholarship. In order to please the scholarship committee, I was taking a challenging course load, trying to validate the committee's faith in me. But now, the added stress of all those difficult courses was more than I could bear. I couldn't focus, and my grades were slipping.

At night, I couldn't sleep. I wandered around campus in the dark, begging God for answers, wanting to know why I was this way and what I was supposed to do about it.

During the day, I daydreamed about ways to kill myself. I didn't really want to die, but I couldn't see any future in this world where I could possibly be happy. I felt like I was staying alive out of obligation to God, not because I had anything at all to live for.

The suicidal daydreams got more regular and more vivid. I started skipping class for the first time in my life. Sometimes I would sit in the floor of my room and just cry. Other times I just felt numb. I'd sit in the hallways late at night, wishing silently that someone would come by and see my pain and find some way to help me. No one ever did. Even if they had, it probably wouldn't have mattered.

Something inside prompted me to confess to my parents that I was depressed and needed help. They immediately offered to pay for whatever therapy I needed and suggested that I find a good psychiatrist to talk to about my depression. I agreed and made an appointment with a local psychiatrist who came with a good recommendation. He was also a Christian, which I hoped would help him understand my dilemma.

My first meeting with the psychiatrist was mostly informational. He asked me some basic questions and then encouraged me to explain my problem in my own words.

I told him that I was depressed and suicidal, and that I felt like my depression stemmed primarily from feeling torn between being gay and being Christian. I told him how important my faith was to me, and that discovering I was gay had turned my life upside down. Now I felt alone and no one seemed to understand.

He nodded slowly. "Well, I can see where that would be a dilemma." He paused. "You know, Justin, the Bible does make it quite clear that God condemns homosexuality, and that being gay is a sin. For example, in First Corinthians, chapter six..."

I didn't return for a second visit.

A second psychiatrist handled the revelation of my dilemma better than the first one, but he still didn't know how to help me.

He prescribed antidepressants, but they were only a stopgap measure; they didn't do anything to help the underlying cause.

My depression wasn't about a chemical imbalance. It wasn't even really about my loneliness. Without realizing it, I had internalized the culture war, and it was tearing me apart inside. I couldn't deny my faith, I couldn't deny the truth about myself, and I couldn't keep living two separate lives.

I made up my mind: Something had to change. It was time for me to stop being afraid and stop letting the culture war define me. With God's help, I was going to find my path in life, regardless of what others might think.

CHAPTER 13

◆

BACK TO THE BIBLE

From the moment I knew I was gay, one question had hung over me like a storm cloud: How did God want me to live? I still didn't feel like I had gotten any definite answers. I had promised God I would stay celibate if that's what I was called to, but I had never felt any confirmation in my spirit as to whether that *was* what God was calling me to. My future options were uncertain.

By now I knew that there were many Christians, gay and straight, who believed that the Bible could be reconciled with same-sex relationships and that the traditional view of them as sinful was based on a misinterpretation of Scripture. They argued that none of the Bible passages apparently condemning homosexuality applied to modern-day monogamous, Christ-centered gay relationships. So far, none of their arguments had convinced me. I suspected this was a case of people trying to justify their own sin, but I wasn't sure.

Conversely, my church taught that gay relationships were always sinful and outside of God's will for humanity, and most of my Christian friends agreed. But these were the same Christians who believed I had chosen to be gay and that I could simply choose not to be—something I already knew wasn't true. How could they base their arguments on a careful and prayerful exploration of the complexities of the issue if they had gotten such basic facts wrong?

If God was calling me to celibacy, I would be celibate, but I needed to be sure. To settle this issue once and for all in my own mind, I had to ignore the half-baked ideas on both sides and go straight to the source—not just a quick perusal of what the Bible had to say, but an honest, prayerful, in-depth study.

THE SODOM STORY

The obvious place to start was with the story of Sodom and Gomorrah.

One of my favorite Christian musical artists at the time was a clever satirist named Steve Taylor. One of his older songs, "Whatever Happened to Sin?," lamented the tendency of some churches to overlook the importance of moral living in their quest to love everyone. I didn't want to be one of those Christians. I wanted very badly to live a moral life in accordance with God's will. Out of the whole song, one verse in particular stuck out for me. In it, Taylor's narrator takes on a gay-affirming pastor, responding to him with the line, "If the Lord don't care and he chooses to ignore-ah / Tell it to the people of Sodom and Gomorrah!"

It was from Taylor's early work—not necessarily indicative of his later views and perhaps not the best rhyme of his career—but the message came through loud and clear: God had destroyed two whole cities because of homosexuality. If that was true, could God's view on the subject have been any clearer?

As I soon discovered, it wasn't quite that clear at all. The only mention of homosexuality in connection with either of these cities was in the story of Sodom in Genesis 19. (There's no mention in the Bible of homosexuality in Gomorrah at all.)

In Genesis 19, we're told that God has already decided to destroy the wicked city of Sodom. At this point, the Scriptures don't specify what's so wicked about it, only that it's a city so wicked that it deserves annihilation. But there is one righteous man, Lot, who lives in Sodom with his family. So God sends two angels to Lot to warn him of the impending destruction.

The angels arrive and decide to spend the night in the city square. But Lot, apparently knowing this is not a safe plan, urges them to spend the night at his house instead. The mysterious travelers follow Lot inside, where they will reveal to him their true identities and intentions. But first, something strange happens.

We're told that *every man in the entire city* surrounds the house and threatens these angels with gang rape. Ultimately, the angels blind the crowd, warn Lot, and escape.

If the angels had taken the form of women, we would be horrified at the wickedness of the city and then move on. Because the angels were in the form of men, however, later readers of the story assumed that the men of Sodom must have been gay. After all, why would straight men threaten to rape other men? And if Sodom truly was a "gay city," it seemed natural to assume that must have been the reason for its destruction. Soon words like *sodomy* and *sodomite* crept into the language based on the idea that Sodom's sin must have been homosexuality.

As I considered the passage, though, numerous questions immediately sprang to my mind.

For one thing, how was it possible that the *entire city* could have been gay? The text was very clear that *every man in the city, young and old*, participated in the attack. I already knew people couldn't *choose* their sexual orientation. I hadn't been able to make myself straight even when I had been desperate to, and I seriously doubted that any straight man could voluntarily turn himself gay, even if he wanted to. But that being true, how could so many gay men end up in one city? Was there something in the water? Were gay people traveling to Sodom in droves to settle there? If so, how did they find out about it? Even today, in the age of airplane travel and the internet, there are no *entirely* gay cities. And if that *had* been the case, why would Lot and his family have moved there? Something about the whole concept just didn't make sense.

That wasn't all. As I quickly discovered, Sodom wasn't alone. In Judges 19, I found the story of Gibeah, eerily similar to the Sodom story in almost every respect. In that story, a male traveler comes to the town of Gibeah and, like the angels, plans to spend the night in the square. A kind man warns him against doing so and ushers him into his house instead. Once again, an angry mob forms, and once again, they threaten to gang-rape the traveler.

What was going on here? Was the ancient landscape dotted with "gay cities" everywhere, populated entirely by men who raped other men?

The end of the Gibeah story held an important clue. In that story, the man's concubine—a woman—is finally sent out to the crowd, and the mob rapes and murders *her* instead.

So maybe the crowd wasn't gay after all. They might have been bisexual, but that was even less likely than all of them being gay. The most likely explanation was that at least most of them were straight. But why would straight men threaten to gang-rape a man?

As I was thinking about this, I remembered one of my history classes in school; we had discussed how rape had been used at times as a symbol of domination, with armies raping the (male) leader of a conquered enemy. I thought, too, about stories I had heard in the news of men being beaten and violently sexually assaulted with broom handles or other objects during fights.

Clearly, in some cultures and contexts—whether in ancient times or in modern-day prisons—male-male rape or the threat of it had been used as a method of violent humiliation and domination. The perpetrators in these cases were usually straight men, not gay men, and their interest wasn't sexual; it was to do harm.

Could this be what was happening in Sodom and Gibeah? I read through the passage again. Which made more sense: that the entire town was gay, or that the entire town was participating in an angry, violent attack against unwelcome outsiders? Could it be that this was the ancient equivalent of a lynch mob?

I considered the evidence.

Every man in the city participated in the attack. It was a lot easier to believe that everyone would be whipped up in a frenzy of hate than to believe that everyone in the town was gay.

Their tone also suggested this was about violence, not sex. They tell Lot that if he gets in their way, "We'll treat you worse than them!" He urges them, "Don't do this wicked thing." This was clearly a threat of rape, not a request for consensual sex, and the threat to treat Lot "worse" suggested that the mob's goal was to inflict harm, not just to satisfy a sex drive.

Lot offers his virgin daughters to the crowd as a distraction, something that (in addition to raising a lot of moral questions) wouldn't make sense if he knew the men were gay. In response, the crowd points out that Lot came to Sodom as a foreigner and therefore has no footing to judge them, suggesting that the angels' outsider status was the real issue and that Lot should feel grateful that they had even allowed *him* into the city.

Clues like these, combined with the Gibeah story, made it seem likely to me that this was a story about a violent threat, not a story about a gay city. It certainly wasn't a story about consensual relationships.

Some Bible scholars have argued that Sodom's sin was "inhospitality." I laughed the first time I read that, because in light of passages about gang rape and murder, to say that the real problem in these cities was about not being *hospitable* sounds like a ludicrous understatement.

Here's what I think they mean.

This was a culture where travelers really did depend on the kindness of strangers. Throughout the Bible, we see that one of the signs of God's people is that they are generous with what they have. For instance, when Jesus tells the story of God separating out the righteous "sheep" from the unrighteous "goats" on Judgment Day, the sheep are those who use their time and resources to help those who are less fortunate. They clothe the naked; they feed the hungry; they visit those in prison. Jesus often entreats his disciples to be more generous than people expect, giving more than asked for and not expecting repayment. Likewise, Job cites his treatment of travelers as evidence of his own righteousness, saying that "no stranger had to spend the night in the street, for my door was always open to the traveler" (Job 31:32).

What we see in the stories of Sodom and Gibeah is the opposite extreme. These cities are not generous and welcoming to strangers; they are cities full of hate, mistrust, and prejudice toward them. These are cities that say to outsiders: "You're not welcome here! We don't want your kind here! If people like you set foot in our town, we will do the most violating things to you we can think of, to send a message to anyone else who might dare to come onto our land." It's the same sentiment that underlies racism, hate between nations, and many other kinds of prejudice.

And in Genesis 19, God is having none of it.

The prophet Ezekiel reinforces this image of Sodom as a city without compassion. Speaking on God's behalf, Ezekiel says:

> Now this was the sin of your sister Sodom: She and her daughters were arrogant, overfed and unconcerned; they did not help the poor and needy. They were haughty and did detestable things before me. Therefore I did away with them as you have seen (Ezekiel 16:49–50).

There are a number of important messages in the Sodom story, but none of them helped me decide what to do about my sexuality. I wasn't trying to choose between celibacy and threatening people with sexual assault! I was trying to find out if it was okay for me to have a romantic relationship someday, and if so, what it might look like.

This passage wasn't helpful in my situation, but maybe one of the other passages on the subject would give me more specific guidance. Confused, I moved on to Leviticus.

LYING WITH A MAN

Leviticus 18:22 was certainly straightforward: Don't lie with a man as with a woman. Period. End of story.

Except that it wasn't the end of the story. Leviticus is in the Old Testament, and as anyone who's been to Sunday school knows, Christians don't typically follow most of the commands in the Old Testament. We do follow some, though, so was this one of the ones we *should* follow or one of the ones we *shouldn't*?

In Leviticus 18–20, God gives Moses a list of rules for the Israelites to keep them separate from the polytheistic cultures around them: "You shall not do as they do in the land of Egypt, where you lived, and you shall not do as they do in the land of Canaan, to which I am bringing you. You shall not walk in their statutes" (Leviticus 18:3 ESV). These aren't just rules for their own sake; these are rules to keep the Israelites set apart for God. So do they apply to us or not?

I read through the list of rules. Some of them were things that certainly seemed just as valid today as when they were written. Bestiality, incest, lying, stealing, and child sacrifice are all condemned in the passage, and Christians continue to condemn them today. But there were plenty of other rules that no Christian I know would preach today. Among other things, Leviticus 18–20 also condemns shaving, wearing mixed fabrics, getting tattoos, sowing different crops in the same field, and sexual activity during a woman's period.

Clearly, just because something was condemned for the Israelites in Moses' day didn't mean it was likewise condemned for Christians today. So if some of these rules applied today and others didn't, how could I figure out which was which? Most important, how could I determine which type the *don't lie with a man* rule was?

Growing up, I had considered that the Old Testament had two types of commandments. *Moral* commandments like those against murder or stealing would apply to all cultures and all situations. They would still be applicable to me today. *Cultural* commandments, like those requiring ritual sacrifice or forbidding certain foods, were only applicable at a time and place in the past. Today's Christians weren't obligated to follow the *cultural* rules anymore. It seemed to me a pretty good way of dividing up the Old Testament, a view held by many Christians I knew, and I had never questioned it. So all I had to do was figure out if this rule was a *moral* commandment or a *cultural* one.

It would be great if it were that simple. As I discovered, it's not.

In this passage, for example, the rule against wearing mixed fabrics seemed pretty obviously cultural to me. I couldn't imagine God condemning a twenty-first-century Christian for wearing a cotton/poly blend. But how did I know it was cultural? Nothing in the passage identified it as such. In fact, nothing in the Old Testament ever differentiates between "moral" and "cultural" commandments.

The New Testament specifically overturns a few Old Testament laws, but the rule about mixed fabrics isn't one of them. Nowhere in the entire Bible does it say that the commandment against wearing mixed fabrics is cultural. So how did I know it was cultural? Sure, it seemed "obvious," but why? Well, because

Christians don't follow that rule anymore. So why don't we follow that rule? Presumably because it was a cultural command. And how did we know it was a cultural command? Because we don't follow it anymore. But—

That approach only led to a circular reasoning loop. Based on that logic, those who believe that the *don't lie with a man* rule should still apply today would identify it as moral, and those who believe it shouldn't apply would identify it as cultural. That didn't help me. I wasn't looking for a loophole to exploit; I wanted to know what God really wanted me to do!

I kept looking. Perhaps there was some other way of differentiating the commands that still should apply from those that shouldn't. Maybe, for instance, I could divide the rules into those pertaining to sex and those not pertaining to sex, and assume that all the sex-related rules were moral commands. This didn't quite work either, however. For one thing, there was nothing in the text to say that; I was just making that leap on my own because there were so many obviously moral commands about sex. For another thing, this didn't address the bigger picture at all; it still left all the non-sex-related commands ambiguous. And for another thing, one of the commands forbade a man from having sex with his wife during the time of her period, and that sounded like a good candidate for a cultural rule, not a moral one. It certainly wasn't something I'd ever heard a pastor preach on, and it didn't strike me as something that God would send people to hell for.

I considered another possibility. Perhaps it was all about the *language*; laws that used the word *unclean* (like those on dietary restrictions and sex during a woman's period) were cultural, and laws that used the word *sin* were moral. But the Old Testament sometimes used the words interchangeably (e.g., Leviticus 5:1–6), and neither word was used to describe male-male sex.

Ultimately, I kept coming back to the word *abomination*. Male-male sex wasn't just condemned in this passage; in many translations, it was called an *abomination*. If anything made this sound like a moral command, that word did. I wondered why it was called that. Was that a sign that this was among the worst sins, something God absolutely detested? (Some translations of the Bible render this word as *detestable*.) I looked up *abomination* and discovered that it was used to describe a number of things in the Old Testament. Among them: forbidden foods, something I knew to be cultural.

But here it got even more complicated. When I looked up the Hebrew text, I discovered that there were different words translated as *abomination*. The "forbidden food" type of abomination was different from the "lying with a man" type of abomination, and the word for the "lying with a man" type of abomination was most often used for things connected to idolatry. But why?

Some scholars, arguing that the Bible doesn't condemn modern-day gay relationships, maintained that this passage was actually intended to condemn ritual cult prostitution, a form of idolatry in that culture that involved male-male sex. In fact, even scholars who did condemn gay relationships admitted that cult prostitution was a relevant factor in understanding this passage. Of the Bible scholars who argue for the traditional view (that gay sex is always a sin), perhaps no one has written as much on the subject as Robert A. J. Gagnon, a professor of New Testament theology who has spent much of his career studying and writing in condemnation of homosexuality. On Leviticus, Gagnon writes:

> I do not doubt that the circles out of which Leviticus 18:22 was produced had in view homosexual cult prostitution, at least partly. Homosexual cult prostitution appears to have been the primary form in which homosexual intercourse was practiced in Israel.[1]

Scholars disagreed on how to apply that knowledge to properly interpret this passage, but it seemed significant that scholars on both sides of the argument agreed that the context for this passage probably had something to do with cult prostitution. That made sense to me, since the rest of the passage was about keeping the Israelites separate from polytheistic cultures. Many of the passage's other rules had similar theological significance: Tattoos, for instance, weren't condemned just because God doesn't like ink on skin; they were apparently part of certain pagan rituals that God didn't want the Israelites associated with. (The verse condemning tattoos also condemns making "any cuts on your body for the dead,"[2] making the theological rationale more apparent.)

If only this passage had said, "Don't lie with a man...because it is connected to idol worship in our culture," I could have put it aside with confidence, knowing that it didn't refer to modern-day committed relationships. But it didn't. Instead, it used a word that *usually* refers to idolatry, but in a context that left the purpose unclear.

If gay sex was being condemned for its connection to idolatry and cult prostitution, that would explain the harsh punishment and the description of it as an "abomination," and it wouldn't apply to modern-day relationships at all. But if gay sex was being condemned because gay sex is inherently sinful in all situations, then that condemnation would still apply today, even in a committed relationship.

I wasn't going to be able to solve this by looking at Leviticus in isolation. I had to consider it in light of the New Testament.

EXCHANGING NATURAL FOR UNNATURAL

In Romans 1, Paul writes about wickedness:

> The wrath of God is being revealed from heaven against all the godlessness and wickedness of men who suppress the

truth by their wickedness. For what may be known about God is plain to them, because God has made it plain to them. For since the creation of the world God's invisible qualities, His eternal power and divine nature, have been clearly seen, being understood from His workmanship, so that men are without excuse.

For although they knew God, they neither glorified Him as God nor gave thanks to Him, but they became futile in their thinking and darkened in their foolish hearts. Although they claimed to be wise, they became fools, and exchanged the glory of the immortal God for images of mortal man and birds and animals and reptiles.

Therefore God gave them over in the desires of their hearts to impurity for the dishonoring of their bodies with one another. They exchanged the truth of God for a lie, and worshiped and served the creature rather than the Creator, who is forever worthy of praise! Amen.

For this reason God gave them over to dishonorable passions. Even their women exchanged natural relations for unnatural ones. Likewise, the men abandoned natural relations with women and burned with lust for one another. Men committed indecent acts with other men, and received in themselves the due penalty for their error.

Furthermore, since they did not see fit to acknowledge God, He gave them up to a depraved mind, to do what ought not to be done. They have become filled with every kind of wickedness, evil, greed, and depravity. They are full of envy, murder, strife, deceit, and malice. They are gossips, slanderers, God-haters, insolent, arrogant, and boastful. They invent new forms of evil; they disobey their parents. They are senseless, faithless, heartless, merciless.

Although they know God's righteous decree that those who do such things are worthy of death, they not only

continue to do these things, but also approve of those who
practice them (Romans 1:18–32 BSB).

Before I knew I was gay, I didn't pay any special attention to
this passage. I didn't worship idols, I wasn't having gay (or straight)
sex, and I'd already understood the basic concepts of humanity's
sin and our need for a Savior. In my mind, this passage didn't really
have anything to do with me.

Now, thanks to the discovery that I was gay, that had all
changed. This was one of the few passages in the New Testament
to mention homosexuality, and it did so in a very negative light. I
needed to understand what it was saying and what that meant for
someone like me.

The passage described people who had turned from God,
refusing to give God honor or thanks, and had worshipped idols
instead. God had responded by giving them over to sexual immo-
rality, resulting in their abandoning "natural" (heterosexual?) sex
in favor of committing "indecent acts" with each other. At the
end of the passage, Paul listed some of the many sins these people
were involved in.

I had always glossed over it before, but now that this passage
seemed directly relevant to my future, I discovered that I had a lot
of questions about it. For example, this passage made it sound like
God had given people over to homosexuality as a result of their
turning from Him. Did that mean that *straight* people had become
gay when they turned from God? Was being gay a punishment for
turning from God?

I hadn't turned from God. I was sure I hadn't turned from God.
I knew I wasn't perfect, but I certainly had never turned away
the way this passage seemed to suggest. How could it say that my
being gay was a punishment for turning from God? And if other
Christians read this, no wonder they thought I was some kind of
apostate.

Did it perhaps mean that they were *already* gay, but that they were celibate—until they turned from God and He gave them over to homosexual *behavior*? But that didn't seem to be what the passage was saying. It said the men had abandoned relations with women *after* they turned from God and *after* God gave them over to impurity. That made it sound like they had been *straight* before, not gay and celibate. Once again I was stuck with the same question as in the Sodom story: Why would straight people choose to have gay sex?

Or maybe I was looking at it all wrong. Maybe this was meant to refer more broadly to all of humanity—that because we, *humanity*, had sinned, God had allowed some kind of corruption of our natural sexual desire to affect us as a species. So perhaps my same-sex attractions were the result of humanity's fall in a broader sense, and not necessarily my own turning from God.

But if this was about all of us, then why did Paul keep saying "they"— "*they* became fools," "God gave *them* over," "*their* women exchanged natural relations," and so forth? It certainly sounded like he was referring to a specific *group* of people, not just humanity in general, and that this group of people had turned from God, worshipped idols, *and* been given over to some kind of unnatural sexual activity. But who were those people, and did they have anything to do with me? Was he talking about gay couples, or was he talking about something entirely different? Whoever "they" were, clearly in Paul's eyes they were sinning. I didn't want to be like them. But what exactly was going on in this passage?

Then I noticed something else curious. When I had skimmed the passage initially, I had read the idol worship and the sexual behavior as two unrelated sins, mentioned to provide examples of wickedness. But as I read the passage more closely, I realized that in Paul's view, these two behaviors were somehow connected. Twice, in fact, he said that the dishonorable sex was a direct result of the idol worship.

In verses 23–24 (Romans 1 BSB), he says:

[They] exchanged the glory of the immortal God for images of mortal man and birds and animals and reptiles.

Therefore God gave them over in the desires of their hearts to impurity for the dishonoring of their bodies with one another.

Then in verses 25–26, he says it again:

They exchanged the truth of God for a lie, and worshiped and served the creature rather than the Creator....

For this reason God gave them over to dishonorable passions.

What was the connection between the idol worship and the dishonorable sex? I could understand saying that sin *in general* is a result of turning from God, which is what I had originally interpreted this passage to mean. But Paul had a long, separate list of sins at the end of the passage. If he intended to mention homosexuality as one of the sins that result from turning from God, why didn't he list it there with all the other sins? Why did he single it out and specifically connect it with the idolatry?

I began to research this question, and it didn't surprise me to discover that in Paul's day, as in the time of Leviticus, some idol-worshipping cults included sex (in sometimes bizarre ways) as part of their worship rituals. Cult temple prostitution, castration, and same-sex sex rites in honor of popular goddesses were all well-known practices of the time.

This explained Paul's connection of idol worship to shameful sexual behavior. With this new information, suddenly the whole passage made a lot more sense to me. The "they" was a reference to people who had turned from God, as represented by the idol worshippers. Paul was using them and their sexual rites as an illustration to make a point to his audience.

In some ways, it was like the strategy the prophet Nathan had used with King David in 2 Samuel 12. David had had Bathsheba's husband, Uriah, killed so that he could have Bathsheba. Rather than directly confronting David about his sin, Nathan told him a story about a rich man who stole from a poor man. After David became angry at the man in the story, Nathan revealed that the man in the story was in fact a representation of David.

Paul's strategy in Romans was similar. He began by talking about wicked people who had turned from God, then discussed how they had begun to worship idols, leading God to give them over to the dishonorable sex rites that accompanied such worship—rites that involved gay sex practiced by otherwise straight people, something Paul knew his audience would find objectionable for many reasons. Furthermore, Paul said, these people had become caught up in all kinds of sins. And just as his audience was nodding in agreement, ready to condemn these people to hell, Paul sprang his trap, catching his audience by surprise:

> You, therefore, have no excuse, you who pass judgment on another. For on whatever grounds you judge the other, you are condemning yourself, because you who pass judgment do the same things (Romans 2:1 BSB).

Paul's entire point in this passage was to show his audience that all of us are sinners in need of a Savior. The idolaters who engaged in shameful sex rites were a perfect illustration of the seriousness of turning from God, a way to get his audience agreeing with him before he unexpectedly turned the tables on them. Read in this light, the purpose of the passage was much clearer.

But it still left me asking, "What does this mean for me?"

If this was about sex rites during idol worship, that didn't seem to have anything to do with committed gay relationships. Even so, Paul's view toward the same-sex aspect of those rites didn't seem very positive at all, and he did call the sex acts (as the NIV puts it) "shameful" and "unnatural." Perhaps he would have condemned the gay sex even if it weren't in the context of idolatry.

Then again, Paul also calls it shameful and unnatural—using the same Greek words—for a man to have long hair: "Doth not even *nature* itself teach you, that, if a man have long hair, it is a *shame* unto him?" (1 Corinthians 11:14 KJV, emphasis mine). Most Christians today understand that passage as referring to the *cultural* standards of that time, and many commentaries point out cultural reasons long hair might have been a "shame" for the men in Paul's audience, even though the passage itself never says it's limited to a particular culture. In fact, of the two of them, it's the *Romans* passage that contains more culture-specific language.

I could argue this either way, but the bottom line was that this passage didn't give me much guidance about how to live as a gay Christian.

THE SINFUL *ARSENOKOITAI*

There was only one other passage in my Bible that seemed to mention any form of homosexuality. It was 1 Corinthians 6:9–11:

> Do you not know that the wicked will not inherit the kingdom of God? Do not be deceived: Neither the sexually immoral nor idolaters nor adulterers nor male prostitutes nor homosexual offenders nor thieves nor the greedy nor drunkards nor slanderers nor swindlers will inherit the kingdom of God. And that is what some of you were. But you were washed, you were sanctified, you were justified in the name of the Lord Jesus Christ and by the Spirit of our God.[3]

In other words, all sinners must be washed and sanctified by Jesus in order to enter God's kingdom. In our sinful states, we cannot do so. This is true of any type of sin, and Paul lists several examples here: Theft. Greed. Slander. Drunkenness. Before we were Christians, our lives might have been characterized by these or other sins, but God wants to cleanse, forgive, and redeem us, at which point our lives will no longer be characterized by sin.

That much I understood. But *what* was a "homosexual offender"?

A friend of mine once joked, "The Bible condemns homosexual offenders, so stop offending the homosexuals." At the time, I wouldn't have found that very funny. This was no laughing matter to me. The options for my future, it seemed, would be determined by this short phrase.

Searches through several reference books taught me that "homosexual offenders" was a translation of the Greek word *arsenokoitai*. To my surprise, one reference book listed the same word as appearing in another passage, 1 Timothy 1:10. I turned to 1 Timothy 1:10 in my NIV Bible and, there, saw that the word was translated simply as "perverts."[4] There's quite a difference between "homosexual offenders" and "perverts." I was even more intrigued: What did this word *arsenokoitai* mean?

In pursuit of the answer to that question, I spent countless hours in the library, read every book I could get my hands on from any perspective, and began studying Greek language and history. The answer that emerged was anything but clear cut.

This word, I discovered, was the source of significant debate among scholars. (No doubt its importance to the gay debate in the church was one of the primary reasons.) Normally scholars researching the meaning of a word in a particular passage look to other uses of the same word in other writings from that era. In this case, there are no other writings that use the word *arsenokoitai* in Paul's day or before Paul; the first surviving recorded usage of the word is in Paul's epistles. This might mean that Paul invented the word, or it might mean that the word was already in common use in his day and his epistles are simply the oldest documentation of it that has survived.

Arsenokoitai is a compound word, made up of the Greek words for "male" (*arsen*) and "bed" (*koite*). The same words appear in the Greek translation of the Leviticus passage, leading some scholars to speculate that Paul could have coined the term in reference to that passage.

Was Paul referring to Leviticus? If so, was he intending to refer to the cult prostitution apparently referenced by both Leviticus 18 and Romans 1? Or was he using the reference to condemn male-male sex in general?

Other scholars believe that *arsenokoitai* is intended to be interpreted together with *malakoi*, the Greek word translated as "male prostitutes" in my NIV and "effeminate" in the KJV. The 1990 edition of *The Catholic Study Bible*, for instance, suggested that:

> The Greek word translated as "boy prostitutes" [*malakoi*] designated catamites, i.e., boys or young men who were kept for purposes of prostitution, a practice not uncommon in the Greco-Roman world. In Greek mythology this was the function of Ganymede, the "cupbearer of the gods," whose Latin name was Catamitus. The term translated "practicing homosexuals" [*arsenokoitai*] refers to adult males who indulged in homosexual practices with such boys.

This practice—married men having sex with boys on the side—was common in Greek culture long before Paul and continued to be practiced in his day. We would certainly condemn that today for a number of reasons, but if *that* was what he was referring to, it didn't tell me anything about the morality of consensual adult relationships in today's society. The New Testament speaks negatively about tax collectors, but we don't view that as a condemnation of modern-day IRS agents; instead, we understand that it's referring to the corrupt practices of the tax collectors of Jesus' day.

The NIV translation of these words was very similar to the Catholic translation. Was that Bible right about what these words referred to? (In 2011, the NIV altered its translation, removing the phrase "male prostitutes" and retranslating *arsenokoitai* and *malakoi* together as "men who have sex with men.")

Whatever *malakoi* meant—"male prostitutes," "boy prostitutes," or even "morally soft," as some scholars suggested—it seemed the easiest one for me to set aside. None of those descriptions were even remotely relevant to my situation. But *arsenokoitai* wasn't so easy. It certainly seemed plausible that it might refer to *any* same-sex act.

Was this passage a condemnation of corrupt same-sex practices in Paul's day—either pederasty or idolatry? Or was it a condemnation of all gay sex for all time? Translation questions aside, I wasn't sure how to answer this question beyond a shadow of a doubt. The passage just didn't give me enough context to be certain.

And so, it seemed, the entire Bible argument came down to this one word. The Leviticus and Romans passages had a clear context of idolatry, not committed relationships. If 1 Corinthians 6:9 was condemning the same things, or something else like pederasty, then the Bible didn't address committed gay relationships at all.[5] If *arsenokoitai*, however, was really a reference to all gay sex in every time and place, then it shed light on the other passages as well, and any other interpretation was just looking for loopholes.

I realized with frustration that neither answer was entirely satisfactory. I could make a convincing argument for either side, but whatever argument I made, how did I know I was right? If I got this wrong, I'd end up either trying to justify sin or unjustly condemning loving relationships that God never intended to condemn.

I tried reading the passage one way. Then I tried the other. They both sounded convincing, yet they both left me feeling thoroughly unconvinced.

THE WINE IN FRONT OF ME

I was disappointed. I had expected that studying these Bible passages was going to clearly answer my question, one way or the other. In my fantasy, there would have been some clear indication that the biblical authors had heard of people like me and had some kind of advice about how we should live.

If any of these passages had mentioned anything, pro or con, about committed gay relationships, or faithful Christians with same-sex attractions, or the importance of mandatory celibacy for people like me, I could have accepted it. But they didn't. Instead, every one of these passages seemed tainted by issues like idolatry and rape, leaving me in serious doubt as to whether they even applied to my situation at all.

On the flip side, if all of these passages had been as clearly irrelevant as the Sodom story, I could have felt satisfied that they *didn't* condemn gay relationships and that I could someday fall in love with a clean conscience. Sadly, it wasn't so simple; as much as I wanted to, I couldn't just brush aside that word *arsenokoitai*. Yes, there was debate about its translation, but the Greek word roots and possible Leviticus connection made a pretty powerful argument for translating it as "men who have sex with men." If that was true, I couldn't ignore it.

But did it really make sense to base such an important, life-altering doctrine—one that could tear relationships apart and destroy families—on one hotly contested word? And how could I ignore the culture in which Paul wrote his letter? If the *arsenokoitai* of Paul's day were married men having sex with boys on the side or participants in fertility rites, shouldn't that affect how we interpreted and applied the passage today?

I was even more confused than I had felt before. I realized that I could easily make a clear, compelling argument for either position. If I chose to pursue a relationship, I could simply focus on the cultural issues and the irrelevance of discussions of fertility rites to committed couples. If I decided to remain celibate, I could focus on the condemnation of the *arsenokoitai*, arguing that every clear instance of homosexuality in the Bible was condemned. I built both of these arguments in my mind, arguing them back and forth with each other like Bobby Fischer playing both sides of a chessboard. Whichever way I argued, I always seemed to end up in a stalemate.

◆

In the classic fantasy film *The Princess Bride*, the mysterious Man in Black challenges the villainous Vizzini to a deadly battle of wits.

Placing two goblets of wine on the table, the Man in Black invites Vizzini to determine which of the goblets is poisoned. Once he makes his selection, each man is to drink—and only one is to survive.

Vizzini prides himself on being a master thinker, and as he thinks through the possibilities, he finds himself drawn first to one goblet, then to the other:

"But it's so simple!" he says. "All I have to do is divine from what I know of you: Are you the sort of man who would put the poison into his own goblet or his enemy's? Now, a clever man would put the poison into his own goblet, because he would know that only a great *fool* would reach for what he was given. I am not a great fool, *so I can clearly not choose the wine in front of you!*"

And then, with barely a pause, he shifts direction: "But you must have known that I was not a great fool—you would have counted on it! *So I can clearly not choose the wine in front of me!*"

Back and forth he goes.

From his knowledge of the poison's origin he deduces that "*I can clearly not choose the wine in front of you.*"

But the Man in Black's penchant for reverse psychology proves that "*I can clearly not choose the wine in front of me!*"

And on and on.

"*. . . I can clearly not choose the wine in front of you!*"

"*. . . I can clearly not choose the wine in front of me!*"

I was beginning to feel like Vizzini. I could argue the passages back and forth to a dizzying degree. Maybe, I thought, I was looking at the whole thing too closely. Maybe I needed to accept my initial impression of these passages—that they condemned all gay relationships—and not think too much about it.

But *not thinking too much about it* was exactly the problem that had caused the church to be so unloving in the first place. We *needed* to think more about it. We *needed* to understand better. And this wasn't just about me; there were lots of happy, committed gay couples out there, some of whom had been together for decades, who truly loved each other. Was I going to be the one to tell them they had to break up if they wanted to be Christians?

I considered, too, what role my own biases played in this. I was attracted to guys, so, by definition, the idea of a God-ordained relationship with one was appealing to me. Did that desire for a companion disqualify me from being objective on this? Was I too blinded by my own loneliness to honestly evaluate what the Bible had to say? Perhaps I should stick with the "safe" position of celibacy, just to be certain. I would never want to let my own desires lead me to justify something sinful.

But, I realized, I also had an *opposing* bias in favor of continuing to believe what I always had believed. I had grown up believing without a doubt that gay relationships were sinful in all cases. As much as I wanted to fall in love, the idea that I had been wrong—and that my church had been wrong—on such a major issue didn't appeal to me at all. Even to *consider* changing my position on this was scary. However much my loneliness might push me in one direction, the security of my long-held beliefs pulled me in the other.

I briefly considered abandoning my quest to figure it all out and going back to just trusting my church and other Christians for answers. But other Christians were divided too, and my church hadn't even understood yet that I didn't *choose* to be gay. How could they adequately advise me when they didn't even understand the key issue at stake?

"God, what do You want me to do?" I prayed. I half expected to hear an audible voice from the heavens answering my question.

Instead, I heard only silence. Where was God? When would He answer me?

CHAPTER 14

◇

WHATEVER COMMANDMENT
THERE MAY BE

After going through all the passages, I felt like I was back where I had started, confused and frustrated. Once more, I reviewed the evidence.

I was torn.

On one hand, yes, there was a potential explanation for each of these passages that meant it wouldn't apply to a modern-day committed gay relationship.

On the other hand, every explicit mention of homosexuality in the Bible was negative. Taken together, the most *obvious* sense of the passages was to condemn gay sex in all contexts. Even if there were other explanations, at some point it just started to feel like looking for loopholes rather than accepting the plain sense of Scripture. I wasn't interested in looking for loopholes.

On the *other* hand, context matters! The Catholic Church

condemned Galileo for insisting that the earth revolves around the sun. Their rationale was based around a "plain-sense" reading of several passages like Psalm 104:5: "[The Lord] set the earth on its foundations; it can never be moved." Today, the poetic imagery is obvious, but at the time, Galileo's interpretation of such passages as metaphors was seen as a weaselly way of trying to avoid the plain sense of Scripture. Similar arguments were made about slavery, hair length, and women's head coverings. In each case, the church ultimately realized that the passages were relevant to a specific context or culture and did *not* apply in the same way to us today. Couldn't the same be true of same-sex relationships?

On the *OTHER* hand, if there was any doubt at all about this, as there certainly seemed to be, wasn't it the best thing to do—the safe thing to do—to count it a sin and stay celibate?

But on the other hand...

I thought of Tevye in *Fiddler on the Roof*, torn between his passion for his traditions and his love for his daughters, throwing up his hands and shouting, "No! There is no other hand!"

I couldn't do this anymore. I couldn't take the constant back and forth, and I was too afraid of talking myself into something wrong. I decided I would have to assume that God required celibacy unless God did something to change my mind—even though something about that approach didn't feel right in my spirit.

◆

At the end of the battle of wits between Vizzini and the Man in Black, after debating at great length between the two goblets of wine, Vizzini attempts to trick the Man in Black into revealing the solution by surreptitiously switching goblets with him. Satisfied he's arrived at the only possible answer, Vizzini confidently drinks from his goblet—only to fall over dead.

"They were both poisoned," the Man in Black admits. "I spent the last few years building up an immunity to iocane powder."

After all that effort, and with all his cleverness, Vizzini had been looking at the puzzle all wrong. His assumptions were faulty, so he never asked the right question.

It wasn't until I stopped focusing on those few passages and went back to studying the Bible as a whole that it began to dawn on me that I had been doing the exact same thing.

I was asking the wrong question. I had been so focused on passages that mentioned homosexuality that I had completely missed the forest for the trees.

The passages I had become so fixated on are *not* the only confusing passages in Scripture. The more I studied, the more I began noticing other passages with the same sorts of problems. For instance, at a time when the term *Scripture* referred primarily to the Old Testament, Paul wrote to Timothy that "all Scripture is God-breathed and is useful for teaching, rebuking, correcting and training in righteousness" (2 Timothy 3:16) and Jesus told his critics, "Do not think that I have come to abolish the Law or the Prophets [that is, the Old Testament]; I have not come to abolish them but to fulfill them" (Matthew 5:17). Yet both Jesus and Paul were accused by their opponents of disregarding the Old Testament Scriptures, and most Christians today feel comfortable ignoring many Old Testament laws. So are we supposed to follow those laws or not?

Even in the New Testament, there are passages I found distressing. For instance:

- "Slaves are to submit to their masters in everything" (Titus 2:9 CSB).
- "Women are to be silent in the churches. They are not permitted to speak, but must be in submission, as the law says" (1 Corinthians 14:34 BSB).

- "If a woman does not cover her head, she should have her hair cut off. And if it is shameful for a woman to have her hair cut or shaved off, she should cover her head" (1 Corinthians 11:6 BSB).
- "Everyone must submit himself to the governing authorities, for there is no authority except that which is from God. The authorities that exist have been appointed by God" (Romans 13:1 BSB).

When examining this last passage, I came across a preacher who argued that civil disobedience such as sit-ins during the civil rights movement was a sin because it opposed "the authorities." But in that case, couldn't you also argue that Christians who helped the Jews escape the Nazis were violating this passage?

I don't know any Christian who would argue for the "plain-sense reading" of all of these passages. Frankly, if they did, I would be concerned about them and their theology. I certainly don't believe that women have to cover their heads or stop talking the moment they enter a church, I don't think for a second that God approves of slavery, and I'm positive that the Christians who fought the Nazis are heroes.

Virtually all Christians recognize that there are passages in the Bible that can't be fairly applied with only a superficial reading. We need context and interpretation, and sometimes that means we need historical insight or other kinds of analysis that come only from a lot of study. For instance, many scholars argue that Paul's prohibition of women speaking in church was a cultural rule related to certain issues of the day. But many of the Christians who argue for a cultural interpretation of *that* passage would argue against the same kind of interpretation for the homosexuality passages.

So how do we know which passages are limited by their cultures and which ones still apply today? If we simply disregard as "cultural" whichever passages we don't agree with, the Bible becomes essentially useless as a moral guide. It's only reaffirming our own views, not challenging us on what we may have gotten wrong.

This leaves us with two options. One option is to throw out the Bible as a moral guide altogether, viewing it as simply a collection of flawed human writings and not expecting it to give us any divine perspective. That is, of course, the approach many non-Christians would take, but that wasn't acceptable to me as a Christian.

The other option is to have a clear, consistent biblical standard for interpreting the text, a principle we can apply to various passages that will help us to determine, fairly and consistently, how to translate them for our culture. This standard could help us make sense of difficult passages without reading our own beliefs into the text.

Such a standard would need to be able to differentiate God's eternal laws—such as those dealing with murder, theft, and adultery—from the *cultural* Bible rules Christians are no longer obligated to follow—such as those dealing with dietary restrictions and head coverings. It would give us a basic yardstick for Christian behavior against which to measure all other actions and interpretations. And, ideally, it would give us a core touchstone by which to judge the many moral questions we face that aren't explicitly addressed in Scripture.

Paul offers just such a standard in his letter to the Romans. In the now-famous epistle, Paul lays out the central message of the Christian faith. People are sinful, he says, and even those who pride themselves on following God's law fall far short of God's expectations. Because none of us can be declared righteous based on our imperfect following of God's law, Paul explains, God offers us grace and a Savior in the form of Jesus, freeing us from the burden of the law without giving us license to sin.

Paul spends a lot of the letter addressing what this means for our relationship with God's law. He uses the term "law" seventy-four times in the letter's first twelve chapters; his final mention of the law comes in this passage:

> Let no debt remain outstanding, except the continuing debt
> to love one another, for he who loves his fellowman has ful-
> filled the law. The commandments, "Do not commit adul-
> tery," "Do not murder," "Do not steal," "Do not covet," *and*
> *whatever other commandment there may be*, are summed up in
> this one rule: "Love your neighbor as yourself." Love does
> no harm to its neighbor. Therefore love is the fulfillment of
> the law (Romans 13:8–10).[1]

The first time I read this passage, I had to read it several more
times to be sure I wasn't misreading it. Was Paul really saying that
whatever commandment there may be—every commandment from
God, including but not limited to the Big Ten—can be summed
up in the rule to love one another? That sounded a little too "hip-
pie liberal" for me. By that logic, couldn't someone use "love" as
an excuse to justify, for instance, cheating on their spouse with
someone more attractive?

No. Paul wasn't talking about that kind of "love." Paul used the
Greek word *agape*, a term that suggested a selfless, unconditional,
sacrificial kind of love, the kind of love that seeks others' good
before our own. *That* kind of love is the fulfillment of God's law,
and, according to Paul, it can be relied upon in any situation.

This didn't start with Paul, of course. Jesus had said that all the
Law and the Prophets hung on the two greatest commandments: to
love God and to love our neighbors (Matthew 22:34–40). In this
context, focusing on interactions between human beings, Paul only
mentioned the second of the two, with the first being implied.

But even so, how could Paul claim that *every commandment* could
be summed up in the rule to love?

I considered this for a moment. If I truly love someone, and
I'm living in love toward that person, I wouldn't kill them. I don't
need a rule to remind me not to murder the people I love; living
out my love for them precludes me from doing it anyway.

Similarly, if I'm living out God's pure *agape* love toward some-one, I wouldn't steal from them. Stealing is an inherently unloving act. If I'm living in love toward my spouse, I wouldn't cheat on them. Cheating is selfish and unloving. If I truly love my brothers or sisters, I wouldn't covet the things they have; I'd be happy for them when good things come their way. That's what love is.

If I were truly filled with God's perfect *agape* love, and if I could live that love out in every moment of my life, I wouldn't need any other commandments written down, because I'd be automatically doing all the right things.

I thought about every example of sin I could come up with. In every single case, Paul was right: Truly living out God's *agape* love for others *always* led to doing the right thing. Sin always resulted from selfish desire in one form or another.

Surely, I thought, there must be more than that. In the past, I had thought of the Bible as a rule book for life. Yes, we're saved by grace, but I'd usually thought of righteous living in terms of fol-lowing rules about what you could and couldn't do as a Christian. Yet Paul seemed to take the opposite view:

> Since you died with Christ to the basic principles of this world, why, as though you still belonged to it, do you submit to its rules: "Do not handle! Do not taste! Do not touch!"? (Colossians 2:20–21)[2]

Well sure, but that was about *the world's* rules, right? What about God's law?

> Before this faith [in Christ] came, we were held prisoners by the law, locked up until faith should be revealed. So the law was put in charge to lead us to Christ that we might be jus-tified by faith. Now that faith has come, *we are no longer under the supervision of the law* (Galatians 3:23–25).[3]

So if we're no longer under the supervision of the law, does that mean Paul was saying we get to sin if we want to?

> What then? Shall we sin because we are not under law but under grace? By no means! (Romans 6:15)

This confused me the first time I read it. It must have confused Paul's audience as well. How can we say that we're not under the law but at the same time say that we're not supposed to sin? How else can we know what sin is, except that it's a violation of God's law?

Paul very carefully explains the distinction:

> You, my brothers and sisters, were called to be free. But do not use your freedom to indulge the sinful nature; rather, serve one another humbly in love. For the entire law is fulfilled in keeping this one command: "Love your neighbor as yourself." (Galatians 5:13–14 TNIV)

Here Paul exposes two theological extremes. First, we are called to be free; we're not bound by the rules and regulations anymore, so the legalists are wrong. By the same token, we must not use that freedom to indulge our selfish desires—our "flesh"—so the hedonists are wrong. The middle way, the way of living out our freedom without sinning, is by serving one another humbly in God's *agape* love. If we live out that love in selfless service of others rather than indulging our own selfish desires, we will automatically do what God has called us to do. Sin comes from our own selfishness, not from selfless love.

And once again, Paul reminds us that the command to love sums up the entire law.

This isn't just Paul's theology. Jesus applied the same principle.

One of the most important rules in the Jewish Scriptures (the Christian Old Testament) was the commandment to observe the Sabbath. From sundown on Friday to sundown on Saturday, Jews weren't supposed to do any work—no cooking, no lifting heavy loads, nothing at all. The day was supposed to be a day of complete rest dedicated to God.

Observing the Sabbath was a sign of allegiance to God (Exodus 31:13). It was one of the Ten Commandments (Deuteronomy 5:12–15). God describes it as a "lasting ordinance" (Leviticus 16:31). Breaking the Sabbath was punishable by death (Exodus 31:14–15; Numbers 15:32–36). Over and over in the Scriptures, whether or not people are keeping the Sabbath is a sign of whether or not they are faithful to God (Nehemiah 13:15–22; Isaiah 56:2, 4, 6; Isaiah 58:13–14; Jeremiah 17:19–27; Ezekiel 20:12–16). Avoiding work on the Sabbath wasn't just *any* commandment; it was one of the *most important* commandments, like a litmus test for whether people were following God or living in sin.

So when Jesus healed people on the Sabbath, it was a big deal. Here he was, claiming to represent God, and yet he seemingly wasn't even following one of the most important of all God's commandments. Not surprisingly, this greatly upset the Pharisees.

It's easy for us to condemn the Pharisees from our perspective today. In the Bible cartoons I watched as a kid, the Pharisees were often depicted as one-dimensional villains, evilly stroking their beards as they plotted ways to oppose Jesus for no reason other than that he was the good guy and they were the bad guys. In fact, though, the Pharisees may have been more like us than we want to admit.

In many ways, these Pharisees were like the pre-Christian equivalent of today's most prominent preachers and Christian leaders. They were devoutly religious, they knew the Scriptures well, and they were very concerned with obedience to God. In addition to any political motives they may have had, one of their strongest objections to Jesus' ministry was that he seemed to be violating God's law and teaching others to do the same. If we'd been in their shoes, many of us modern Christians might have had the same concerns.

When Jesus publicly healed a man's withered hand on the Sabbath, the Pharisees were furious. Jesus knew they would be, and he made a point of letting the Pharisees see what he was doing. What fascinates me most, however, is Jesus' *justification* for his action.

Growing up, I always assumed that Jesus *wasn't* really breaking the Sabbath by healing someone, because perhaps God didn't count supernatural healing as "work" on the same level with cooking or heavy lifting. If I had been Jesus, that's the argument I would have made: "The Bible says not to *work* on the Sabbath. I'm not working; I'm healing. This isn't work for me."

Jesus doesn't make that argument. Instead, he asks something that seems like avoiding the question:

> Then Jesus asked them, "Which is lawful on the Sabbath:
> to do good or to do evil, to save life or to kill?" (Mark 3:4)

This used to puzzle me.

Students of logic would call this argument a false dichotomy. Good or evil, saving life or killing, aren't the only options. No one was asking Jesus to *kill* anybody, and he was healing a man's hand, not saving his life.[4] He surely could have waited until the next day to heal the man; there was no reason he *had* to do it on that particular day. The question was about the morality of healing on the Sabbath, and Jesus seemed to be avoiding it.

From a rule-following perspective, Jesus' argument makes no sense. But from a love-your-neighbor perspective, it makes perfect sense. What's the most loving thing to do: to help someone in their time of need, or to pass them by? If given the choice between the loving option and the unloving option, isn't it always right to do the loving thing? If love is the fulfillment of the law, shouldn't that take precedence over everything else?

The Pharisees were obsessed with following the Scriptures to the letter. In their zeal to obey God's law, they had become legalistic, debating questions like what did or didn't count as work on the Sabbath. If Jesus had defended his actions by saying, "Healing isn't work," he would have been validating their legalistic letter-of-the-law approach to the whole issue. Instead, he suggests there's something much bigger at stake here: an underlying principle that is greater than the letter of the law.

On another occasion, Jesus and his disciples are walking through a grain field, and as they do, they pick some kernels to eat. Once again, the Pharisees are incensed. The Sabbath law forbade harvesting grain, and according to the Pharisees' strict interpretation, this included even picking a few kernels to eat.

> Some of the Pharisees asked, "Why are you doing what is unlawful on the Sabbath?"
>
> Jesus answered them, "Have you never read what David did when he and his companions were hungry? He entered the house of God, and taking the consecrated bread, he ate what is lawful only for priests to eat. And he also gave some to his companions" (Luke 6:2–4).

Notice what Jesus doesn't say. He doesn't say, "We're only picking grain, not harvesting, so we're not technically breaking the rule." That's what I would have said, and it's the sort of nitpicky argument the Pharisees were used to having.

Instead, Jesus gives them an even *clearer* example of a violation of God's law—and from the Scriptures, no less! In 1 Samuel 21, David is on the run from King Saul, and the only food he is able to get is the "bread of the Presence," which he is forbidden by God's law to eat, but he eats it anyway. Jesus approves of this, arguing that sometimes violating the letter of the law is necessary in order to do the right thing and support the spirit of the law.

After healing on the Sabbath on another occasion, Jesus makes another argument to the Pharisees:

> Then he asked them, "If one of you has a child or an ox that
> falls into a well on the Sabbath day, will you not immediately
> pull it out?" And they had nothing to say (Luke 14:5–6).

Over and over, Jesus provides examples of the spirit of the law superseding the letter of the law. It's clear that pulling a child out of a well *is* work; there's no getting around that. It's equally clear that it would be the right thing to do, even on the Sabbath. What loving parent would allow their child to lie in a well overnight in order to follow the letter of the Scriptures?

When the Pharisees challenge Jesus about breaking the Sabbath, he doesn't argue with them about whether the Sabbath law still applies. Nor does he argue with them about whether healing or picking grain is *really* a violation of the law (even though he would have a good case that it's not). He doesn't fall into the trap of debating about, for example, how much grain someone can pick before it counts as harvesting. These are exactly the sorts of arguments Christians often get into about homosexuality, debating to what extent certain passages apply to us today and whether they condemn a particular behavior in a particular situation or not. They are the arguments I had been agonizing over for months, feeling torn between different almost-convincing explanations.

Instead, Jesus gives the Pharisees examples of even more drastic violations of the law that would still be the right actions to take in their circumstances. Then he says:

> The Sabbath was made for man, not man for the Sabbath
> (Mark 2:27).

Considering how important a part of the law the Sabbath was, we might interpret Jesus' words this way: "The law was made for people; people weren't made for the law."

Or, as Paul put it, "The law was put in charge to lead us to Christ." Christ did not come to lead us to the law.

Throughout his ministry, Jesus emphasizes the spirit of the law over the letter of the law, and often this means that Jesus' way is more difficult. When the law says not to commit adultery, Jesus says not to commit it even in your heart. When the law says to give and pray and fast, Jesus says to do these things for the right reasons and avoid doing them for praise from people. On the other hand, sometimes Jesus' way gives the freedom to set aside legalistic restrictions in favor of doing the loving thing, like pulling a child out of a well even when it violates the Sabbath law.

It is this approach that gets Jesus accused of abolishing the Law and the Prophets, which is why he says:

> Do not think that I have come to abolish the Law or the Prophets; I have not come to abolish them but to fulfill them. (Matthew 5:17)

If Jesus had said that he *did* come to abolish the Law and the Prophets, we might just write all this off as proof that Old Testament laws such as the Sabbath law don't apply to Christians. But we still do follow some Old Testament laws (like the Ten Commandments), and Jesus said he came not to abolish, but to *fulfill* them. What can he mean?

From a Christian perspective, everything in the Bible—Old and New Testaments—points toward Jesus. The sacrifices, the rituals, the rules—all of these are just shadows of the reality in Christ (Colossians 2:17). What Jesus brings us isn't just a new set of laws; he brings us something completely different from what we had before.

If you've ever had to supervise young children, you know that sometimes kids need things spelled out for them. "Hey, Billy! You know the rule: Don't hit!"

"Well, you didn't say, 'Don't kick.'"

"Don't kick either, Billy. Hey! What did I say?"

"You said, 'Don't hit' and 'Don't kick.' You didn't say, 'Don't push.'"

"Don't hit, kick, *or* push."

As adults, we understand the purpose behind these rules. We don't need to be told not to hit or kick or push; we understand that the point is to be kind to one another, and that these rules are a way of approximating that for children. We know that the rules don't really cover everything, and that there may be times when the rules must be violated in order to follow their spirit (say, to push someone out of the way of a truck). Rules have a purpose, but they don't exist for their own sake.

Medicine bottles tend to have a lot of rules on them. They're there for our protection. But have you ever had a doctor tell you to disregard those rules? If so, which did you follow—the rules or the doctor?

Once, when I was sick, the doctor advised me to take an over-the-counter medication in a way that contradicted the instructions on the bottle. "On the bottle it will tell you to take only two tablets," she said. "But for the next week, I want you to take four instead." I followed her advice. Why? Because I trust the doctor. She knows why that rule is on the bottle, and she knows that in certain circumstances, it makes sense to disregard it. On my own, I would never make that decision, but led by someone who understands the underlying purpose of the rules and has my best interests at heart, I have the freedom—even the responsibility—to do so.

I believe the Holy Spirit functions in that capacity for us as Christians. Christians usually understand the Holy Spirit as the "Helper" Jesus promised to send, the indwelling of God in the hearts of all believers. The Holy Spirit knows the purpose of God's laws and can guide us in interpreting and applying them to our situations, superseding the letter of the law when appropriate, and fulfilling God's ultimate desire for us on earth: not to be slaves to a set of rules, but to live out God's unconditional *agape* love in every moment of every day.

That's why Paul says:

> If you are led by the Spirit, you are not under the law (Galatians 5:18).

Of course, anyone can *say* they're being led by the Spirit. Thankfully, the Bible gives us a reference for what it should look like when we are. Jesus tells us that bad trees bear bad fruit and good trees bear good fruit (Luke 6:43–44), so while we can't judge people's hearts, we *can* see the results of their actions.

Meanwhile, Paul tells us that every commandment from God can be summed up in the rule to love one another. As I mentioned, I could easily see how this was true for every sin I could think of: murder, theft, adultery, coveting, and so forth. Sin *always* results from a failure to act out of God's perfectly selfless love, and in the end, it always bears bad fruit.

With these standards in mind, it became much easier to interpret Scripture's difficult passages consistently. Yes, there were slaves in Bible times, but doesn't selfless *agape* love demand their freedom? Rules about head coverings and hair length had a purpose in Paul's culture, but if they have no ultimate bearing on our commission to selflessly love God and our neighbors, then, led by the Spirit, we can safely set them aside today.

I then tried applying these standards to the question of homosexuality. Undeniably, there were many types of homosexual behavior that were driven by selfishness, not by *agape* love. Behaviors like rape, idolatry, prostitution, and child exploitation were all clear examples of the results of selfish, fleshly motivation, not love for God or others. They were sinful, and their bad fruit bore that out.

But suppose two people loved each other with all their hearts, and they wanted to commit themselves to each other in the sight of God—to love, honor, and cherish; to selflessly serve and encourage one another; to serve God together; to be faithful for the rest of their lives. If they were of opposite sexes, we would call that holy and beautiful and something to celebrate. But if we changed only one thing—the gender of one of those people—while still keeping the same love and selflessness and commitment, suddenly many Christians would call it an abomination deserving of hell.

As I read and reread Romans 13:8–10, I couldn't find any way to reconcile that view with what Paul tells us sin is. If every commandment can be summed up in the rule to love one another, then either gay couples were the one exception to this rule, and Paul was wrong—or my church had made a big mistake.

A TERRIFYING PROPOSITION

The more I studied the Bible, the more I found myself coming to the conclusion that my church had gotten this issue wrong.

Because of Paul's teachings about grace and sin, and because of the way Jesus read and applied Scripture, I could no longer justify condemning a loving, committed, Christ-centered relationship based solely on gender. The bad fruit I saw coming out of my church's current approach and the good fruit I saw in Christ-centered gay couples I met only further reinforced this for me.

The standards Jesus and Paul applied—the same standards that allowed me to put aside culture-based biblical rules about food or hair length or head coverings—didn't just *allow* me to do the same on this issue; they *required* it. To do otherwise was being inconsistent.

As I considered this, I realized that my view had completely changed. Studying the Bible had convinced me of something I would have thought impossible only months before: that God would bless gay couples. For a lot of gay Christians, coming to that conclusion would have been a happy ending. For me, it was terrifying.

Yes, if my studies had reinforced the traditional view, I had known I'd have to endure the loneliness of celibacy, but at least that had felt like a "safe" position within established Christian tradition. Coming to a conclusion that supported gay relationships was uncharted territory. If I was wrong about this, I was moving in a sinful direction, and if I told anyone else what I believed, I could unwittingly lead people into sin. That was something I just couldn't risk! I would much rather be single and celibate—even if God didn't require it—than risk sinning against God and leading others down a sinful path.

And yet the more I studied these passages and the more I prayed about this, the more I found it impossible to return to my former way of thinking. It was like the famous illustration that appears to be an old woman when viewed one way and a young woman when viewed another way. At first, you may only see one image, but once you've seen the other one, you can't go back and unsee it. Try as I might, I could never go back.

Still, I was terrified of being wrong, especially since I had such a personal stake in the matter. How could I ever be sure that I wasn't just seeing what I wanted to see? Maybe, I thought, I should say I still believed gay relationships were sinful, even though that now seemed to me in conflict with the Scriptures. I didn't want to risk being wrong.

But there was another thought I just couldn't shake: What if I was *right*? What if the majority of Christians had interpreted these passages incorrectly? What if we had allowed our own prejudices to cloud our judgment? What if we were turning people away from God by misapplying the Bible? If so, that wouldn't just be a grave injustice; it would be a sin against God!

Now I had a real dilemma.

Studying the Bible had brought me to a conclusion that was different from the one I had learned growing up. And if I was wrong and I spoke out, I could be sinning and leading others into sin. But if I was right and I *didn't* speak out, then I was allowing the church to be an active participant in a terrible sin, one that was not only destroying lives and families but was also turning countless people away from the unconditional love of Christ.

The early church dealt with a similar dilemma. Today, Christians debate whether *gays* can be members of the church and, if so, whether they have to be celibate. Then, Christians debated whether *Gentiles* could be members of the church and, if so, whether they had to be circumcised. Circumcision was required according to the Scriptures, and a split formed between those who believed it was still required and those who believed it no longer was. Not surprisingly, many of the Gentiles were on the side of not requiring circumcision anymore. I don't blame them!

Paul argued against requiring circumcision, but he went even further than that:

> Mark my words! I, Paul, tell you that if you let yourselves be circumcised, Christ will be of no value to you at all (Galatians 5:2).

Paul didn't just believe circumcision wasn't *necessary*. He believed that doing it in order to be on the "safe" side was actually a *sin*. It was putting oneself back under the law and nullifying the grace that comes from Christ.

By that standard, I realized, there was no "safe side" on this issue. If I *supported* gay relationships and was wrong, I would be sinning by encouraging people to do something wrong, but if I *opposed* gay relationships and was wrong, I would be sinning by putting myself and others back under the law and making Christ "of no value."

Either way, these were big stakes, and I couldn't afford to keep quiet. I had to do my best to live according to what I believed, remaining open to God's leading and trusting in God's grace if I made a mistake.

And I had to speak up about the biggest thing the church was missing.

CHAPTER 15

◇

LIGHTNING ROD

G race. We had missed the point of grace.

In his book *What's So Amazing About Grace?*, evangelical author Philip Yancey takes the church to task for failing to embody the very grace we sing about. He tells the story of a prostitute in Chicago, enduring horrible conditions and desperate for help. A friend of Yancey's asked whether she had considered turning to a church for support.

"'Church!' she cried. 'Why would I ever go there? I was already feeling terrible about myself. They'd just make me feel worse.'"

This, Yancey points out, is a far more common problem than most Christians would like to admit, and it has colored the world's view of Christians:

> These characterizations of Christians are surely incomplete,
> for I know many Christians who embody grace. Yet some-
> how throughout history the church has managed to gain a

reputation for its ungrace. As a little English girl prayed, "O God, make the bad people good, and the good people nice."[1]

Whether I was right or wrong in my interpretation of Scripture about gay marriage, one thing was clear: We Christians were failing to show grace to the gay community the way Jesus would. At the very least, Christians ought to be listening to their gay friends, seeking to understand them, to know their joys and their struggles. If we couldn't do that much, how could we hope to be vessels for God's lavish grace and unconditional love?

I was sure most Christians were under the impression that they were extending grace. Nevertheless, even I as a fellow Christian was experiencing grace from them only rarely. If I, who was actively seeking grace from the church, wasn't finding it, then it almost certainly wasn't being felt by those gay people who had turned their backs on the church.

Jesus radiated grace and compassion in such a way that people came to him to hear his views on things. By contrast, we Christians were so focused on preaching our views on things that we were driving people away, turning them off to church, Jesus, and everything we had to say. If we didn't fix this soon, the damage to the church's reputation might be irreversible.

I had started this journey in search of answers for my own life. I had continued it because I wanted to fit in and be understood. Now I was moving into a completely new chapter: This was about stopping the misinformation cycle so the church wouldn't treat anyone else with such unintentional ungrace. And maybe, just maybe, helping to save the church from itself.

But why should anybody listen to me? I was a nobody. I wasn't a preacher or a theologian or a scholar. There were lots of things about the Bible I didn't understand and lots of theological questions I didn't have answers to. I did have a different take on the Bible passages in question, but I wasn't ready to go public with that yet. There was just one thing I had that qualified me to address this subject, and it was something no one could take away from me: my story.

I typed up a short version of my story—growing up in the church, wrestling with my sexuality, and ultimately realizing I was gay—and posted it to a Christian internet group I was part of. The responses I got were surprisingly positive. One guy, who had only days before been railing against the evils of homosexuality, wrote to me to tell me that he had been deeply moved by my story and was now having to reconsider his approach to the issue.

Encouraged, I built a simple website for myself and posted my story there as well, sending the link to several of my close friends as a way of helping them better understand me. Those friends, too, sent me positive responses, indicating that I had made them rethink things.

What happened next stunned me. One by one, emails started trickling in from people I'd never met before. Many of them were closeted and scared gay Christians who had somehow found my website and, with it, the first story they'd ever read from someone whose experience was similar to theirs.

At first, most of the emails were from teenagers and young adults, many of them going through the very same emotions I had been through. They wrote about feeling scared and alone, wanting to serve God but being afraid of rejection by the church. They wrote about how emotional it had been for them to find my story and know there was someone else out there like them, someone who loved God as they did and knew what it felt like to be attracted to the same sex. They asked for my advice on coming out to their parents and their pastors. They wanted to know if I thought there was any chance that, someday, they could fall in love. I tried my best to offer encouragement without claiming to have the answers.

Then other emails began to come in from people of all ages. A mom wrote to ask about how to respond to her gay son. A pastor wrote, saying that I was the only person in the world he'd told about his true feelings; he was afraid of losing his congregation if they knew. A seventy-year-old woman wrote, saying that all her life, she'd never told anyone her secret—not her husband, not her kids, not her grandkids. She wanted to encourage me not to make the same mistakes she had. "Tell the truth," she urged.

Then came the email I can never forget. "I was going to kill myself tonight," it said. "I told God He had one more chance to give me a reason not to. Somehow I found your website.... You will never meet me, but tonight you saved my life."

As the emails continued to pour in, a few of us began meeting regularly in an internet chat room, where we discussed the challenges of being gay in the church. I encouraged the others to write out their stories and post them online too.

◆

Meanwhile, on campus, tensions between GALBA and CCF were at an all-time high. GALBA students had shown up to protest CCF's latest ex-gay speaker, and the resultant shouting match had pleased no one on either side. One of my GALBA friends and I began meeting with two CCF members to discuss a better way for CCF to address the relevant issues. From what I could tell, it seemed that CCF's members and leadership were split about how to handle the question, but eventually they agreed to host a symposium to discuss it.

There were some conditions: The symposium would be planned and hosted entirely by CCF; GALBA was to have no involvement. (This was all just as well, since I'm not sure GALBA would have wanted any involvement anyway.) At the symposium, three speakers would be given ten minutes each to tell their stories, followed by Q & A with the audience. I was to be one of the speakers, to represent a gay Christian viewpoint; my friend Jordan, a CCF leader, was to represent a straight Christian viewpoint; and a representative of an ex-gay organization was going to come to campus to represent an ex-gay viewpoint.

I groaned inwardly at the inclusion of the final speaker. CCF had already had multiple ex-gay speakers come to campus. If the goal of this symposium was supposed to be building bridges between CCF and the gay students on campus, the dialogue could have taken place between a representative of each of those communities. There was no reason to bring an out-of-town ex-gay leader to campus to add to the mix. This arrangement was a reminder of the underlying gays-vs.-Christians dynamic—the speakers were being set up as competing points of view rather than as participants in a dialogue for greater understanding.

Reservations aside, I knew this was a huge step forward for CCF, and I jumped at the chance. The three of us sat onstage in front of an auditorium full of CCF students. It was the first time I had spoken in front of so many people. With only ten minutes to speak, I knew I didn't have time to represent the concerns of GALBA or talk about Bible interpretation; instead, I just focused on telling my story as I had told it now to so many others. The Christians sat transfixed, and afterward, most of the questions were for me.

"You've really never been attracted to a woman?"

"Has it been difficult to hold on to your faith through all this?"

"What are some practical things I could do to better support the gay students on campus?"

This last question caught me by surprise. It was exactly the right question to ask, and yet I suddenly realized I didn't have a good answer ready. I tried my best to answer off the top of my head, while mentally filing this goof away. *Next time I speak to a Christian audience*, I thought, *I'll have some practical tips ready.*

When the symposium ended, I was suddenly the man of the

hour. CCF members lined up to thank me and to tell me how much my story meant to them.

One wide-eyed girl shook my hand as if I were her favorite movie star. "When you apologized for going over by a couple of minutes, I just wanted to say, 'Don't apologize! Keep talking! Keep talking!' I could have listened to you all night."

That bit of praise felt a little overboard to me, but I realized what she meant. It wasn't that I was such a compelling speaker; I had been nervous and awkward. The big deal was that the story I had to tell was a story these kids had never heard before. For some, I was telling their story, though they might never admit it. For others, I was telling the story of their friends or family members. Fundamentally, I was telling the story of people the church had wronged, and that mattered to them.

I went to bed that night with my mind racing. This was the way to change the world: Combat the misinformation with personal stories.

LIGHTS, CAMERAS, ACTIVIST

Our campus had a closed-circuit TV station, accessible in all the dorm rooms. Perhaps the most popular show aired at midnight, a campus issue discussion/call-in show hosted by two conservative Christian students. As GALBA was gearing up for a week of activities to bring attention to its cause, we got a call asking if we'd like to discuss our plans on the show. I volunteered along with Martin, a fellow GALBA member, and that evening, we were miked up and staring into TV cameras as midnight hit and the show went live.

This was it. If anyone on campus didn't know I was gay by now, they were about to.

Sitting there under the bright lights and fielding questions from the hosts and the disembodied voices of the show's callers, it hit me that I was in way over my head. The hosts began by asking us about GALBA and our upcoming activities for the week, but the questions quickly turned to topics like the long-term impact of gay couples adopting or how we could know definitively if a certain historical figure was gay.

I didn't have answers to these questions. I couldn't speak for the American gay community. I was just Justin, a Southern Baptist college student who had figured out he was gay only a few years earlier. Yet in a lot of people's minds, merely admitting that I was gay was a political statement.

Lesson learned: Being out didn't make me an expert on all things gay. It only made me an expert on my own story. Like it or not, though, people were going to ask me those kinds of questions. If I was going to keep speaking out, I was going to have to study, and I was going to have to learn how to set boundaries and graciously decline to answer questions outside my area of expertise.

A hundred miles away, my parents were fast asleep when the phone call came, startling them from their slumber.

My mom answered.

"Do you have a son named Justin Lee?" the voice on the other end asked.

Her heart dropped. She was sure something horrible had happened. People don't call you in the middle of the night and ask you about your child unless something is wrong.

"Yes," she said, fearing the worst.

"Did you know he's a homosexual?" the caller asked.

Never have I been more glad that I told my parents the truth before starting college than I was when she told me about this conversation the next day. I can only imagine how it would have affected them and my relationship with them if this had been how they'd learned the truth.

Thankfully, they already knew.

"Who is this?" my mom asked.

"I'm a student at your son's school," he said. "I'm watching him on TV right now."

I hadn't told her I was going to be on TV.

Mom was confused, worried, and probably more than a little irritated that I hadn't told her I was going to do this. But she was *not* going to let someone speak badly of her son. As the anonymous caller proceeded to disparage me, telling her how disgusted he was that I would call myself gay while claiming to be a Christian, she stuck up for me, telling him that he didn't know what he was talking about and that she was proud of me for being honest. Whatever disagreements she and I had, in this moment, she was my mother. And that was all that mattered.

Later, my parents and I realized that the caller must have gotten my home phone number from the campus directory, where that information was listed for every student. But we never knew who the mysterious caller was, leaving me wondering who on campus would harass my parents in the middle of the night, and what else they might do.

The incident shook me up. I realized that taking an unpopular stand could cost not only me, but my family as well. In spite of that, it brought my mom and me closer together. I knew she didn't want me going on TV and taking public stands. When I had first come out, she had begged me not to tell anyone about my sexuality. She worried it would follow me forever, and that people would only see me as a gay man, no matter what I might otherwise accomplish. Even so, she never fussed at me for that late-night campus TV appearance. She was angry at whoever would say such horrible things about me. We didn't stop disagreeing after that, but it reminded us both that we were family before anything else. We were all going to get through this together.

Shaken but undeterred, I continued speaking out and telling my story whenever I could. I made more campus TV appearances, published my story in a book of campus essays, and helped organize another seminar on homosexuality and Christianity, this one with GALBA's help. The more I told my story, the more positive feedback I got. There were always detractors, but in general, other Christians seemed genuinely moved by my story, and many of them thanked me for changing their attitudes toward gay people.

All this time, emails kept pouring in from around the world, and I spent more and more of my time answering them, offering to pray for people and letting them know they weren't alone.

Like it or not, I was becoming a lightning rod for the gay/ Christian controversy, not only on campus but around the internet. Other people were turning to me as an authority, even though I was still very aware of how much I had to learn. I studied the Bible regularly and devoured every theological work I could find on the subject, but I always found myself with even more questions. What I knew for sure was what I had experienced, and that was what I told people about.

SIDE A AND SIDE B

The more time I spent on this subject, the more I kept being drawn back to the need for *grace* in our conversations. This terrible divide between gays and Christians was tearing a lot of people apart; that was clear from every email I received and every story I heard. But everyone saw it as someone else's fault. To my gay friends, this was all about Christians attacking them for no reason, so why shouldn't they attack back? To many Christians I knew, this was all about gay people rebelling against God and spreading sinful teachings throughout society, so they had a moral obligation to take a stand against it! The pastors, the activists, the ex-gays, the parents— everyone I met seemed convinced that they were doing the right thing, but few of them seemed to have much understanding of what people on the other side were going through.

But I believe the grace of Jesus Christ can bridge any divide. I'd already seen hints of that, but what would it take for it to happen between gays and Christians on a much larger scale? What if we could actually talk to each other?

Imagine my delight, then, when I stumbled upon an internet discussion group called Bridges Across the Divide. Bridges Across wasn't a Christian group, but it had been started by two Christians with very different views on homosexuality—Maggie, a straight mother who supported her gay daughter's committed relation- ship, and Steve, an ex-gay man who viewed such relationships as contrary to God's will. The two had begun a dialogue about how people with such opposing viewpoints could understand one another and work together for respect and peace in the midst of the culture war.

Their dialogue had attracted a small but dedicated group of "bridgers," people on both sides who had made a commitment to have gracious dialogue with each other across their lines of disagreement. These weren't just lovey-dovey let's-all-get-along chats; their discussions were passionate and meaningful, and they often disagreed (even argued) about important issues on which there could be no compromise. These weren't perfect people; sometimes, even in this space dedicated to gracious dialogue, things got too heated and people would need to take a break to cool off. But in general, the tone of this dialogue was surprisingly kind and civil, especially considering how different the views were among its participants.

One of the early problems Bridges Across had faced was trying to find a way to refer to the two primary positions—the "sides" of the divide they were bridging.

Maggie's position in favor of same-sex relationships might be called "pro-gay," but did that make Steve's more traditional posi- tion "anti-gay"? That didn't sit right, and since there were celibate gay people who agreed with Steve, it didn't make sense. They might call them "liberal" and "conservative" views, but those terms already had too much political baggage. (What of those who agreed with Maggie, for instance, but had conservative political and theological stances?) Similar problems plagued every other pairing of terms they could think of.

Eventually, the group settled on something completely different: *SideA* and *SideB*. They explained the terms this way on their website:

> SideA: There are people from many backgrounds who for religious or other reasons believe that homosexual relationships have the same value as heterosexual relationships.
>
> SideB: And there are those of many faiths who disagree, believing that only a male/female relationship in marriage is the Creator's intent for our sexuality.

In essence, SideA holds that gay sex (like straight sex) is morally acceptable in the right circumstances. SideB holds that gay sex is inherently morally wrong.

Each of these groups might have many subgroups. For instance, two SideA people might disagree on what the "right circumstances" are. One might say that gay sex is only acceptable within a same-sex marriage, while another might argue that it only matters that the partners are consenting adults. Similarly, two SideB people might disagree on how a same-sex-attracted person should live. One might argue for ex-gay therapy of some kind, while another might strongly oppose that and push for celibacy instead.

SideA and *SideB* were just broad terms, but they gave the group a way to talk about the issues. Eventually, the terms began to pop up in other places as well, with people discussing whether they held a Side A or Side B (now usually written with the spaces) view of homosexuality.

The Bridges Across project made a huge impression on me. As

I read and participated in some of the conversations the group was having, I was struck by the respectful tone of the dialogue between such different people. I saw Christian ex-gay leaders having productive conversation with gay Wiccans, and that floored me.

I also saw the limitations of such dialogue. In order for this kind of thing to be successful, it seemed that the group had to be small and intimate enough for people to really get to know and trust each other. If the group got too large, the respectfulness of the dialogue seemed to suffer. Personalities made a difference; so, too, did the existence or nonexistence of shared values between people.

Bridges Across functioned primarily as a training ground, bringing people with different viewpoints together to dialogue and take what they learned to their respective walks of life. As an organization, Bridges Across didn't really do work "in the world." The success of its dialogue made me wonder, though: Could this model of bridge building be practically applied to other kinds of organizations as well?

A SPACE FOR GRACE

By the time I graduated college, I was receiving more emails than I could answer from gay Christians in need of support and someone to talk to. Some of the people who had contacted me were in favor of same-sex marriage (Side A), while others believed celibacy was God's call for gay Christians and were committed to living that out (Side B). But both groups felt ostracized and misunderstood in their own churches. Both were struggling and in need of some kind of Christian community where they could be honest about what they were going through.

I knew I couldn't keep being the sole support system for all these people, so I prayerfully considered ways they could support each other. Was it possible that they could be a support network for each other, despite the disagreement on marriage? I decided there was only one way to find out.

I bought some social networking software, configured it for our needs, and launched an internet community space in which my newfound gay Christian friends could gather and support one another. As I responded to emails from gay Christians, I mentioned this new online space to them. Soon there were about a dozen of us posting messages each day, praying for each other, chatting, becoming friends, rediscovering how good it felt to be part of a community that loved you as you were.

Then there were a hundred of us.

Before long, there were a thousand.

As this little pet project of mine grew, I realized how deep the need was for this kind of connection, drawing people from very different places in life. Some came looking for friends. Some came looking for love. Some came looking for God. Some came because they wanted to offer their support to others. Most came because they were desperately in need of that support.

We were all over the world. We crossed all denominational lines. We were diverse in age, gender, and race. Some of us hadn't decided yet whether we thought it was okay for gay Christians to be in committed, consummated relationships. Those of us who *had* made up our minds didn't all fall on the same side. Yet in the midst of all our disagreements, we were united by two things: our passion for Jesus Christ and our conviction that the church needed to do a much better job of supporting gay people.

For the first two years, I paid all the organization's expenses out of my own pocket. I designed and maintained the website, wrote the computer code to make it work, approved and followed up on new member registrations, moderated discussions to ensure everyone was heard, answered all the emails that came in, and so forth, all while working a full-time job. As the community continued to grow, it got to be overwhelming. So great was the need for this kind of resource that I found myself requesting fewer hours at work and spending every moment of my free time just trying to maintain the website.

After a while, people began asking spontaneously whether they could write me checks in gratitude and to support the future of what they had come to see as an important ministry. I didn't want the burden of handling people's money without some kind of oversight, so after further prayer and reflection, I suggested something else: We should incorporate. People pitched in the money for a lawyer and filing fees, and a year later, we were officially a nonprofit organization.

As we became a nonprofit, our focus changed. Together, we had the power to do much more than provide prayer and encouragement to individual hurting gay Christians. We could work to help the church understand how it was missing the mark. Our ultimate goal, then, was to help transform the church into an institution that would be doing the kind of supportive ministry work we had so needed and found lacking—and in so doing, to make the existence of our own organization someday no longer necessary.

Growth happened quickly. What had begun as an internet project morphed into something more. People were forming strong bonds with their new friends from the website, and it wasn't long before they were talking about getting together in person for local Bible studies and social events. Then someone asked: What if we set a date and place for a national gathering?

Our first conference was in 2005 at a small church in Dallas, Texas. Forty people attended, not just from across the United States but from other countries as well. A volunteer named Danny and I pulled together a bare-bones agenda, but we didn't really know how to plan a conference, and the end result was about the least polished, least professional event you can imagine. Nothing started on time, the audio system didn't work, and it wasn't until I was set to take the stage with a video presentation that I discovered I had forgotten the video cables.

In the end, none of that mattered. We began singing songs of worship, and in that moment, every one of us knew we were home. Some people raised their hands in praise; others swayed back and forth; still others stood quietly and mouthed prayers. Something I cannot describe filled the room—an overwhelming experience of the peace and joy and warmth of the love of God—the moving of the Holy Spirit in all of us in a way that took my breath away and reduced people to tears. This was undeniably God's work.

We set up an open mike so people could share the things God was doing in their hearts that weekend. One after another, people came forward to tearfully pour out their gratitude for the existence of a group like this. A young man's voice cracked as he told us all this was the first time he had felt the Holy Spirit in his life since coming out and being forced to leave his home church. Another man broke down as he shared how members of our community had been there to pray with and support him after his partner of fifteen years had died in a hiking accident. A Southern Baptist woman beamed with joy at the experience of being in such a community of support and seeing God work in so many lives.

The next year, the conference doubled in size. Then it doubled again.

At first, my primary focus had been on *gay* men and women in the church. Soon, though, I was meeting Christians who were bisexual and transgender,[2] and learning from them about some of the other kinds of experiences that can make people feel like outcasts. We welcomed them into our group and began using the then-common acronym *LGBT*—lesbian, gay, bisexual, and transgender—to talk about challenges all of us shared. (Today, the acronym is more typically written as *LGBTQ*, with the last letter standing for *queer*—or, less commonly, *questioning*.) I also began meeting a lot of straight Christians who cared deeply about these issues and wanted to be part of helping make change. We welcomed them, too, with open arms.

News of what we were doing made it out to the media, and then things really exploded. The *New York Times* called. *Dr. Phil* called. CNN called. Reporters wanted to come interview me in our office, and I was embarrassed to tell them that we didn't even have an office; I was still working out of my apartment. I did TV, radio, and newspaper interviews for markets across America. It was amazing; we were this little nonprofit with hardly any money at all, no staff, and no office, but the media was fascinated by us. Gays and Christians are supposed to be enemies. Side A and Side B are supposed to be enemies. Yet here we were, cats and dogs, living alongside each other and supporting one another in good times and bad.

Over a period of sixteen years, I had the privilege of seeing firsthand what can happen when Christ is lifted up and Truth and Love come together to create a space for grace in the midst of disagreement.

Of course, we made plenty of mistakes along the way, and not everything was perfect. Among other things, I think we ultimately tried to take too much on; the gracious dialogue that worked well for a small, close-knit community of shared values was much harder to maintain when we were suddenly being inundated by so many people from around the world with different needs and many fewer values in common. It was a learning experience for me, to be sure, and I could probably write an entire book on things I wish I'd known beforehand and pitfalls I wish I'd avoided. But no matter what else I do in life, one thing I hope I never forget is the look on people's faces when they first realized there was a place for them to worship Jesus with a community of fellow believers who wouldn't push them away—and the tears in their eyes as they sang and prayed and discovered together what it meant to be the church.

❖

Then Peter said, "Surely no one can stand in the way of their being baptized with water. They have received the Holy Spirit just as we have." So he ordered that they be baptized in the name of Jesus Christ (Acts 10:46–48).

◆

Today there are multiple places for LGBTQ Christians and those who love them to connect for worship and community. (You can find some of my own personal recommendations on my website at geekyjustin.com.) But my prayer continues to be for *every* church to meet that need, and we still have a long way to go.

We're all still learning and growing and changing each day, and we're never going to do everything perfectly. Not in this life. But I've now had the opportunity to meet so many amazing Christians who are committed to fixing our mistakes and getting this right. They've proven to me that the Holy Spirit is still alive and well in the church and that underneath all the ugliness our fallen humanity has brought to the name of Christ, there is plenty of hope for the future. That mission doesn't belong to any person or organization or denomination. It's about all of us as the Body of Christ—imperfect but bound together by the grace of God.

Christians will not all agree on this or any issue anytime soon. But living together in a loving Christian community is possible in the midst of those challenging disagreements. It's not easy, and we will all make mistakes. But it's what God calls us to.

It is, I believe, even more than our doctrine, the thing that most demonstrates our commitment to Christ.

CHAPTER 16

◆

THE MORE YOU KNOW

'd always thought there would be some pivotal moment, some threshold to cross, to take me from *ignorant child still learning about the world* to *mature adult who knows all the answers*. So it was something of a shock, after all those years of feeling like I was too young and unimportant to make a difference, to wake up one morning and realize that people were now looking at me not only as an *adult* but also as an *expert*. I didn't quite feel like either. In my mind, I was still that scared kid wrestling for the first time with his sexuality and realizing how much he still didn't know.

It turns out that being an adult is just an extension of the same growth process that starts when we're young and continues all our lives. As long as we're living, we're learning and growing. We're never finished.

God knows everything. The rest of us are just big kids.

Even if I didn't see myself as an expert, though, other people clearly saw me as one. I was invited to speak in churches and universities across the country. I met with parents seeking to understand their kids and pastors seeking to handle conflict in their congregations. In my spare time, I did some writing online and started a YouTube channel.

Eventually, at the urging of several people close to me, I wrote a book about my journey so far—what became the first edition of *Torn*—and almost couldn't believe it when a Christian publisher wanted to print it. When the book came out, I was like a kid on Christmas morning. I went to several local bookstores just to see if they had my book in stock. I'd go to the Christianity section, and there it would be, this book with my name on it, filled with the stories I had once thought I would take to my grave. It was surreal.

Even more surreal was learning that people in other countries were reading my book and that it was being translated into other languages. As more people discovered the book, I was asked to speak not only across the U.S. but also around the world. Sometimes, large audiences would turn out to hear me, and I couldn't believe they even knew who I was.

Often at these events, people wanted me to make a biblical case for same-sex marriage. I understood why; for me, too, the possibility of a relationship had been a huge question, and it certainly affects a lot of people's lives. But that wasn't my primary focus. "Expert" or not, I wasn't trying to set myself up as the Bible Answer Man. I couldn't be—and didn't want to be—the final authority on what the Bible does or doesn't say.

What I wanted was for the entire Body of Christ to have this conversation with more grace and understanding. If I was right about what the Bible said, I had confidence that the Holy Spirit would lead others there, too. And if I was wrong about some of these things, we would still need that grace and understanding to help us get it right.

Even if I didn't see myself as an expert, though, other people saw me as one, and they continued to turn to me for advice and answers. I realized that I had a platform now, a gift from God, and I wanted to use it well. I thought often of the words of Spider-Man's Uncle Ben, "with great power comes great responsibility"[1]—themselves an echo of Jesus' words in Luke 12:48, "From everyone who has been given much, much will be required" (BSB). That responsibility weighed on me, and I did my best to offer thoughtful, well-researched advice to everyone who asked.

But there were times I had no idea what advice to give. On one occasion, a woman named Gail contacted me about her husband, Hank. They had been married for more than fifteen years, but Gail had recently learned that Hank was gay and had never been attracted to her. She was still reeling from this revelation and wanted my advice on what to do next. On one hand, her husband seemed unhappy in the marriage, and she didn't relish the idea of spending the rest of her life with someone who could never have romantic feelings for her. On the other hand, she was terrified of being alone again at this point in her life, and she felt certain that God frowned on divorce in all but the most extenuating of circumstances. She wondered if there was any way to save her marriage, and if so, what that might be.

I knew it had taken her much courage to tell me all this, but I felt completely unprepared for this sort of question. I had never been married. I had never counseled a married couple. I could certainly quote Bible passages on marriage or divorce, but as a young, single man, I had never given much thought to this sort of thing. I felt sure it would have been better if Hank had been honest with Gail from the beginning, but there was no way to undo the decisions of the past. Given their situation now, what advice could I possibly give that wouldn't lead to heartache?

Gail and Hank were far from the only couple I encountered in this situation. Many others sought my advice after that, and every time, I felt out of my depth. I urged them to pray, to communicate with each other, and to seek the advice of others with more expertise in this area, but I always felt like I was failing them by not being able to give a better answer. The reason they were coming to me, after all, was that so many other experts—their pastors and Christian marriage counselors—believed that people like Hank could simply choose to stop being gay. These couples were seeking me out because they knew I understood that it was more complicated than that.

As overwhelmed as I was by these stories, though, at least I felt like I had a good handle on the basics of these situations. I knew from personal experience what it felt like to be gay, and I knew what it was like to be in a relationship without mutual feelings.

But there were other stories I felt far less prepared to address. Some of them, like my friend Eric's, ripped me right out of my comfort zone just as I was starting to think I knew what I was doing.

ERIC'S STORY

It was early in my ministry career, and I was still getting used to being publicly known as a gay Christian. Eric was a friend I'd known for just over a year. I knew he'd been struggling some with his faith, and in recent months it had become clear to me that something in particular was bothering him, but he hadn't wanted to talk about it, so I hadn't pushed. One day, though, he was visibly upset by a conversation he'd had with his dad, and when I asked what it was about, he grew quiet. In the silence that followed, he seemed to be considering whether this was a story he was ready to tell me. Eventually, he decided that it was, and he began to explain.

Eric hadn't been born "Eric." He'd been born with a female name and a female body. He described himself with the now-outdated term *FTM*—meaning *female to male*. Today, we would simply describe Eric as a *transgender man*. This had been the subject of Eric's argument with his father, who still saw Eric as his "little girl" and continued to refer to him as such.

This news took me completely by surprise. I'd heard of transgender people, but as far as I knew, I'd never met one before, and I'd certainly never suspected that *Eric* might be transgender. My initial gut reaction was to try picturing him as a girl, imagining what he might have looked like growing up. I couldn't do it. He was Eric, the guy I'd been good friends with for the past year! He had facial hair and a masculine voice! How could he have once been—

I suddenly realized that this was exactly why he'd been reluctant to tell me and others. He didn't *want* us to think of him the way he'd once been. He wanted us to think of him the way he was now. He wanted us to think of him as *he*, just as I always had, not as *she*.

This was going to take some time for me to process. I silently nodded for him to continue his story.

From his earliest memories, he said, he'd never felt right in a female body. He described his childhood as years upon years of daily torture, feeling trapped in a body that wasn't his—but not, at the time, having the words to explain this to anyone or knowing what to do to make it better.

"It was like having a boy's brain stuck in a girl's body," he said, a heavy note of shame in his voice.

That shameful tone was familiar. It reminded me of how I'd felt when I'd had to admit the truth about myself to my parents—ashamed of this secret I'd spent so many years fighting to suppress.

Eric had spent years fighting his secret, too. Growing up with a girl's body, he'd tried to fit in with other girls, but he wasn't like them at all, and he hadn't known why. He'd tried therapy, but it hadn't helped. He'd tried just thinking of himself as a "tomboy," as a nontraditional girl, but it had always just felt wrong on some fundamental level.

Eventually, he had grown so depressed that he was barely able to function. It wasn't until he'd learned about other transgender people, changed his name, and begun living as a boy—now a man—that he'd finally felt happy. His life now wasn't perfect, and he still had bad days, but it felt like *his* life for the first time.

But there was a cost to all this, he told me. His conservative family and friends hadn't been supportive. After he'd started hormone treatments to bring his outer self in line with his inner self, he'd cut most people from the past out of his life and started fresh with new friends who only knew him as Eric. He was more fortunate than many transgender people, he said, because it wasn't usually obvious to the general public that he was trans; he just looked like any other guy.

For younger readers who grew up in a world where these sorts of things were already being openly discussed, it may be difficult to understand just how overwhelming this information felt to me at the time. I didn't grow up with terms like *gender identity* or *LGBTQ*. When I'd joined GALBA in college, the *B* was still a recent addition; the group had until then been GALA, and no one had apparently even thought about adding a *T*. Despite often being lumped together, *sexual orientation*—who you're attracted to—is a very different subject from *gender identity*—your internal sense of maleness or femaleness. My journey had forced me to learn a lot about sexual orientation, but that didn't make me any kind of expert on gender identity. This was all very, very new to me.

Eric finished what he was saying and looked at me to see how I'd respond. I hesitated for a moment, trying to decide what to say.

A million practical and theological questions ran through my head. On one hand, I wanted to show the love to him that others hadn't always shown to me. On the other hand, there is a big difference between blurring gender lines—which this seemed to do—and my journey, in which the *difference* between men and women was an essential component. After all, for both gay and straight people, gender plays a major role in whom we find attractive.

And I had another concern: Critics of gay affirmation had often claimed that the LGBTQ umbrella, if left unchecked, would eventually expand to include all manner of strange and deviant behavior. "If two men can marry," they'd say, "why not a woman and her dog? It's a slippery slope." I had always countered that these two situations were nothing alike, and that the best way to avoid a slippery slope was to consider every issue separately, on its own merits.

Well, this was a new issue. I had to consider it on its own, starting from square one. I didn't want to set us on a slippery slope, and I didn't want to hurt my friend. I felt like I was back in the high school cafeteria where I'd started this whole journey, searching once more for the perfect Christian response to a new, complicated issue.

Except, in that case, I thought I knew the answers. This time, I was quite sure that I didn't.

❖

My fourth-grade teacher had a sign hanging on his classroom wall. It said: "The more you know, the more you know that you don't know."[2]

To fourth-grade me, that was profound enough to be worth remembering.

As I got older, though, it slipped out of my mind. By middle and then high school, the people I admired most were the ones who seemed to know *all* the answers—especially in matters of faith. I looked up to those pastors and other Christian leaders who were so confident in their knowledge, they had an instant answer for any spiritual or moral question.

"How can a good God allow evil in the world?" Boom. They had an instant answer.

"What does the Bible say about this complicated dilemma I'm facing?" Boom. They had an instant answer.

"What should the Christian position be on the hot-button political issue of the moment?" Boom. They had an instant answer.

I saw their *confidence* as *wisdom*. They didn't say, "My view is..." or "Some experts believe..."; they just confidently asserted, "Here's the answer to your question." Their certainty made them seem trustworthy and authoritative, as if every word they said *must* be true because they were so sure that it was. To me, that was the point you were supposed to get to once you'd studied the Bible long enough. You should be able to answer any question without doubt or hesitation, citing chapter and verse to prove your point.

This is what I thought the Bible meant when it said that Christians should "always be ready to give a defense to everyone who asks you a reason for the hope that is in you" (1 Peter 3:15 NKJV). This verse was often quoted in my church to encourage us to have a strong, confident argument ready to defend our beliefs—not only our belief in Jesus as the Son of God, but also our beliefs on any issues that might bring us in conflict with the world.

That's why I loved debating people like my high school classmate Sean. I was a good debater, and I knew the Bible well. Every time someone threw a tricky question at me and I was able to instantly make the case for why my position was right and everyone else's was wrong, I felt like I was proving myself as a good Christian.

But the ugly truth is that the confidence I saw as wisdom was too often a sign of something else: a *lack of humility*. I was *proud* of my Bible knowledge, and I was arrogant enough to think I had all the answers to questions with complexities I wasn't even aware of. I thought I was serving God with those conversations. In truth, I was serving my own ego. My faith was sincere, but my actions were foolish.

Now, don't get me wrong. I'm not saying we Christians *shouldn't* study the Bible or have answers to questions. We absolutely *should* do those things! Wisdom is a virtue, one that is certainly nourished by prayer and Bible study. And with wisdom often comes increased confidence in our answers to certain questions. All of that is good. But my fourth-grade teacher was right. The more we know, the more we know that we don't know. The confidence that comes with wisdom must also come with an equal amount of *humility*. Confidence without humility is just arrogance.

This becomes especially clear when we're talking about other people's lives. I might know a lot about a situation you're facing. I might have good advice and wisdom to share. But I will never know your story as well as you do, because you've lived it and I haven't. You may have experienced things I've never considered. No matter how confident I am that I'm right, I need to have enough humility to first admit that I'm fallible and that my knowledge is still growing. Perhaps I'm right about everything. But even if I am, what that means in the context of *your* specific life situation is always going to be uncharted territory.

◆

As I considered how to respond to Eric, I stopped and thought back to all those Christians I'd come out to over the years. So many of them, I realized, had immediately responded by trying to give me *answers*. As soon as they'd heard I was gay, they'd felt compelled to tell me their position on homosexuality, recommend an ex-gay ministry, or ask if I'd read certain Bible passages. All of these things were done with the best of intentions and a desire to help me follow Jesus on my journey. But in most cases, I hadn't asked for their opinion or advice; I was just trying to share my story with them. I was trying to open up to them about something I'd been going through—something that had shaped me in profound ways—because I wanted them to understand me better. I wanted to be able to be more transparent with them and not have to keep secrets. When they responded to that very personal gesture by giving me unsolicited opinions and advice, it felt as if they were treating me and my journey as an issue to debate or a problem to solve. I know that wasn't their intent, but it was absolutely how it felt. Those moments created distance between us when I'd been trying to draw us closer.

With those experiences in mind, I quickly realized I'd been about to make the same mistake with Eric. He hadn't asked me for my opinion on choices he'd made or my advice on future choices. He hadn't asked me to take a position on the state of transgender people in society today. He was just telling me his story. And if he felt anything like the way I'd felt when I came out to people, I imagined he was putting on a brave face but was secretly terrified of how I'd respond.

After so many years of trying to have immediate, theologically accurate answers to every question, I had just automatically jumped to trying to figure out my position on this "issue" and all my answers to any possible related questions. I was panicking because I didn't actually have all those answers yet. But that wasn't what Eric wanted or needed in that moment anyway. What he wanted was simply to be *known* and *loved*.

This is what we all want. As influential pastor Tim Keller once said: "To be loved but not known is comforting but superficial. To be known and not loved is our greatest fear. But to be fully known and truly loved is, well, a lot like being loved by God. It is what we need more than anything."[3]

Although Keller was writing about marriage, his words are just as true in other contexts. People were created with connection in mind. We yearn to be both *known* and *loved* for who we are—just as God knows and loves us even with all our faults. As a gay man, I often worried that I wouldn't be truly *loved* if people really *knew* me. I hid the truth about my sexuality because being loved but not known, as superficial as that was, seemed better than being known but not loved. This is the fear that keeps many people in the closet, and it doesn't only affect LGBTQ people, either. Many of us have been afraid to be honest with others about parts of ourselves—our mistakes, things in our past, areas of disagreement, whatever it may be—because we think that being more *known* will result in being less *loved*.

But if Christian love is supposed to be like God's love, it should be a love with no conditions. I didn't need to know everything about gender identity, or have an opinion on every decision Eric had ever made in his life, to simply show him love. All I had to do was let him know that I was his friend, and that, as his friend, I wanted to know and love him just as he was.

So I did. I thanked him for sharing and told him how honored I was that he trusted me enough to tell me this. I reaffirmed my love for him as a friend and promised that nothing would change that. And then I did something that didn't come as naturally to me. Instead of trying to be the guy with all the answers, I just admitted my ignorance.

"I don't know much about this subject," I said, "but I'm going to do my best to learn."

BACK TO SQUARE ONE

In the weeks that followed, I rounded up the most helpful books I could find on the biology and psychology of gender. A lot of the terms inside were new to me, and even the ones I knew weren't always used the way I expected.

One book, in its opening pages, said that there was a difference between *sex* and *gender*. Traditionally, they had meant pretty much the same thing—which was how I'd always been taught. But in the mid-20th century, some researchers began to distinguish the two, using *sex* to refer to our biology and *gender* to refer to our internal sense of maleness or femaleness.

Ugh, I thought at first. *Why make it so complicated?* I liked being able to use *gender* instead of *sex* to avoid confusion with the "intercourse" meaning of *sex*.

But as I thought about Eric's situation, I could see where the distinction would come in handy. For me, the distinction had never mattered, because for me, as for most people, everything about my sex and gender had always been aligned.

When most of us were born, the doctor looked at our naked bodies and said, "It's a boy" or "It's a girl," and that simple statement accurately predicted a lot of things about us and our future life. If the doctor says "boy," that usually means that the child has XY sex chromosomes, will have higher levels of testosterone, and will one day develop facial hair and a deeper voice, among other things. If the doctor says "girl," that usually means that the child has XX sex chromosomes, will have higher levels of estrogen, and will one day develop breasts and begin menstruation, among other things. Because all these parts of our biology usually line up in the same way, we're used to looking at a person and instantly sizing them up as male or female and having all kinds of assumptions about them. And those assumptions are usually right.

But *usually* isn't *always*. And this is where I encountered a word I'd never heard before: *intersex*, a term for people whose bodies don't fit our usual expectations for males or females.

See, while all these things—genitals, sex chromosomes, hormones, etc.—usually line up together in a particular way, sometimes they don't. Some people's sex chromosomes are atypical—XXY, say, instead of XX or XY. Some people are born with genitals that aren't typically male or typically female. Sometimes things appear typical at first but actually aren't, such as when people are born with external anatomy that appears female despite their having typically male XY sex chromosomes and other internal differences from most girls. The books went on and on about the causes and details of various *intersex conditions* like these, and a lot of it went over my head. One thing was clear, though: For many people, life wasn't as simple as *male* or *female*.

In the past, intersex people were sometimes described with

words like *hermaphrodite*, now widely considered an offensive term. The reality is more complicated than that, though. Being intersex isn't halfway between being male and being female; many intersex people would firmly classify themselves as one or the other, even though their bodies might be atypical in some ways. But with some conditions, that kind of classification isn't so easy. So in cases where a child's sex is ambiguous, who decides whether they're a boy or a girl?

This is apparently not a simple question. In the past, doctors would look at the infant and make a recommendation to parents about what medical treatments the child should have and whether the parents should raise them as a boy or a girl. But this didn't always go well. Some of those children grew up deeply unhappy, feeling as though their brains didn't match their bodies even though their parents had never told them they were born intersex.

Reading about their tragic stories really made me rethink a lot of my assumptions about gender, and it convinced me that something of our gender must be in our brains, even if we can't pinpoint exactly where. That was enough to convince me that intersex people ought to be able to make those sorts of decisions for themselves whenever possible. How could anyone else—even their well-meaning parents or doctor—make such a critical decision for a baby just by looking at them, without knowing what was going on inside their brain?

But that immediately raised another question. Was it possible for a person's *brain* to be atypically gendered or otherwise out of alignment with their body, the same way their sex chromosomes, hormones, or genitals might be? Might their body's observable sex characteristics line up with each other but not with their brain? Such a case wouldn't be considered an *intersex* condition; it would be an example of being *transgender*—having an internal gender identity that is different from what the doctor said when the person was born.

I didn't know if that was how it worked, but it sounded plausible. Perhaps Eric really was born with a male brain in a female body. If so, I couldn't begin to fathom what that must have been like for him.

Thinking about it that way helped me begin to understand how complicated life could be for people like Eric. Even this, though, would turn out to be an oversimplification. Scientists don't have an easy way to separate "male brains" from "female brains," and not every transgender person would describe their experience as that of being "trapped in the wrong body" anyway.

For instance, when I asked my friend Gabe—another transgender man—whether he resonated with Eric's image of a male brain trapped in a female body, he had to think for a moment before responding.

"I just have my Gabe brain," he said. "I don't know if I have a 'male brain,' because I wasn't socialized as a boy growing up." Until he said that, I hadn't even thought about the impact of upbringing. And Gabe was right; how can any of us really know what it feels like in other people's brains? We only know our own experience. Even so, Gabe knew he felt more comfortable with a male identity and male pronouns than with the female ones he'd had growing up.

And then there's my friend Christopher, one of a growing number of people who identify as *nonbinary*. Nonbinary people often describe themselves as existing somewhere on a spectrum between male and female without exclusively identifying with either.[4] Like many nonbinary people, Christopher prefers the pronouns *they* and *them* rather than *he* or *she*.

"It's hard to explain, and there are parts of it I'm still trying to figure out," Christopher said to me. "Because it's not as simple as feeling like I have the wrong parts. It's more that I just don't feel like I fit into 'I'm male' or 'I'm female,' and saying I'm nonbinary takes some of that pressure off. It allows me to just *be* and not feel like I have to fit into existing labels."

If I had a hard time wrapping my mind around Eric's experience, I had an even harder time wrapping my mind around Christopher's. Was *nonbinary* simply a new way of expressing that people don't always fit into stereotypical gender boxes? Or was it something different and deeper? Just as Eric's experience doesn't represent all transgender people, Christopher's experience doesn't represent all nonbinary people. Others might describe things very differently. But for Christopher, at least, there seemed to be something important and powerful about being free from the expectations associated with gendered language. I wasn't sure I fully understood it, but I didn't have to understand it all to respect my friend's wishes with the words I used.

WHEN WE FEEL OVERWHELMED

If this conversation sometimes feels overwhelming to you, you're not alone. It's overwhelming to me sometimes too.

Even just keeping up with the terminology can be overwhelming. The first time I heard the term *cisgender*—which refers, essentially, to someone who *isn't* transgender—I had no idea what it meant and was afraid to ask, for fear of looking stupid. (Thank goodness we have mobile internet these days to let us discreetly look things up in the moment!)

And, sometimes, the right term for something *changes*. When I was a kid, I used to roll my eyes when my parents or grandparents used an outdated term. Now, however, I have a bit more empathy for their situation. Some of the "correct," forward-thinking terms I learned when I started this work are now considered hopelessly outdated, and it can be hard to unlearn them. When I wrote the first edition of *Torn*, the acronym *LGBT* was the most widely used. Not long after it was published, though, someone commented on one of my old blog posts asking why I was still using that outdated acronym instead of the now-standard *LGBTQ*—a term designed to be more inclusive of those who are *questioning* their identity or fall under the broad umbrella term *queer*. (Even that acronym might be outdated by the time you read this.) Every year, it seems, there are new terms replacing old terms, and other new terms describing things we didn't have a term for before.

So I'll admit, there are times when keeping up with new ideas and terms gets to be overwhelming, and it can be tempting to do my best impression of a crotchety old man, waving my fist in the air and shouting, "Why do these young kids have to keep making up new terms? We were fine with the old terms!" But that's been the challenge of every generation in human history—not just with new language but with new ideas and new ways of doing things. We're all still learning, still growing.

I believe that living out the love of Christ means that we keep pushing ourselves to see things from others' perspectives, learn their language, and meet them where they are. It's what Jesus did, after all.

At the same time, we also need to acknowledge the reality that we are all only human, and sometimes, trying to absorb too much new information at one time can be too overwhelming to process, especially when it means rethinking the way you've seen things—or people—in the past. I felt overwhelmed many times on my journey to make sense of my faith and sexuality, and I felt overwhelmed as I wrestled with the things I learned from Eric and others about their experiences with gender. Sometimes, when learning about some new concept, I've found myself thinking, *No! No! This is all too complicated! I just want to go back to a simpler time when everything made sense and it was easy to understand! This is too much!*

I think it's normal to feel that way, especially for those of us who feel more settled when we know we have all the answers. But the truth remains that the more we know, the more we know that we don't know. It was much easier to feel certain that I understood everything back before I knew about gay people, transgender people, or intersex people, but that didn't mean that those people didn't exist; it just meant I wasn't *aware* of them or the things they were going through.

I remember having similar feelings as a kid when I first learned about fractions. Until then, math had always been about whole numbers. But now we were supposed to deal with *partial* numbers that could be represented in different ways, where everything was more complicated and even the rules for addition and subtraction were different. (*I have to create a "common denominator"? What?*) All those complexities felt very unnecessary, and I remember wishing we could just go back to whole numbers and stick with those. But whether we studied them or not, fractions are part of the real world. Without them, a lot of things in our world wouldn't work, from baking to banking.

It's okay to feel overwhelmed sometimes and admit that we're confused and don't understand everything. That's human. And there may be some things we'll never understand. We just have to remind ourselves that even when we feel overwhelmed or don't understand something, those complicated realities still exist in the world. Even if I'd never studied fractions, there would still be fractions all around me. And even if I never think about intersex or transgender people, there will still be intersex and transgender people in the world who don't have the luxury of saying, "This is too complicated," because it's the only body and the only life they have.

So what can we do in those moments when we feel overwhelmed by new information, new concepts, or new terminology?

We can humble ourselves, admit our ignorance, and show *love*.

Recently, at one of my speaking engagements, an older woman raised her hand and explained that her grandchild had recently been asking to be referred to as "they."

"I don't understand it," the woman said. "I love my grandchild, but this 'they/them' stuff just doesn't make any sense to me."

I did my best to explain to her what I had learned from Christopher, but I confessed that I, too, still struggled to say "they" without feeling awkward when referring to a known person. It goes against the way I was taught to use English and the way I've spoken it for decades—and that woman has had many more years of that than me.

"I can't speak for your grandchild," I said, "but I think it's okay if you don't fully understand it and don't always know the right thing to say. Just making the effort, being a good listener, and keeping the lines of communication open shows that you love them."

You don't have to agree with someone on everything—or even understand it all—in order to show them your love.

That's why, for me, it's been so important to get comfortable with saying, "I don't know." For someone who's always been obsessed with having the answers, that's been a difficult lesson to learn. But I've come to realize that the Christian leaders I look up to today aren't the ones who pretend to know everything; they're the ones who have enough humility to know that they *don't* know everything. When a leader isn't afraid to admit, "I don't know the answer to that question," it gives me more confidence that they know their own limitations—and that they're more likely to know what they're talking about on other issues when they say they do. Those are the people I most aspire to be like now—not the ones who are fastest to answer, but the ones who show humility and patience with the learning process. They realize that God is the ultimate source of answers, not us, and God never asked any of us to have every answer to every question. What God did ask us to do was show love, even to our enemies and cultural opponents. And that's something we can do whether or not we have the answers. Even when we're feeling totally overwhelmed.

WHEN WE DISAGREE

Of course, *showing love* doesn't mean we're always going to agree, and *being humble* doesn't mean we can never take a stand. There will be times when our love—for God and others—means we can't agree with someone on something even though they very much want us to.

This has been true from the beginning of the Christian church. The New Testament is filled with examples of ways the early Christians disagreed with one another. Sometimes, the best thing was to put the disagreement aside and simply agree to disagree. Other times, it was important enough for Christians to take a strong public stand, as with combatting heresy. In either case, though, it's important to show grace to one another in those times of disagreement.

Easy to say. But how do we actually do that without compromising our values? What if someone asks you to attend a wedding ceremony you don't feel comfortable attending or to use pronouns you don't feel comfortable using? What if someone in your church doesn't agree with something you believe or decisions you or your family members have made?

What if you *want* to love someone, but you're also very sure that they're very wrong about something important?

Thankfully, the Bible gives us some great advice on this. In the final two chapters, we'll put it into action.

CHAPTER 17

◆

WE NEED TO TALK

Have you ever heard a movie line so bad, you literally groaned out loud?

For me, it was a line in 2023's *Indiana Jones and the Dial of Destiny*. As he reflects back on all the amazing, miraculous things he's seen through the film series, Indy utters this line as if offering profound wisdom:

"I've come to believe it's not so much *what* you believe, it's *how hard* you believe it."

But that's not true at all, is it? It absolutely does matter *what* you believe! Some things are *true* and some are *false*. Some things are *right* and some are *wrong*. If I go to the bank to withdraw money, it doesn't matter *how hard* I believe there's money in my account; what matters is if it's true or not. I could believe with all my heart that there's money in there, but if the bank's computers say that's not the truth, I'm walking out empty-handed.

On matters of taste or opinion, everyone has a right to their own point of view. If you like *Star Wars* but I prefer *Star Trek*, maybe we just won't go to the movies together. No big deal.

But when it comes to matters of right and wrong, every opinion *isn't* equally valid. Believing the wrong thing can be dangerous. It can lead to sin or other types of harm. Surely Indiana Jones should know this. He did, after all, witness God's graphic vengeance on the villains of *Raiders of the Lost Ark*—Nazis who presumably didn't *believe* the Ark of the Covenant would harm them. (Spoiler: It did.)

This creates a challenge for us when we disagree on issues like the ones in this book. Whether we're talking about sexual orientation, gender identity, or something else entirely, there will be times when you think something is *right* but someone else thinks it's *wrong*, and there will be times when you think something is *wrong* but someone else thinks it's *right*. You may believe someone else's teachings or actions are causing great harm, maybe even leading people away from God. So what do you do then?

Indy is wrong. It *does* matter what we believe. But when we find that we can't agree, it also matters that we treat each other with the love of God—both with our *words* and with our *actions*.

We'll get to *actions* in the next chapter. In this chapter, let's talk about words. How do we talk to each other about our disagreements without ending up in arguments all the time? What if you want to try to change someone's mind, but you're afraid of offending them or hurting your friendship? What if your family or church is divided and you're struggling to find a way to communicate because people on both sides are so frustrated?

I'd like to recommend to you an approach that has been incredibly helpful for me over the years—something you can use whether you're talking to a church leader about homosexuality, talking to your child about gender identity, or just working through a personal dispute with a friend. It's a process of *loving, gracious dialogue* that has four main steps. (By the way, if you find this helpful, my book *Talking Across the Divide* offers lots more tips on applying this approach to a range of issues.)

STEP 1: BEGIN WITH EMPATHY.

The words *sympathy* and *empathy* sound very similar, but they don't mean quite the same thing.

Sympathy most often refers to a kind of compassion or pity you feel for someone who's going through a rough time. When someone experiences a loss, for instance, we might send a sympathy card to say, essentially, "I'm so sorry you're going through this. I hope you feel better soon."

Empathy, though, requires more effort. It's when you go beyond just pity or compassion to mentally *put yourself in the other person's shoes* and imagine life from their perspective. Empathy doesn't just hold people at arm's length and hope things will get better for them; empathy tries to see life *through their eyes*. A biographer writing about someone might feel *sympathy* for their situation. An actor playing that person in a movie, though, would try to feel *empathy* for them, to fully get into their head and ask, "What must it feel like to be this person in this situation?"

As Christians, we serve an empathetic God.

We believe that God loved us enough to literally walk in our shoes, live life with us, and experience our pains and struggles as one of us. The Bible doesn't depict God as sitting far away in heaven, sending us sympathy cards when we have hard times; the Bible depicts God as crying right along with us, sharing in both our joys and our sorrows. God doesn't just love us with sympathy. God loves us with empathy. And that is the love the Bible teaches us to practice and share with others.

Of course, this doesn't mean that God is always pleased with our decisions. We are all sinners, and our sin wounds God. But the grace of God through Jesus Christ means that even when we get things wrong, God continues to love us with that incredible empathy—for "while we were yet sinners, Christ died for us" (Romans 5:8 KJV). Following that example, you can show empathy and grace to others even when you disagree strongly with their views, words, or actions.

In practice, that requires starting with the understanding that this issue *matters to both of you* and that you're both *sincere in wanting to get it right*, even though (in most cases) *you can't both be right*.

Sometimes, people think that having gracious dialogue on an issue means saying that everyone's opinion is equally valid, much as Indy does at the beginning of this chapter. If we're truly talking about opinions—like "What color should the church carpet be?"—then sure, everyone's got a right to their own opinion (even if their taste is terrible). But that approach doesn't work on issues of truth or morality. If God tells us to do something or not to do something, then the people who say otherwise are *wrong* and *sinning*. On these issues, everyone can't be right. And I find that acknowledging that up front in a gracious way can actually help put people's minds at ease.

When I speak to Christian groups about LGBTQ issues, people in the audience are often nervous about two things. Some are afraid that I'll take a position they disagree with and that they'll have to spend the entire time listening to me insult their point of view and lecture them about how wrong they are. No one wants to sit through that! But others are afraid I *won't* take a position and that I'll say, "Let's all just get along" without acknowledging that some issues *matter* and not everyone can be right. On important issues, that's not a helpful approach either!

The solution is to simply admit up front that "this issue matters and we can't both be right," but to do it in a way that shows empathy—acknowledging that the people who disagree with you are still *sincere* people who *care* about getting it right, even though you disagree with them about what the right answer is.

The apostle Paul demonstrated this beautifully in Athens (Acts 17:16–34).

The Athenians had a polytheistic culture with all sorts of temples and shrines to various gods. I can just imagine Paul, this passionate man of God who had grown up with the commandment to have "no other gods before me" (Exodus 20:3), looking around and seeing idol after idol. He must have been tempted to get up and start preaching fire and brimstone, lecturing the Athenians about worshipping false gods! Instead, though, he wisely recognized that these people might be wrong in their beliefs, but they were *sincere*. They were trying to get it right. So rather than lecture them, he found another way to begin the conversation.

There was an altar there "to an unknown god" because the people of Athens were worried about accidentally offending some god they didn't know about. So when Paul got up to speak, he said,

> Men of Athens, I see that in every way you are very religious. For as I walked around and examined your objects of worship, I even found an altar with this inscription: TO AN UNKNOWN GOD. Therefore what you worship as something unknown, I now proclaim to you. (Acts 17:22–23, BSB)

Think about what a remarkable, empathetic approach that is—especially from someone as headstrong as Paul. Rather than condemning them for their error, Paul compliments them for being "very religious." He realizes that they're sincere in wanting to get things right, and he latches on to the good things he knows they're going for. He of course goes on to talk about Jesus, which was his point all along, but by approaching the topic this way, he builds a bridge to his listeners. Now they are on a journey together, instead of his coming in shouting and putting them on the defensive.

STEP 2: LISTEN TO THEIR STORY.

In an episode of the popular TV series *Ted Lasso*, the title character wisely recommends, "Be curious, not judgmental" as a good approach to handling conflict.[1] In other words, before we jump to conclusions about someone, we ought to take the time to be curious about them and ask questions—to learn more about where their views come from and what makes them tick. When we do, we'll often find that our assumptions about them were wrong. We might still disagree with their views, but our curiosity can help us *understand* them better, and that's a vital part of practicing empathy.

In the same vein, James 1:19 tells us we should be "quick to listen, slow to speak and slow to become angry." Too often, though, we're the opposite.

When we're sure someone is wrong about something, our first instinct is usually to start *talking*, trying to convince the other person to change their mind. We might cite Scripture or make persuasive arguments, debating more and more passionately—as if we expect them to suddenly say, "Oh, that's a good point; never mind, I agree with you now." But that's not usually what happens, is it? Instead, the other person just ends up arguing back, just as passionately, and we both wind up frustrated with no one having budged an inch.

When this happens, it's tempting to say, "They're just stubborn. They'll never listen." Maybe that's true. But we might have a lot more success if we tried being curious and *listening to them first*.

Productive dialogue, as Stephen R. Covey reminds us, requires that we "seek first to understand, *then* to be understood." We can't skip the first step in order to get to the second. If we approach others the way pushy salespeople do, rushing to get to our own ideas in order to convince them to do what we want, they're not likely to care about anything we have to say. Who wants to be pressured by a salesperson who doesn't listen? On the other hand, when you take the time to genuinely ask someone about their feelings, opinions, and experiences, it makes them feel good, and it proves to them that they aren't going to have to fight with you to be heard.

This kind of listening isn't easy. When the other person says things you strongly disagree with, you'll be tempted to jump in and correct or argue with them. Resist that urge. This isn't a race. Instead, ask open-ended questions to learn more about what they believe and why it matters to them.

And as much as possible, choose questions that can be answered with a *story*. Don't just ask, "What's your view on this topic?" or even, "Why do you have that view on this topic?" Instead, ask, "Do you remember when you first encountered this topic?" and, "Are there events since then that have shaped your perspective?" Then as the other person answers, try to listen so well that you're ultimately able to tell their story back to them in your own words: "It sounds like when you went through such-and-such, that made you feel such-and-such, which now has you concerned about such-and-such..." It might sound corny, but if you do it sincerely, telling someone else their own story can be a powerful demonstration of love and understanding.

It reminds me of Jesus' encounter with a Samaritan woman in John chapter 4—an encounter that makes such an impact on her that she can't stop talking about it. "Come, see a man who told me everything I ever did," she says. "Could this be the Christ?" (John 4:29 BSB).

It seems to me that there are two big things going on here. First, of course, is that Jesus has once again proven his identity by performing a miracle; he's told this woman things he couldn't otherwise have known, and that's convinced her that he is who he claims to be.

But I also think it's significant that the way Jesus proves himself to her is by showing her how well he knows her story. Jesus' miracles always seem to have some purpose beyond the miracle itself, typically providing something *needed*—something *lacking*. He provides healing to those in need of healing. He provides food when there's a lack of food. And in this case, he provides this woman with the gift of being *known*.

As we saw earlier, there's something incredibly powerful about being both known and loved. And one of the best ways to make someone feel known and loved is to *tell them their own story*. We may not be able to do it miraculously as Jesus did, but we can do it by being good listeners, and that kind of care can feel miraculous in its own way.

When you make someone feel known and loved, they often relax and open up about other stories and concerns they wouldn't otherwise have shared. Just keep listening and asking follow-up questions—not "gotcha" questions designed to put them on the defensive, but empathetic questions to help you understand them better. Questions like, "What was that experience like for you?" "How have you been feeling about this discussion in our church?" "What parts of this dialogue have been most painful?" "Are there times I've ever made you feel like you weren't being heard or respected?"

Obviously, questions like these can be great ones to ask an LGBTQ person, as long as they're comfortable answering. But they can be useful in plenty of other situations. As a gay man, I often ask these questions of straight conservative Christians who disagree with me, because I want them to know that I care about their feelings too, even though others like them may have caused me pain in the past. The truth is, we're all sinners and we're all still learning. I've made plenty of mistakes and hurt people in my life, and I hope they'd show me grace and give me the chance to learn too. That kind of empathy is one of the best gifts we can offer one another. It's one of the wonderful things Christianity has to offer the world.

STEP 3: SHARE YOUR STORY.

I usually recommend listening and asking questions for as long as you can, making sure the other person feels fully heard and understood before you start trying to give your side of things. Eventually, though, when they're ready to hear your perspective, I suggest doing something else that might not come naturally: Instead of giving them an *argument* for your position, give them *your* story.

Again, this may be counterintuitive at first. You might wonder, why would you tell a *story* when the disagreement is about facts or Bible interpretation? What story could you possibly have to tell? Especially if it's an important moral issue, telling stories might feel like a waste of time.

But in my experience, if you really want to get someone to listen, stories are the most powerful way to go.

There's a reason the Bible is filled with stories and not just a list of rules. There's a reason Jesus, too, taught so frequently in parables. (Well, there are multiple reasons, but I'm pretty sure this is one of them.) Stories have power. Memorable stories stick with people and continue to make them think long after they've forgotten everything else you said. And unlike most other kinds of arguments, stories speak to our hearts as well as our heads.

At first, you might not think you have a story to tell. But you do. It's the story of the event or events in your life that caused you to care so much about the disagreement at hand.

If you're a parent of an LGBTQ kid, share what that's been like. If you're a pastor wrestling with questions because of people you know in your congregation, share that experience. Whoever you are, you have a story. When we're able to be vulnerable about our pain as well as our joy, that vulnerability has great power to open hearts and change minds. Jesus often modeled how apparent weakness and humility can actually bring tremendous strength, and that's definitely true here.

Some LGBTQ people are worried about sharing the painful parts of their journeys because they don't want to come across as victims. I definitely understand that fear. But I believe it's important for us to be honest about the good *and* the bad in our stories. Pretending we haven't been hurt—if indeed we have—doesn't help people understand us. Being honest about our emotions, our mistakes, our pain, our confusion, and everything else allows people to see us as the human beings we are instead of seeing us as just an issue.

By telling your story, you're not just making a case the other person can argue with. You're humanizing yourself and your position in their eyes, helping them to understand *who* you are and *why* this is important to you. They might still disagree, but now at least they know what's motivating you, and that allows the two of you to move together to step 4.

STEP 4: PRAYERFULLY SEEK GOD'S WILL TOGETHER.

In John 17:21, Jesus prays for the future Christian believers, "that all of them may be one, Father, just as you are in me and I am in you." In praying for that unity, Jesus certainly knew that we weren't always going to agree on everything. We're only human, after all. But there is a way for us to be united even in our disagreement. *We can seek God's will together as allies rather than enemies.*

This rarely happens in our polarized world. In America's two-party politics, for example, each party seems to rejoice when bad things happen to the other, because a loss for their opponent is a gain for them. But as Christians, we shouldn't have that attitude toward trying to serve God. If you and I are both Christians but we disagree on what God wants us to do about something, that doesn't mean we're enemies. We're still two members of the same Body who, despite our disagreement, have a shared goal: to serve God. We don't "win" by defeating each other. We succeed together if we can support each other in putting our egos aside, joining hands, and taking the journey together to try to figure out what's true and what God wants us to do.

This can be easier said than done, though. When we disagree strongly with someone, we can get so focused on that disagreement that it becomes the only thing we think of when we picture that person. And that can destroy a relationship.

In Gary Chapman's popular book *The Five Love Languages*, he imagines each person with an emotional "love tank" that can be filled by another person's loving words and deeds—or emptied by that person's criticisms and thoughtlessness. Other writers have described this as an "emotional bank account," an image my mom often used when I was growing up. To maintain a happy relationship with someone—whether they're a spouse, a family member, or a friend—it's important to put more into that tank than we take out, even in times of disagreement. And because a single negative interaction can outweigh multiple positive ones, we need to be intentional about including as many positive shared experiences as possible in these discussions to prevent our disagreements from permanently damaging our relationships.

A great way to do that is to *focus on our common ground and shared values.*

Any time you discuss a disagreement, begin by talking about whatever values or beliefs you do have in common—a desire to be kind to one another, to do God's will, to solve a shared problem, etc.—and come back to those things as often as you can throughout your conversation. Don't use them as weapons: "I thought you believed in being kind, but you're not being very kind!" Instead, use them to draw the two of you together as often as possible: "Because we both value kindness, I would love to find a way forward on this that we can both agree is kind, even if we end up disagreeing on the particulars."

This is easiest to do if the person you disagree with is a fellow Christian; you can begin with your shared commitment to Christ and your shared Christian values. But it's possible even if they're not a Christian, as Paul demonstrated in Athens with the common ground of being "very religious." Always look for the good in the other person. You may not agree with their conclusions, but is there anything about their *intent* or *approach* that you can agree with? Take the time to appreciate those things and compliment them aloud. Do your best not to let the disagreement outweigh the things that hold you together.

This is a radical departure from the way the world handles conflict. In the culture wars around us, people draw battle lines and race to see who can get enough power to overwhelm their opponents and force things to go their way. But if, through empathy, we can come to *understand* our opponents—not to agree with them on everything, but to learn to see the world through their eyes—and we're able to patiently help them understand us in return, we can build the trust it takes to stop aiming our weapons at each other and start seeking truth together.

To do this requires the work of all the fruits of the Spirit—love, joy, peace, patience, kindness, goodness, faithfulness, gentleness, and self-control (Galatians 5:22–23 BSB). We have to keep our tempers in check when the other person says something hurtful and show grace when we see the evidence of their sin. Some days will be frustrating. We may take two steps forward and one step back—or one step forward and two steps back. When that happens, we just have to ask God for strength and keep going.

Along the way, it's important to work together to cultivate an atmosphere of mutual care in the discussions. Be willing to be transparent about your weaknesses and uncertainties, and don't be afraid to admit when you need to step away from the conversation for a while to avoid getting too upset. If you lose your temper, be the first to apologize, even if the other person was more at fault.

And pay attention to how they're feeling too. If they're getting emotional, don't use that against them; be gracious and treat them as you'd want to be treated in that situation. This isn't a competition. It's a journey together.

Through it all, don't forget the importance of maintaining your relationship with this person outside of this particular discussion. Don't let one disagreement be the central point around which your whole relationship revolves. Spend the bulk of your time on other things.

Have meals together. Get ice cream. Take hikes together. Go to movies. Play games. Do things you both enjoy that allow you to talk about totally unrelated subjects. Listen to the details of their day and find points of common interest to bond over. If possible, go out of your way to do thoughtful things for them just to show you care.

These kinds of things are especially important with someone you don't know well, but they're also important for family members you've known your whole life. It can be easy to let this one disagreement take over your relationship and make you forget what you love about each other. Don't let that happen. Being intentional about building your relationship outside of this disagreement is a big part of what makes the difference between treating someone as an issue or opponent and treating someone as a beloved child of God who, like you, wants to know what's true.

CHAPTER 18

◆

PRACTICING LOVE

Two millennia ago, a man called Jesus of Nazareth changed the world forever.

Born in the humblest of circumstances, he devoted his life to the service of others. He socialized with outcasts and sinners. He had compassion for those who were hungry and sick. He preached about God's plans for our future, but he preached even more about grace, humility, and forgiveness in the here and now. His followers rightfully proclaimed him a king, yet *he* was the one who washed *their* feet. He lived every moment as a servant, and then he gave up his life for the sake of those who killed him.

I believe that man was and is the Son of God. I am a Christian because of *him*, and I believe that we as Christians are called to follow in his footsteps. When we do, we make the world a brighter place. When we fail, we can destroy lives. Tragically, our treatment of LGBTQ people is one place where we've failed over and over again, and the neighbors Jesus taught us to love are the ones who have paid the price for our sins as a church.

But what will our future be? Will we continue to be known for which people we're "against"? Will our behavior reflect the worst of the world around us? Or is there another way—a way in which we might once again be known for reflecting the One we serve?

LOVING THE SINNER

When I discussed homosexuality with my high school friend Sean all those years ago, I thought that "Love the sinner, hate the sin" was the perfect summary of Christian grace in the midst of disagreement. Now I cringe when I hear people say that.

The basic point of the phrase is true. But "Love the sinner, hate the sin" feels very different depending on which side of the table you're sitting on. To the person doing the "loving," it feels very generous: *Even though this person is a sinner, I'm going to treat them with love and compassion!*

However, it doesn't feel very generous at all when someone is saying it about you. Yes, I know I'm a sinner, as we all are, but something about the phrase feels condescending and dehumanizing, as if I'm now "the sinner" rather than the person's friend or neighbor, and "loving" me has become the new project they've taken on out of obligation to God rather than a genuine interest in my well-being. For this, it seems, I am supposed to feel grateful, as if this were a great imposition on someone who could easily have passed me by and left me in my sinful state.

When someone says they're "loving the sinner," it sounds as though the person being referred to is a "sinner" in some sense that the speaker is not. That's not a biblical picture. According to the Bible, all of us are sinners, equally fallen in God's eyes, and all of us have been shown so much grace by God that we have absolutely no right to look down on anyone else.

Baptist minister Tony Campolo had this response to the phrase:

> I always am uptight when somebody says…"I love the sinner, but I hate his sin." I'm sure you've heard that line over and over again. And my response is, "That's interesting. Because that's just the opposite of what Jesus says. Jesus never says, 'Love the sinner, but hate his sin.' Jesus says, 'Love the sinner, and hate your *own* sin. And after you get rid of the sin in your own life, then you can begin talking about the sin in your brother or sister's life.' "[1]

Jesus was known for his grace and mercy. His friends were widely known as outcasts and sinners, yet he treated them as his friends, not as "sinners" or projects. When other people were ready to stone a woman caught in adultery, he stood in her defense. When he met another woman with a live-in boyfriend and a long string of husbands, he acknowledged her situation without lecturing her about it. Jesus knew that most of the people he encountered were already painfully aware that "people like him" looked down on them as sinners. Rather than adding to their shame, Jesus met them as friends, treating them as equals even though they were in no way his equals, and showing them love and grace even when they didn't deserve it.

If anyone had a right to lecture people about their sin, it was the sinless Son of God. If even he could meet sinners as equals, how much more should we Christians—all sinners ourselves—treat as equals the people we encounter in our lives?

Jesus saved his lecturing and anger exclusively for the self-righteous and those who put barriers in the way of others trying to come to God. When greedy and unscrupulous money changers set up shop in the only space reserved for Gentiles to worship, Jesus turned over their tables in disgust. His most famous frustration, however, was with the self-righteous Pharisees.

As I mentioned earlier, I believe the Pharisees of Jesus' day had a lot in common with today's Christian leaders. Whenever Jesus addresses the Pharisees in the Bible, I think we Christians need to sit up and take notice to see if in some ways he may be talking to us. In Matthew, he says of them:

> Do not do what they do, for they do not practice what they preach. They tie up heavy, cumbersome loads and put them on other people's shoulders, but they themselves are not willing to lift a finger to move them....
>
> Woe to you, teachers of the law and Pharisees, you hypocrites! You shut the door of the kingdom of heaven in people's faces. You yourselves do not enter, nor will you let those enter who are trying to.
>
> Woe to you, teachers of the law and Pharisees, you hypocrites! You travel over land and sea to win a single convert, and when you have succeeded, you make them twice as much a child of hell as you are....
>
> Woe to you, teachers of the law and Pharisees, you hypocrites! You give a tenth of your spices—mint, dill and cumin. But you have neglected the more important matters of the law—justice, mercy and faithfulness. You should have practiced the latter, without neglecting the former. You blind guides! You strain out a gnat but swallow a camel. (Matthew 23:3–4, 13–15, 23–24)

It's remarkable to me how much this passage resonates with many LGBTQ people I know who grew up in church. Many of them felt that church leaders put heavy burdens on them—such as by expecting them to abstain not only from sex but even from romantic relationships in a way few straight Christians would be able to do—but that those leaders gave comparatively little thought to showing empathy or finding ways to help ease that burden. In too many cases, Christians have had a reputation for prioritizing following the rules over caring for the people.

For those Christians who believe we've gotten the rules wrong, the obvious solution here is to correct our misunderstanding of Scripture so that we stop putting unnecessary burdens on people. But the solution may not seem as obvious for Christians like Martin, the pastor I mentioned at the beginning of this book. Martin is firmly convinced that the Bible is clear in not allowing for same-sex marriage or sexual activity, and as a pastor, he has a responsibility to teach what he believes the Bible says—even though this is undeniably a burden for any gay people in his congregation. Given what he believes about Scripture, then, what could Martin and his church do to actively demonstrate the love of Christ without taking a condescending "love the sinner" approach?

This is a question we all face as Christians. We may disagree on what God's rules for us are in this or that situation, but we all agree that God does have expectations for us. Not everything is good. Sooner or later, we will all encounter situations in which someone is living in a way we disapprove of. What does it look like to show those people Christian love?

THE PATH OF ACTIVE LOVE

As Christians, we believe that we are saved by grace through faith, not by works (Ephesians 2:8–9). We don't have to be "good enough" to earn God's grace. But that doesn't mean we get to just coast through life, taking the easy road, knowing that we're saved no matter what. If our faith is sincere, it should be evident in the things we do.

The Bible reminds us of this:

> What good is it, my brothers and sisters, if someone claims to have faith but has no deeds? Can such faith save them? Suppose a brother or a sister is without clothes and daily food. If one of you says to them, "Go in peace; keep warm and well fed," but does nothing about their physical needs, what good is it? In the same way, faith by itself, if it is not accompanied by action, is dead....Show me your faith without deeds, and I will show you my faith by my deeds (James 2:14–18).

We could substitute the word *love* for *faith* in this passage, and it would be just as true. If we claim to love someone but don't show it through our actions, that love is dead. We can't just offer simple solutions, tell people to "go in peace," and take no action to care for them and tend to their wounds. Our love must be active.

In the classic musical *My Fair Lady*, Eliza Doolittle spends her days taking English lessons from a man who treats her like an academic puzzle to solve but never shows her any affection. When a young suitor named Freddy finds a moment alone with her, he *does* express affection, and he begins to sing a flowery love song to her. But this isn't what she wants. She hilariously interrupts his song with one of her own, saying, "Words, words, words, I'm so sick of words...if you're in love, *show me!*"

As Christians, we must heed this message. The path toward becoming the church we're called to be is a path of *active love*, a love that *shows* itself by its actions instead of just *telling* people that we love them—or, worse, criticizing them and calling it "telling the truth in love."

Yes, when you love someone, it is sometimes necessary to tell them an uncomfortable truth. But this can be painful, and it requires a major withdrawal from your emotional bank account with them. You must have built up a *lot* of trust and goodwill between you—and be continuing to show active love in many other ways—for your criticism to be received as loving. Otherwise, you run the risk of coming across like a Christian character in the satirical film *Saved!* who shouts, "I am *filled* with Christ's love!" while throwing her Bible at someone. If we lecture people, quote Bible passages at them, or even wish them well without doing anything about their needs, it doesn't matter if we say we're doing it all "in love"; they won't experience it as love. Our love must be active. We must show, not tell.

Showing love can take many forms, depending on the person and their situation. In general, it means empathetically listening and caring about their story and the challenges they're facing. Are they feeling lonely? Invite them to do things with you. Has their partner been sick? Ask about them—even if you don't approve of the relationship. Have they had a difficult time fitting in at your church? Offer to introduce them to people, and pay attention to whether there might be opportunities for your church to better minister to their needs. Of course, these are just a few basic examples; far better is to get to know the person as an individual—one of the purposes of the gracious dialogue in the previous chapter—and find out what their specific needs might be. The question isn't "What makes LGBTQ people feel loved?" It's "What would make *this person* feel loved?"

One loving act that does apply to many LGBTQ people, though, is to use the terminology they prefer when talking to or about them. If someone prefers the term *pansexual* rather than *bisexual*, that's the appropriate way to talk about them—even if it's not *your* preferred term. For many younger people, the term *queer* is an encouragingly diverse word, and they may prefer it over any other LGBTQ term. For many others—especially some folks my age and older—it's still a hurtful and divisive term, not only because of its long use as a slur but because of its history as a word meaning "odd" or "strange." The word that makes one person feel seen can make another feel othered; what matters is, as much as possible, to use the word that makes a particular person feel known and loved.

The words we use for someone are powerful indicators of our level of respect for them. Suppose my friend is named Horace, but he's always hated that name, and he goes by "Bud" instead. It doesn't matter whether I like the name Bud or whether I think it's an appropriate nickname for someone with the birth name Horace. If he introduces himself to me as Bud and asks me to call him Bud, the respectful thing for me to do is to call him Bud. If I were to keep calling him Horace instead, that wouldn't cause him to change his mind; it would only cause him to feel disrespected by me and no longer be very interested in being my friend.

In the same way, I believe that when a transgender person shares their preferred name or pronouns, it's very important to hear that and use them. As I write these words, there's a lot of cultural debate about the idea of "preferred pronouns"; it's become a point of political division, and I know a lot of Christians who are uncomfortable with the idea of someone using pronouns based on their internal gender identity. As I shared in an earlier chapter, adjusting to some of these new terms and ways of using language has been a challenge for me, too, and I haven't always agreed with everyone's choice of terms. But I believe it's important to use the name and pronouns someone asks you to use, as a simple sign of respect and love—even if you don't personally approve of their choices. To refuse to do so isn't going to cause them to change their mind or live any differently; it's just going to cause them to distance themselves from you. On the other hand, to use someone's pronouns, ask about their partner, or share in their joys and sorrows doesn't imply that you approve of everything they do; it just demonstrates that you love them enough to show that you care.

MAKING JUDGMENT CALLS

There are times, though, when the line between showing *love* and showing *approval* may not be so clear. Suppose you're invited to a same-sex wedding, but you don't approve of the relationship. Should you go?

It's a challenging question, and I can't answer it for you. If it's a wedding for someone very close to you, like your child, choosing not to attend can cause lasting damage to your relationship with them. For this reason, I know many parents who choose to attend as a sign of love, just as they would any other significant event in their child's life. Their reasoning is that their attendance isn't an endorsement; it's simply a reflection of their desire to remain in their child's life even when that child makes decisions they disapprove of.

Others feel they can't attend such a wedding in good conscience, so instead, they seek out other ways to actively demonstrate their love—attending the reception, say, or sending a thoughtful gift. Whatever you choose, do your best to keep the focus on the love and support you want to show rather than on any areas of disapproval. There are plenty of other times to talk about your differences; you don't want that to be the thing they most remember from an important occasion in their lives.

If *you're* the one getting married and you're struggling with what to do about a friend or family member who doesn't approve, I advise showing them as much grace as possible. Just as we don't want others trying to pressure us to follow their consciences, we can't ask others to follow ours. Consider offering several options to allow them to participate or attend without violating their conscience. Of course, they may ultimately choose not to be involved at all, and that may be very painful. Try to show them grace anyway and see it as a sign of their love for you rather than a rejection. (And, after all, would you really want someone there who's unhappy on your happy day?) In all things, do your best to focus on the positive and show the grace and mercy to others that you'd want them to show to you.

EASING THE BURDEN

For churches and Christian institutions, an important part of showing love is working to help ease the burden LGBTQ people often feel in church. This includes tending to their spiritual wounds and offering opportunities for community and connection.

This is especially important in Side B churches that preach celibacy for gay people.

Eve Tushnet, a celibate gay Christian, once wrote that the church too often comes across as giving gay teens only a "No"—telling them what they can't do—instead of giving positive guidance about what they *can* do. As she puts it, "You can't have a vocation of not-gay-marrying and not-having-sex. You can't have a vocation of No."

Another celibate Christian I know put it this way: "My experience with a lot of churches is that they will say, 'Gay people should be celibate,' but then leave you out in the cold to figure out what that means."

The path of celibacy is remarkably difficult for even the most committed people, and celibate people of any orientation can have a very difficult time meeting their needs for human connection. Unfortunately, in many churches, programming and classes for singles are either nonexistent or designed around meeting the needs of "pre-married" people, with little thought given to the unique needs of those celibate for life.

Although I don't believe celibacy is required for all gay Christians, some gay Christians do believe that's what they're called to, and I want to support them in following their consciences. If their churches want to support them, too, they must take an active role in learning what kinds of support their celibate members need and then working to ease their burdens—providing family, community, and love while charting a path for what an abundant life might look like for them—a path of Yes, not merely of No.

WHAT ABOUT CHURCH DISCIPLINE?

When it comes to showing active love in the midst of disagreement, some of the most challenging questions concern church policies. What happens, for instance, when a Side A gay couple in a committed relationship attends a Side B church that believes such relationships are sinful? Should they be fully embraced even though the church believes they're living in sin? Should they be held at arm's length? Disciplined? Kicked out?

Churches continue to wrestle with this question. Some have responded as my old church did, telling gay Christians they are welcome to attend only as long as they are celibate. Their rationale for this comes from 1 Corinthians 5, where Paul chided the Corinthian church for failing to take a stand when a man in their congregation became well known for having an incestuous relationship with his own stepmother. The relationship was one that was universally recognized as sinful not only within the Christian community but also throughout the whole society. Paul described it as something that "even pagans do not tolerate."

Paul had good reason to be concerned: Not only was the church failing to offer the moral guidance it should, but this man's behavior also risked seriously harming the reputation of the church in the broader culture. In Paul's day, this "Christianity" was a mysterious new thing most people didn't yet understand, and false rumors about what Christians believed dogged the church for centuries. As Denver Seminary professor Bruce L. Shelley notes:

> [One] cause of persecution of early Christians were the slanders disseminated about them. Once these were started, they could not be halted. The suspicion that the Christian gatherings were sexual orgies and cover for every kind of crime took hold of the popular imagination with a terrible vehemence.[2]

As the church was just starting to make its mark, it was vital that Christians distance themselves from the appearance of condoning sin, and Paul advised them to do so. In some ways, though, that situation was the exact opposite of the one faced by the American church today, where the prevailing view of us is that we are unkind, judgmental, and homophobic, and where distancing ourselves from gay people only damages our reputation even more.

There's another critical difference here. Paul was describing a situation where there was essentially universal agreement that the behavior in question was sinful: The church knew it, the culture knew it, and presumably the man knew it as well but simply didn't see any need to repent. Paul hoped that by taking a strong stand against his sin, the church could demonstrate the seriousness of the problem and move him to repent. That does not, however, describe the modern-day situation involving gay relationships. There is widespread disagreement—both within the culture and within the church—about the morality of these relationships, with honest, sincere, committed, Bible-believing Christians on both sides of the argument. The gay couple attending church is likely doing what they believe to be the right thing, not living in open and sinful rebellion, and as I've tried to demonstrate in this book, the questions are difficult, complex, and hotly disputed among Christians.

Paul's advice for situations like these is completely different from his advice in 1 Corinthians 5. In Romans 14, Paul addresses a similarly hotly disputed question of the day, the question of whether it was participating in idolatry for Christians to eat food that had been sacrificed to an idol. Because of the widespread availability of such food in that culture, it had become a major issue. Some Christians argued that eating such food was idolatrous and sinful, while others argued that it was acceptable if one did it with the right heart. In his response, Paul wrote:

> Accept the one whose faith is weak, without quarreling over disputable matters. One person's faith allows them to eat anything, but another, whose faith is weak, eats only vegetables. The one who eats everything must not treat with contempt the one who does not, and the one who does not eat everything must not judge the one who does, for God has accepted them. Who are you to judge someone else's servant? To their own master, servants stand or fall. And they will stand, for the Lord is able to make them stand.
>
> One person considers one day more sacred than another; another considers every day alike. Each of them should be fully convinced in their own mind....
>
> You, then, why do you judge your brother or sister? Or why do you treat them with contempt? For we will all stand before God's judgment seat....
>
> Therefore let us stop passing judgment on one another. Instead, make up your mind not to put any stumbling block or obstacle in the way of a brother or sister....
>
> So whatever you believe about these things keep between yourself and God (Romans 14:1–5, 10, 13, 22).

When everyone was in agreement, Paul encouraged the church to take action. But when there was serious disagreement within the Body of Christ, Paul encouraged people to follow their consciences and allow other believers to do likewise. I believe the situation we're facing today is the latter type.

Of course, no matter how welcoming a congregation is, many gay couples will feel unable to attend a church that cannot honor their relationship as blessed by God. A while back, I participated in a Christian dialogue on gay issues that was held at a church with a traditional Side B viewpoint. One of the pastors from that church spoke movingly of his desire to reach out to and welcome gay people, even though he and his church officially considered gay relationships to be sinful. He pointed out that although that was the official view of the church, it was not a regular sermon topic, and he felt the environment of the congregation was warm and loving for *all* people, regardless of their background. We had discussed some of the hurt that gay people have faced at the hands of the church, and this pastor was clearly brokenhearted over the pain. He wanted to do his part to change things.

In response, a partnered gay man spoke up. "I hear your earnestness," he said. "I see that you want to welcome me. But I have to tell you that I just couldn't sit Sunday after Sunday in a church where my relationship with my partner—the most important person in my life—is viewed as something sinful. Could you be a member of a congregation that said your relationship with your wife was really just living in sin? My integrity and respect for my partner and myself won't allow me to do that."

The exchange continued for quite some time, and it affected all of us. That couple won't be attending that church, but the honest conversation that took place—with grace and love on both sides—helped to build a vital bridge of understanding that may transform how both sides see the issue.

Each gay person has a different perspective. Celibate gay Christians may well feel at home in that church, and I know many gay couples who have chosen to attend churches because of other things about them or about their theology, in spite of a lack of support for their relationships. Others say that's just something they could never do. Each of us must make our own decision, and each church must carefully examine the issue and decide what sort of place there is for LGBTQ Christians in the congregation.

I would encourage churches to err on the side of welcome in these cases. But whatever the church policy may be, each of us as individual Christians can make a choice about how we respond to the people we disagree with in our lives. Do we throw the Bible at them and lecture them about every disagreement "in love"? Do we keep a polite distance and wish them well without lifting a finger to help them? Or do we love them with our actions, getting invested in their lives, following the example of a Savior who washed his own sinful followers' feet?

THE OBSTACLES AHEAD

When CCF leader Warren invited me out to lunch only to preach at me, I'm sure he meant well, but I didn't feel very loved. A year later, he and his wife moved to another position, and a new couple, Brent and Jennifer, took their places. By this point, it was common knowledge within the group that I was gay, so I knew it was only a matter of time before Brent and Jennifer found out. I was tired of feeling like a victim, waiting for other people to figure things out, so during one of my first conversations with them, I found an excuse to mention my involvement with GALBA. Sure enough, Brent responded almost immediately by asking me to meet him for lunch, just as Warren had done before him, "just to talk."

I accepted the offer, but this time I came prepared. The day of the meeting, I made a list of the questions I thought he was likely to ask, and I rehearsed short, simple answers to all of them so that I could explain myself before he could interrupt. I bookmarked all the relevant passages in my Bible and packed it into my backpack. Then, with a deep breath and a silent prayer, I was off to meet Brent for lunch.

As Warren had done before him, Brent started out with small talk: "How are you?" "How are your classes going?" "Do you have plans for the future?" I sat there stiff as a board, keeping an eye on the time and keeping my answers short, making sure we'd have plenty of time to talk about the real issue at hand.

About halfway through lunch, there was a lull in the conversation. I was worried we wouldn't have time if we didn't get a move on, so I spoke up: "So, Brent, what did you have in mind to talk about today?"

"What do you mean?" he asked.

"Well, I mean, you invited me to lunch. I assume you had a reason for inviting me. What did you want to talk about?"

He looked confused. Then—what? Hurt? Offended? I couldn't tell. "I didn't have anything in particular in mind," he said simply. "I'm new to the group, so I'm trying to get to know everyone, and you're active in the group, so I just wanted a chance to meet you and have lunch."

As soon as the words came out of his mouth, I knew it was true. I had assumed he was just the same as Warren, and with all my emotional armor on, it had never occurred to me that he might just be a nice guy who wanted to get to know me for me, not because he wanted to preach at me. In my haste to keep him from stereotyping me, I had stereotyped him.

That was over twenty years ago, and Brent still stands out in my mind as one of the examples of straight Christians in the world who know how to love people as Jesus loved, not with an air of condescending paternalism, not with pride in themselves for "loving the sinner," but with genuine humility and caring. If only all Christians were like Brent.

But with every negative encounter LGBTQ people have with Christians, it gets that much harder for the Brents of the world. I went into the conversation with Brent ready for a battle because my past experience had led me to believe that this was what I was going to get. When Christians try to mask a condescending attitude with politeness and faux friendliness, LGBTQ people begin to suspect that all supposedly friendly Christians are really hiding judgmental attitudes toward them. Eventually, they try to avoid Christians altogether.

If you've ever had a sunburn, you know the feeling of being so raw that even the lightest touch—a friendly pat on the back—can feel like an attack. When you've been "burned" by one encounter after another with unloving Christians, you can wind up so emotionally raw that even someone who does everything right feels like an enemy.

It's important to understand this when you try to reach out to the LGBTQ people in your life. Some of them may respond badly even if you don't do anything wrong. It's worth listening to their criticisms to make sure you haven't unintentionally caused offense, but sometimes, it's not about you at all. It's about all those who came before you. This is one of the big challenges we have to overcome as a church. We're not just starting from zero with a goal of being loving; we have to make up for our own past mistakes and the mistakes of other Christians.

This kind of pain doesn't just make non-Christians wary of Christians; it also affects LGBTQ people who are already Christians. My friend Michael once confessed to me that he would sometime catch himself wanting to avoid "the sort of people who like going to church" even though he also liked going to church. Michael had heard so many anti-gay remarks from other Christians that he found himself dreading conversations with Christians *even though he was one of them*!

Aaron, another gay Christian friend of mine, shared with me that his experiences with other Christians were seriously damaging his faith. In one chat, he wrote to me, "With all that I've been going through these last few years, I'm having trouble trusting Christianity. Like I don't know if I can ever trust a pastor ever again." LGBTQ people are not pulling Aaron away from the church. Christians are.

And it doesn't only affect LGBTQ people; it also affects those who care about them. Recently, after I spoke at a church event that was advertised in the local community, a mom with a transgender child shared that although she'd come to hear me speak, it was the first time she'd been in a church building in years. She'd grown up a devout Christian and had raised her children in the church. But the unloving response of so many Christians to her trans child had left her lifelong faith badly shaken. "I just thought, 'Something this hateful can't be of God,'" she told me. "I don't know what to believe anymore. I don't know if I'm still a Christian."

Many people on both sides have imagined that this kind of fallout is a result of disagreement over the morality of gay relationships or theological understandings of gender. It isn't. Those disagreements are important, but Christians are able to disagree on many theological and moral issues without causing this kind of turmoil. What makes this situation unique is the level of venom and ungrace people are feeling from the church, and it is that—not merely the disagreement—that people are responding to in such strong ways.

So what can we do? We can show active love.

There's no step-by-step guide for how to do that in every situation. There's not a list of rules to follow. Active love is about letting the Holy Spirit work through us to care for people and show them understanding and grace instead of judgment. When people wrong us, we can be merciful and forgiving instead of trying to get even. When we disagree with someone's decisions, we can choose to show even more grace rather than less. And when our attempts to love people aren't warmly received, we can show patience and understanding, knowing that God's timetable isn't ours and God hasn't abandoned anyone. In every moment of every day, we can just keep treating people the way we'd want to be treated.

Rather than loving the sinner and hating the sin, we can love everyone and hate our own sin.

OUR SECRET SUPERPOWER

I spent years thinking that something was wrong with me because I was gay and that in order for God to use me, I'd have to become straight. I now realize God's been able to use me even more because I'm gay.

In a culture that sees LGBTQ people and Christians as enemies, LGBTQ Christians are in a unique position to bring peace and change minds. We're like the church's secret weapon or untapped superpower. We're Christians who know firsthand what it's like to feel like outcasts and to be hurt by the church, and that gives us important perspective that the church needs. We've become very aware of our reliance on God's grace at a deep, personal level in a way that many Christians haven't. We've had to fight for our faith, questioning everything and rebuilding our faith from the ground up, truly claiming it for ourselves and not just accepting what we were always taught. We've had to evaluate what works and what doesn't in the church, and that's made us stronger and made our faith stronger. We've had to learn to put our ultimate trust in God instead of in the human institutions of the church.

When it comes to sharing our faith, we have more credibility because of what we've been through, and we know the reasons many people outside the church are so resistant to our culture's version of Christianity. If Christians in our culture are killing Christianity, the LGBTQ Christians just might be the ones who are able to save it.

For these and dozens more reasons, I think God wants to use gay Christians, bi Christians, trans Christians, and other LGBTQ Christians to help the church become what it's supposed to be.

That means that we who are both LGBTQ and Christian must accept the calling and take our place in the church, working in the various ways we're led to make the world and the church a better place.

It also means that Christians who aren't LGBTQ must work to ensure that those who are can be welcomed and supported at all levels of the church, and that their unique experiences and insight are honored. But regardless of what anyone else does, we LGBTQ Christians must not wait for someone else's permission to do the work God has called us to.

So often, when LGBTQ Christians get together, we end up talking about what it would take for us to be truly welcomed in the churches that we love. Like all of us, I've felt the sting of rejection too many times! But I think it's time for us to stop focusing on that and start reminding ourselves that we already *are* God's children. We're not standing outside the doors of the church knocking and waiting for permission to enter; we already are part of the church. As 1 Corinthians 12:21 reminds us, "The eye cannot say to the hand, 'I don't need you!'" Every part of the Body of Christ is essential, and we are part of that Body. We are necessary.

Despite all the frustrating stories I have about the past and the frustrating news we see around us in the present, I'm hopeful for the future. I see more and more LGBTQ Christians confidently taking their places as needed members of the Body of Christ, doing the work God calls them to, often quietly and without any fanfare, but with the knowledge that our Savior has accepted us no matter what anyone else says. And I see more and more churches and individual Christians working to undo the damage of the past and counter the harmful message that the Bible is "against" LGBTQ people. Whatever our theology on marriage, sex, or gender, the reminder that God loves and has grace for us all is something we can all get behind.

We still have a long way to go. Some churches, afraid that we're becoming too accepting of sin, keep using hurtful rhetoric that dehumanizes LGBTQ people. Other churches, eager to get away from the sins of the past, have too quickly abandoned core Christian doctrines and diluted what it is that made us Christians to begin with. Both, I believe, are critical mistakes. But I see a growing third group that is finding a middle way, combining Truth and Love, showing grace in disagreement, and boldly recommitting itself to follow Jesus. The members of this group may not always get attention for their good work, but they are steadily, faithfully seeking God together and shaping the future of Christianity in our world. My prayers are with them, because I know that God can use the least expected people to make the biggest difference.

A SHINING EXAMPLE

When I was still in college, at the height of my struggles to figure out my place in the world, our campus was visited by Baptist minister and author Tony Campolo, the one with the quip about loving the sinner and hating your own sin. Dr. Campolo's position at the time was that the Bible limits sex to the marriage of a man and a woman. His wife, Peggy, held the opposite view; she supported same-sex marriage, and the two of them had delivered a number of joint public presentations in which they discussed their differences of opinion and how they were still able to love each other and respect each other's faith in spite of such a significant theological disagreement.

I had read about the Campolos and their presentations, so when I heard Dr. Campolo was going to visit the CCF weekly meeting while he was on campus, I knew I had to be there.

The room was busy with activity when he entered the room. The meeting hadn't started yet, so he walked around, greeting people warmly. I realized this was my chance to meet him and thank him in person for his work building bridges in the church on the issue that was changing my life.

I nervously made my way through the crowd in his direction. Then he turned around, and I found myself standing face-to-face with him.

"Dr. Campolo," I blurted out, "my name is Justin Lee. I'm part of the gay student group on campus here, and—"

I had intended to tell him that I was also a member of CCF, that I had been studying the Bible debate, and that I respected him and his wife for their willingness to talk publicly about the need for greater understanding and patience. All of that was in my head, but I didn't get that far.

Before I could get another word out, he was giving me a warm embrace, saying, "Well, I'm glad you're here!"

I was stunned. This man knew nothing about me except that I was gay. He didn't know if I was a Christian, if I was having sex, or anything else about my life. He didn't ask. He simply made me feel welcome and unconditionally loved.

Nearly speechless, I managed to tell him that I was a Christian who had been struggling with what it meant to be gay and Christian.

"Tell me all about it!" he said, leading me to two chairs in the corner of the room and inviting me to sit next to him. For the next few minutes, he ignored the crowd just to hear my story. He didn't offer any advice or judgments, and he didn't ask whether I shared his view that gays should be celibate. He just listened and affirmed me. He made me feel important and heard as a human being. He showed me love. And when he had to get up to speak to the crowd, I realized that it didn't matter whether he and I agreed theologically or not. He loved me as I was, just as Christ would.

In that moment, I knew one thing for certain. No matter what theological views Christians might ultimately hold on gay marriage, sex, or relationships, if all Christians loved as Dr. Campolo loved me in that moment, this world would be a completely different place.

Many years have come and gone since that event. Dr. Campolo eventually felt convicted to change his own views and ultimately affirmed same-sex marriage. But no matter what else happens in my life, that moment—the moment when a straight Christian man who didn't agree with me embraced me without question— will remain one of the most powerful images of Christian love. Dr. Campolo was representing Jesus to me that day.

It's not always as simple as a hug. And sometimes it is.

In the years to come, we may sometimes get our theology wrong—though of course we should try our best to get it right. And we may sometimes make the wrong choices—though of course we should try our best to make the right ones and live sinless lives.

But if, by the grace of God, we could someday be known not for whom we're against or for what positions we hold on this or that issue, but, first and foremost, for how much we are like Jesus—

If we could be known for being always ready to embrace the hurting, the sinner, and the outcast without question—

If we could be known for the ways we forgive those who've wronged us—

If we could be known for the genuine, active love we show even to our greatest enemies—love that is not merely spoken but truly experienced—

If that could be our reputation, *we could be the generation to transform the church*. And we could see the church, in turn, become the transformative influence on our society that we were always called to be.

Will there come a time in this life when every Christian does this all the time? No. As long as Christians are human, we will be sinners.

But there is no need to wait for some future perfect church. You and I—right here, right now—are the Body of Christ. We who've been hurt. We who've had our hearts torn. We who know how it feels to be pulled apart by sin and put back together by the grace of Christ.

Today—this very moment—we can take that first step. We can reach out to someone with forgiveness or compassion or connection, ready to listen and love with our actions. We can practice it until it becomes habit. We can recommit ourselves each day to keep going, asking God for the strength and grace we need.

And together, working as the Body of Christ in the world, we can mend what's been torn—in our own lives and in the lives of others.

May it be so, and may we be the ones to make it happen.

NOTES

Chapter 1. Battle of the Century

1. Lesbian, gay, bisexual, transgender, and queer. More on this terminology in later chapters.
2. "Changing Attitudes on Same-Sex Marriage," Pew Research Center, May 14, 2019, https://www.pewresearch.org/religion/fact-sheet/changing-attitudes-on-gay-marriage/.
3. "Global Views of Same-Sex Marriage Vary Widely," Pew Research Center, November 27, 2023, https://www.pewresearch.org/short-reads/2023/11/27/how-people-around-the-world-view-same-sex-marriage/.
4. "Religion and Congregations in a Time of Social and Political Upheaval," Public Religion Research Institute, May 16, 2023, https://www.prri.org/research/religion-and-congregations-in-a-time-of-social-and-political-upheaval/.
5. David Kinnaman and Gabe Lyons, *unChristian: What a New Generation Really Thinks About Christianity...and Why It Matters* (Grand Rapids: Baker Books, 2007), 92.
6. Matthew 11:19.
7. Romans 3:9–31.

8. Matthew 18:23–35.
9. Luke 18:9–14.
10. Dan Savage, "In Your Image," Savage Love, October 14, 2010.

CHAPTER 4. THE TRUTH COMES OUT

1. Luke 15:11–32.
2. E.g., John 3:19–21; Ephesians 5:8–13.
3. Thanks to my friend Peggy Campolo for this analogy.

CHAPTER 5. WHY ARE PEOPLE GAY?

1. Dr. R. von Krafft-Ebing, *Psychopathia Sexualis*, trans. Charles Gilbert Chaddock, M.D. (Philadelphia: The F. A. Davis Co. Publishers, 1892).
2. These aren't the only terms you'll encounter in this conversation, but they're currently some of the most common; we'll talk about some others in later chapters. Language is changing all the time, though, so if someone close to you uses a different term, I recommend asking them what it means to them, to help avoid any potential misunderstandings.
3. For the sake of simplicity, I'm not addressing some of the more complicated gender questions in this section, and I will be using the terms *sex* and *gender* interchangeably.
4. Irving Bieber et al., *Homosexuality: A Psychoanalytic Study* (New York: Basic Books, 1962), 310–313.
5. Elizabeth Gilbert, "Queer and Loathing," *Spin*, June 1996, 78.
6. From a November 1999 Exodus fundraising letter.
7. Joseph Nicolosi and Linda Ames Nicolosi, *A Parent's Guide to Preventing Homosexuality* (Downers Grove, IL: InterVarsity Press, 2002), 86.

8. Simon LeVay, *Gay, Straight, and the Reason Why: The Science of Sexual Orientation*, 2nd ed. (New York: Oxford University Press, 2017), chap. 12, Kindle.

CHAPTER 7. HOW DID WE GET HERE?

1. Okay, technically, Humpty Dumpty isn't in Wonderland; he's in the looking-glass world. If you're the sort of person who cares about such distinctions, we'd probably make good friends.

2. Elizabeth R. Moberly, *Homosexuality: A New Christian Ethic* (Cambridge: James Clarke & Co., 1983), 40.

3. Erik Eckholm, "'Ex-Gay' Men Fight Back Against View That Homosexuality Can't Be Changed," *New York Times*, November 1, 2012, https://www.nytimes.com/2012/11/01/us/ex-gay-men-fight-view-that-homosexuality-cant-be-changed.html.

4. Frank Worthen, "History of Exodus." Recorded at the Exodus International North American Conference, July 25, 2000.

5. Colin Cook, "Church Funds Program for Homosexuals," *Spectrum*, April 1982, 46–48.

6. Ann Japenga, "It's Called Change Counseling: Troubled Pioneer Maintains His Faith in Program," *Los Angeles Times*, December 6, 1987.

7. Virginia Culver, "Sessions with Gays Criticized: Former Minister's Counseling Methods Brought Reprimands," *Denver Post*, October 27, 1995.

8. There has been some debate as to whether Gary Cooper's behind-the-scenes role in organizing and convening the group that became Exodus qualifies him to be called a "cofounder." By all accounts, though, he was part of the initial founding group, co-organizer of the conference that started everything, and one of the earliest public faces of the group.

9. E. Mansell Pattison and Myrna Loy Pattison, "'Ex-Gays': Religiously Mediated Change in Homosexuals," *American Journal of Psychiatry* 137, no. 12 (December 1980): 1553–1562.

10. John Paulk, *Not Afraid to Change* (Mukilteo, WA: WinePress Publishing, 1998).

11. Katie McDonough, "Conversion Therapy Advocate Issues Formal Apology, Renounces 'Ex-Gay' Past," *Salon*, April 25, 2013, https://www.salon.com/2013/04/25/conversion_therapy_advocate_issues_formal_apology_renounces_ex_gay_past/.

12. "The Berkeley Symposium on Same Sex Marriage: Law & Politics," University of California Television, filmed April 19, 2004, 18:12, https://www.youtube.com/watch?v=9dIfRoVW6Js.

13. Michael Majchrowicz, "Conversion Therapy Leader for 2 Decades, McKrae Game Disavows Movement He Helped Fuel," *Post and Courier*, August 30, 2019, https://www.postandcourier.com/news/conversion-therapy-leader-for-2-decades-mckrae-game-disavows-movement-he-helped-fuel/article_fb56dcfc-c384-11e9-970d-bb9a2a8656c5.html.

CHAPTER 8. THAT THE MAN SHOULD BE ALONE

1. Roger Ebert, "All the Lonely People," *Chicago Sun-Times Online*, November 5, 2010.

CHAPTER 9. *SOUTH PARK* CHRISTIANS

1. This wording is from the NIV's 1984 edition.
2. NIV 1984 edition.

CHAPTER 10. THE POISONED YEAST

1. Stephen R. Covey, *The 7 Habits of Highly Effective People: Restoring the Character Ethic* (New York: Fireside, 1990), 30–31.

2. Bruce Bawer, *A Place at the Table: The Gay Individual in American Society* (New York: Touchstone, 1993), 47.

Chapter 11. Faith Assassins

1. Philip Yancey, *What's So Amazing About Grace?* (Grand Rapids, MI: Zondervan Publishing House, 1997), 31.

Chapter 12. The Other Side

1. Bawer, *A Place at the Table*, 18–19.
2. The story of GALBA's name is more evidence of how rapidly things have changed in our society! Today such a group would almost certainly include a *T* for *transgender*, but at that time, terms like *LGBT* and *LGBTQ* were not yet in widespread use, and many organizations that had been founded as "gay and lesbian" groups were just beginning to rethink their names. GALBA had originally been founded as GALA, the Gay and Lesbian Issues Awareness Group—which still, weirdly, didn't fit its acronym.

Chapter 13. Back to the Bible

1. Robert A. J. Gagnon, *The Bible and Homosexual Practice: Texts and Hermeneutics* (Nashville: Abingdon Press, 2001), 130.
2. Leviticus 19:28, ESV.
3. NIV 1984 edition.
4 This was changed in the 2011 edition.
5. I did read Bible commentaries that suggested romantic relationships between figures such as David and Jonathan or the centurion and his servant, but I wasn't convinced that these were romantic/sexual relationships or that there was enough there on which to hang a theological argument about sexual morality.

Chapter 14. Whatever Commandment There May Be

1 NIV 1984 edition, emphasis mine.

2. NIV 1984 edition.

3. NIV 1984 edition, emphasis mine.

4. The Pharisees, by contrast, did have murder in their hearts.

Chapter 15. Lightning Rod

1. Yancey, *What's So Amazing About Grace?*, 11, 32.

2. More on the term *transgender* in the next chapter.

Chapter 16. The More You Know

1. This line has taken various forms in different tellings of the Spider-Man story—and it hasn't always been spoken by Uncle Ben—but this particular wording is most famous from the 2002 film starring Tobey Maguire.

2. Versions of this quote have been wrongly attributed to a number of historical figures, but it's fair to say that the general idea has been around for a long time.

3. Timothy Keller, *The Meaning of Marriage* (New York: Penguin Books, 2011), chap. 3, Kindle.

4. Again, this is just one of many possible ways of describing the concept, and not all nonbinary people would agree with this way of putting it.

Chapter 17. We Need to Talk

1. Ted incorrectly ascribes the quote to Walt Whitman; it may have originated with an advice column in the *Charlotte Observer*. Regardless of who said it first, though, it's excellent advice.

CHAPTER 18. PRACTICING LOVE

1. Tony Campolo, *Bridging the Gap: Conversations on Befriending Our Gay Neighbours* (New Direction Ministries of Canada, 2009), DVD.

2. Bruce L. Shelley, *Church History in Plain Language*, updated 2nd ed. (Nashville: Thomas Nelson, 1996), 41.

ABOUT THE AUTHOR

For more than twenty-five years, Justin Lee has been an influential Christian voice in the LGBTQ conversation, best known for helping families and churches navigate areas of disagreement.

Justin is the founder of Nuance Ministries and the author of *Talking Across the Divide: How to Communicate with People You Disagree with and Maybe Even Change the World*. He speaks regularly to both Christian and secular audiences around the world, using humor and personal stories to bring grace to challenging issues.

A self-proclaimed geek, Justin enjoys unwinding with board games and infusing his writing with pop culture references. He makes educational videos on the Bible and addresses a variety of other subjects on his @GeekyJustin YouTube channel and his website at GeekyJustin.com.